A
TEXTBOOK
OF MODERN
WESTERN ARMENIAN

BY KEVORK B. BARDAKJIAN
AND
ROBERT W. THOMSON
Harvard University

CARAVAN BOOKS
DELMAR, NEW YORK
1977

First published in 1977 by
Caravan Books, Delmar, New York 12054

First Edition

Made and printed in the United States of America

Library of Congress Cataloging in Publication Data

Bardakjian, K   B
Textbook of modern western Armenian.
1. Armenian language, Modern—West Armenian—Grammar.
I. Thomson, Robert W., 1934-   joint author.
II. Title.
PK8373.B37   491'.992'82421   77-1774
ISBN 0-88206-012-0

iii

PREFACE

This textbook of modern Western Armenian is designed as a first year course at the undergraduate level. It is specifically aimed at students with no prior knowledge of Armenian, and emphasis has been placed on the numerous subtleties and nuances of Armenian which might seem strange or difficult to English speakers. In the textbook, stress has been put on explaining the grammar and syntax; for practice in speaking, the lessons are provided with tapes which elaborate on the material in the exercises.

The vocabulary is based on the thousand most frequent words in Armenian. These were compiled from word frequency lists available for Western European languages, so the authors do not claim scientific accuracy. But at least none of the vocabulary is obscure or useless.

A greater problem was that of the norm of expression. Modern Western Armenian having no Academy to regulate usage, the authors opted for spoken Beirut Armenian as the most acceptable form where alternatives existed. This textbook reflects recent linguistic trends in spoken Armenian; a deliberate attempt has been made to disregard literary and stylistic archaisms. Furthermore, the English of the exercises has not been simplified. Users of the book are therefore warned to seek idiomatic translations and to avoid literal renderings from one language into the other.

This textbook is the result of collaboration between a native speaker of Armenian and one of English. The format and choice of topics are primarily those of RWT, while the grammatical and syntactical usages were provided by KBB. But this is a joint venture, and the authors accept equal responsibility for faults and defects.

The Office of Education gave a grant (1975-76) for the preparation of the final form of this textbook. We are also grateful to Linda Malkasian and Matthew Der Manuelian for their assistance, and to Carol Cross for typing several recensions. Mrs. K. Tololyan assisted in the preparation of the tapes. But not least we must thank those students who in several classes were subjected to this textbook at various stages in its preparation, and whose comments proved most salutary. Their remarks have not been recorded individually, but we are indebted to them collectively.

K. B. Bardakjian

R. W. Thomson

INTRODUCTION

The Armenian language

Armenian is a branch of the Indo-European family of languages; its closest affinities are with Greek and Iranian. Armenian was not indigenous to the Armenian plateau, but was introduced by newcomers during the first millennium BC. After the fall of the Urartean kingdom (circa 600 BC) Armenian gradually spread. By about the second century BC it had become the common tongue of the inhabitants of Armenia.

Armenian was first written in the fifth century AD after a monk named Mashtots (later also known as Mesrop) had invented a national script. Immediately an extensive literature developed of both original compositions and works translated from Greek and Syriac. The common literary language is called *grabar*, meaning "written." It is still debated whether this was the accepted medium of a certain class or one of the more widely spoken dialects. For over a thousand years *grabar* remained the standard form of written Armenian, although after the twelfth century some works, such as law-codes, fables, poetry, were written in forms of Armenian closer to the spoken vernaculars. *Grabar* was no longer spoken, but served until the nineteenth century as a common medium of written expression, much in the same way as Latin in early modern Europe or classical Arabic in the modern Middle East.

By the nineteenth century the old language was incomprehensible to the public, nor was there a common vernacular used by all Armenians. Many of the Armenian people had long since been dispersed far from their homeland; Armenian colonies now reached from Europe to the Far East. But the main political and cultural centers of Armenian life came to be Constantinople - for the Armenians of the Ottoman empire - and Tiflis - for the Armenians of the Caucasus.

1

In the nineteenth century new political and social ideas from the West were reaching the Armenians in the Ottoman and Russian empires. The leaders of Armenian society were anxious to bring these ideas to the masses, to raise the level of general Armenian culture, and to instill in their fellow-countrymen concepts of liberty and patriotism.

Here the popular press was to play the major role. But first an acceptable literary medium had to be forged. On the one hand it had to be more universally acceptable than one of the local dialects, and on the other hand it had to be more comprehensible than the classical language. So it was that primarily in Constantinople and Tiflis there developed standard written forms of Armenian. These were purged of much of the foreign influences of Turkish, Arabic, Persian and Russian, yet they did reflect the basic differences between the spoken Armenian of these two cities. The standard literary form of Armenian developed in Constantinople is known as modern Western Armenian, and is the form presented in this textbook. The standard literary form of Armenian developed in nine-teenth century Tiflis is known as modern Eastern Armenian. Western Armenian is spoken in the Armenian diaspora that stems from the Ottoman empire: the Medi-terranean, Europe, the Americas and Australia. Eastern Armenian is spoken in the Armenian SSR, and in the diaspora of the Soviet Union and Iran.

In view of the origin of modern literary Armenian, it is not surprising that Armenian literature of the 19th and 20th centuries is rich in many fields not represented in the classical literature. Plays, novels, essays and purely secular poetry are the most outstanding new directions in which Armenians have expressed their concerns and aspirations.

Modern Armenian literature

The literary works of the Mekhitarist Fathers in the eighteenth and nineteenth centuries marked the beginnings of modern Armenian literature. Their writings, mainly in the form of plays and poetry, gave rise to the Classical School, which was followed by Romanticism and Realism in the second half of the nineteenth century. The traditions of the Mekhitarists, extolling patriotism and human virtues, were inherited by subsequent Armenian writers and integrated with the themes and techniques acquired from European authors. Armenian *belles-lettres* by the end of the nineteenth century included all the usual genres.

In addition to the themes of the earlier generations, writers such as Abovian, Alishan, Beshigtashlian, Nalbandian, Turian, Raffi, Sundukian, and Baronian reflected and evaluated the political and social realities of Armenian life. Their literature stimulated patriotism, enhancing the national awareness and sense of political unity of the Armenian people. Towards the end of the nineteenth and at the beginning of the twentieth century Armenian verse attained unprecedented expression in the poetry of a number of very talented writers - Tumanian, Isahakian, Medzarents, Siamanto, Varuzhan, Terian, and Charents. The national and human concerns expressed in these writings, the brilliance of their techniques, and the elegance of their styles certainly warrant a significant place for their works in the literary heritage of mankind.

After the 1915 massacres, Armenian literary life resumed in the diaspora. Besides Soviet Armenia, the Armenian communities of the USA, France, Italy, Egypt, Syria, Iran, and particularly of Lebanon, have been the major centers of Armenian culture and literature to the present day.

Modern Western Armenian

Modern Western Armenian was a literary medium even from the early decades

of the eighteenth century, which marked the initial stages of the Armenian
Awakening. Its distinct literary features took shape as it began to be used
widely in books intended for public circulation and in the periodical press.
By the middle of the nineteenth century, Western Armenian was a developed
literary language comprehensible to almost all Western Armenians. Although it
was based on the dialect of Constantinople, in due course numerous features of
other Western Armenian dialects were incorporated by Armenians who had emigrated
to Constantinople from Armenia proper.

In the second half of the nineteenth century, Modern Western Armenian pre-
vailed as the literary standard, despite strong opposition from the admirers of
Classical Armenian. The modern vernacular was purified, it acquired fixed
linguistic patterns, and was molded into an extremely flexible linguistic tool,
expressed in a remarkable body of literature. In the twentieth century Modern
Western Armenian underwent considerable changes, both in its spoken and written
versions. If Modern Eastern Armenian has been subject to the strong influence
of Russian, Modern Western Armenian has, to a lesser degree, been influenced by
several Eastern or European languages, due to the world-wide dispersion of the
Western Armenians. Modern Western Armenian, unlike Modern Eastern Armenian,
did not become a state language and has, therefore, never been subject to control
over those aspects of the language that can be regulated through uniform instruc-
tion and academic institutions.

Capital		l.c.		Armenian name	guide to pronunciation	numerical value
Ա	*Ա*	ա	*ա*	այբ	a as in far	1
Բ	*Բ*	բ	*բ*	բեն	p as in pen	2
Գ	*Գ* (Գ)	գ	*գ* (Գ)	գիմ	k as in kid	3
Դ	*Դ*	դ	*դ*	դա	t as in top	4
Ե	*Ե*	ե	*ե* (Ե)	եչ	e as in pen; *initial*: ye as in yes	5
Զ	*Զ*	զ	*զ*	զա	z as in zoo	6
Է	*Է*	է	*է*	է	e as in pen	7
Ը	*Ը*	ը	*ը*	ըթ	as in about	8
Թ	*Թ*	թ	*թ*	թո	t as in top	9
Ժ	*Ժ*	ժ	*ժ*	դէ	s as in leisure	10
Ի	*Ի*	ի	*ի*	ինի	ee as in meet	20
Լ	*Լ*	լ	*լ*	լիւն	l as in low	30
Խ	*Խ*	խ	*խ*	խէ	ch as in German Aachen	40
Ծ	*Ծ*	ծ	*ծ*	ծա	dz as in adze	50
Կ	*Կ*	կ	*կ*	կեն	g as in goose	60
Հ	*Հ*	հ	*հ*	հն	h as in hat	70
Ձ	*Ձ*	ձ	*ձ*	ձա	tz as in blitz	80
Ղ	*Ղ*	ղ	*ղ*	ղատ	γ as in modern Greek γάλα	90
Ճ	*Ճ*	ճ	*ճ*	ճէ	j as in joy	100
Մ	*Մ*	մ	*մ*	մեն	m as in mat	200
Յ	*Յ*	յ	*յ*	յի	y as in yes; *initial*: h as in hat; *final*: silent, except in monosyllabic nouns	300
Ն	*Ն*	ն	*ն*	նու	n as in no	400

5

Շ	*Շ*	շ	*շ*	*շա*	sh as in <u>sh</u>ip	500
Ո	*Ո*	ո	*ո*	*վո*	o as in <u>o</u>pera; *initial:* <u>vo</u> as in <u>vo</u>lley, except when followed by *վ*	600
Չ	*Չ*	չ	*չ*	*չա*	<u>ch</u> as in chur<u>ch</u>	700
Պ	*Պ*	պ	*պ*	*պէ*	b as in <u>b</u>et	800
Ջ	*Ջ*	ջ	*ջ*	*ջէ*	<u>ch</u> as <u>ch</u>urch	900
Ռ	*Ռ*	ռ	*ռ*	*ռա*	r (rolled) as in <u>r</u>oyal	1,000
Ս	*Ս*	ս	*ս*	*սէ*	s as in <u>s</u>eat	2,000
Վ	*Վ*	վ	*վ*	*վեւ*	v as in <u>v</u>olley	3,000
Տ	*Տ*	տ	*տ*	*տիւն*	d as in <u>d</u>eep	4,000
Ր	*Ր*	ր	*ր*	*րէ*	r as in <u>r</u>est	5,000
Ց	*Ց*	ց	*ց*	*ցո*	tz as in bli<u>tz</u>	6,000
Ւ	*Ւ*	ւ	*ւ*	*յիւն*	v as in <u>v</u>olley; <u>oo</u> after *ի*, except in final position or when followed by a vowel	7,000
Փ	*Փ*	փ	*փ*	*փիւր*	p as in <u>p</u>en	8,000
Ք	*Ք*	ք	*ք*	*քէ*	k as in <u>k</u>id	9,000
Օ	*Օ*	օ	*օ*	*o*	o as in <u>o</u>pera	
Ֆ	*Ֆ*	ֆ	*ֆ*	*ֆէ*	f as in <u>F</u>rench	
ու					<u>oo</u> as in g<u>oo</u>se; before a vowel, v as in <u>v</u>olley.	

In modern Western Armenian numerous distinctions of the classical tongue have been lost, and important changes in the pronunciation of some vowels and consonants have taken place. This poses problems for spelling, since the same sound may reflect one of two different letters. Thus:

Vowels: [ա, ե, է, ը, ի, ն, o, ու]: ե and է are identical, except in initial position; e.g. գետ (river) and սէր (love) have the same vowel sound; but in երես (face) there is an initial glide, absent in էշ (donkey).

ո and o are identical, except in initial position. E.g., սով (famine) and մօտ (near) have the same vowel sound, but in որ (which) there is an initial /v/ *(vor)* absent in oդ (weather). [However, before վ ո is pronounced /o/, thus ով (who) *ov* (not */vov/*).]

ը is rarely written except in initial position, when words are hyphenated, or in some compounds. However, it is a very common vowel in spoken Armenian. The position of this unwritten vowel is not always obvious; for details see the Appendix on *Consonantal Clusters*.

Consonants: The following pairs have identical pronunciation:

 պ and փ: պարեկամ (friend), փառք (glory)

ք and բ: գայլ (wolf), քաղաք (city)

 դ and թ: դէմք (face), թատրոն (theater)

ծ and գ: ծեւ (form), գուցակ (list)

չ and ջ: չորս (four), ջուր (water)

վ and ւ: վաղը (tomorrow), լաւ (good)

Diphthongs:

ւյ   pronounced /ay/ Հայկ (proper name), except in final position, when

it is pronounced /a/ արքայ (king), կու լայ (weeps). But monosyl-

labic nouns (not verbs) retain the pronunciation /ay/ Հայ (Armenian).

եա   pronounced /ya/ սենեակ (room)

իւ   pronounced /iu/ միւս (other), but /iv/ in final position թիւ (num-

ber) and followed by a vowel դիւան (archive)

ոյ   pronounced /ui/ լոյս (light); but /o/ in final position ժողովածոյ

(collection), except /oy/ when followed by a vowel and in monosyllabic

nouns գոյական (substantive), խոյ (ram)

Syllables:

In Armenian syllables begin with a single consonant - except for words

beginning with a vowel. Note that the unwritten ը must often be inserted in

pronunciation. Syllables may end in an open vowel, a single consonant, or a

cluster.

Thus: Հարուստ   (rich):   Հա-րուստ

       անիկա   (he, she, it):   ա-նի-կա

       ամպոտ   (cloudy):   ամ-պոտ

       մարդ   (man):   մարդ

       նման   (like):   ն (ը) -ման

       գիրք   (book):   գիրք

       ինչպես   (how?):   ին չ-պես

       գեղեցիկ   (beautiful):   գե-ղե-ցիկ

Note that if a word begins with the combinations գբ, գգ, սթ, սկ, սպ, ստ,

սփ, սբ, the unwritten ը is pronounced *before* the initial consonant.

Thus: *qpwnwծ* (busy): *բq-բw-nwծ*

uկիqբ (beginning): *բu-կիqբ*

For full details see the *Appendix on Consonantal Clusters.*

Stress:

The stress in Armenian is placed on the last *full* syllable of a word: *բարեկա́մ, բաղա́բ* (but *բաղաբի́, բաղաբական, բաղաբակրութիւ́ն)* , *մէ́կբ,* *հա́յրս* (pronounced *հայ-րբ́u*).

Punctuation:

The following signs are specifically Armenian:

Period, Full Stop	*w:*	(*վերջակէտ*)
Colon or Semi-colon	*w.*	(*միջակէտ*)
Stop less than a comma; also used when phrases are in apposition, and when the repeated verb is omitted.	*w՝*	(*բութ*)
Exclamation	*ẃ*	(*երկար*)
Stress, sign of imperative	*ẃ*	(*շեշտ*)
Question mark	*w̃*	(*պարոյկ*)

The other signs have the same use as in English.

———————

Note to the reader

Words used as examples but not in the exercises are enclosed in brackets [ ].

1. *Personal Pronouns*

In Armenian there is no grammatical distinction of gender. The personal pronouns in the third person thus render the English *he/she/it*.

Nominative case

	Singular	Plural
1st person	ես	մենք
2nd person	դուն	դուք
3rd person	ան, անիկա, ինք(ը)	անոնք, իրենք

2. *Present Indicative of the verb "to be"*

	Singular	Plural
1st person	եմ	ենք
2nd person	ես	էք
3rd person	է	են

a) As in French or German, the 2nd person singular is only used to address friends or relatives.

b) The personal pronouns are not necessary with verbs except for emphasis or clarity.

E.g.   Հոս եմ: I am here.

Ան հոս է: *He/She* is here.

Note that the verbal forms եմ etc. are not stressed and that the ե has no initial glide: *hoś em*.

10

3. *Interrogative sentences*

The usual word order is Subject, Interrogative, Copula.* The question

mark ⌢ is placed over the stressed syllable of the interrogative word.

    E.g. *(Դուք) ի̂նչպես եք:*   How are you?

        Անոնք ու̂ր են: Where are they?

When there is no interrogative adverb, questions are rendered by a change

in stress, reflected in written Armenian by the ⌢ over the stressed word.

    E.g. *Անոնք հ̂ոս են:*   Are they *here?*

        Անո̂նք հոս են: Are *they* here?

For greater emphasis, the word order may be changed:

        Հ̂ոս են անոնք: Are they *here?*

4. *Negative*

The negative particle is *ոչ* "no, not." With verbs this reduces to *չ*,

prefixed to the verbal form.

    E.g. *Հոս չէ:*   He is not here.

        Հ̂ոս են: Ո́չ, հոս չեն: Are they here? No, they are

                                      not here.

Note the use of *չէ* as a general negative:

        Հ̂ոս են: Չէ́, հոս չեն: Are they here? No, they are

                                        not here.

        ճիշդ է, չէ̂:   That's right, isn't it?)

    (In this phrase, *չէ* cannot be replaced by *ոչ*.)

Cf. also Lesson II 4.

*I.e. the appropriate part of the verb "to be."

5. *Articles*

a) There is no separate form for a definite article in Armenian. Instead, the suffix -ը (-ն after a vowel) is used.

E.g.   հայրը   the father

         գիրքը   the book

         կատուն   the cat

         թիւը   the number

After a diphthong in monosyllabic nouns, -ը is used.

E.g.   հայը   the Armenian

         [հաւը   the chicken]

[This rule also applies to compounds if the last component is monosyllabic and ends in a diphthong.

E.g.   մակբայը   the adverb]

But if the original diphthong is pronounced as a simple vowel, i.e. in nouns of more than one syllable (except as just noted), -ն is used and the -յ is dropped.

E.g.   տղայ   boy   տղան   the boy

     cf. also երեկոյ   evening   երեկոն   the evening

Even after a consonant or diphthong -ն is used if the following word is a form of the present or imperfect indicative of the verb "to be" (եմ etc.) or ալ ("also") or ու ("and").

E.g.   Դուն հայրն ես: You are the father.

         հայրն ու մայրը   the father and the mother

         Հայրն ալ հոս է: The father also is here.

Before other following vowels hiatus occurs.

E.g.   Օրը ամպոտ է: The weather is cloudy.

         հայրը եւ մայրը   the father and the mother

Vocabulary: Lesson I

ալ	also, too	*ինք (ը)*	he, she, it
աղէկ	good; well	*իրենք*	they
ամպոտ	cloudy	*իրիկուն*	evening
այո	yes	*լաւ*	good; well
ան	he, she, it	*լոյս*	light
անիկա	he, she, it	*բարի լոյս*	good morning!
անձրեւոտ	rainy	*կատու*	cat
անոնք	they	*հայ*	Armenian (person)
ասիկա	this (pron.)	*հայր*	father
ատիկա	that (pron.)	*հոն*	there
արեւոտ	sunny	*հոս*	here
բարեւ	hello!	*ճիշդ*	right, correct; exact
բարի	good		precise (adj. & adv.)
գէշ	bad	*մայր*	mother
գիշեր	night	*մարդ*	man
գիրք	book	*մենք*	we
գործ	work,job,task,business	*մնաս բարով*	good-bye (said by
դուն	you (s.)		person leaving)
դուք	you (pl.)	*շատ*	very; (too) much, many
ես	I	*շնորհակալութիւն*	thanks
երթաս բարով	good-bye (response)	*ոչ*	no
եւ	and	*ու*	and
թիւ	number, figure	*ո՞ւր*	where?
ինչպէս	how?	*չէ*	no

պաղ	cold (adj. & noun)	ցտեսութիւն	good-bye; au revoir
տաք	hot	քանի մը	some, a few
տղայ	boy, son	օդ	air; weather

Greetings

Բարեւ:	Hello
Բարեւ:	(Response)
Բարի լոյս:	Good morning
Բարի լոյս:	(Response)
Բարի իրիկուն:	Good evening
Բարի իրիկուն:	(Response)
Գիշեր բարի:	Good night
Լոյս բարի:	(Response)
Մնաս բարով:	Good-bye
Երթաս բարով:	(Response)
Ցտեսութիւն:	Good-bye (au revoir)
Ցտեսութիւն:	(Response)

Ինչպէս ես:	How are you?
Աղէկ չեմ:	I am not well
Շատ աղէկ չեմ:	I am not very well
Լաւ չեմ:	I am not well
Շատ լաւ չեմ:	I am not very well
Աղէկ եմ, շնորհակալութիւն:	I am well, thank you
Լաւ եմ, շնորհակալութիւն:	I am well, thank you
Շատ լաւ եմ, շնորհակալութիւն: Դուք ինչպէս էք:	I'm very well, thank you; how are you?
Գործերը ինչպէս են:	How are things? (How is business?)
Շատ լաւ չեն:	Not very well
Գէշ չեն, շնորհակալութիւն:	Not bad, thanks
Լաւ են, շնորհակալութիւն:	Good, thank you
Շատ լաւ են, շնորհակալութիւն:	Very good, thank you

Weather

Հոս օդը տաք է:	Օդը ամպոտ է:
Հոն օդը տաք չէ:	Օդը արեւոտ է:
Հոս օդը պաղ է:	Օդը անձրեւոտ է:
Հոն օդը պաղ չէ:	

1.   Կատուն ո՞ւր է:

2.   Անիկա հոս չէ:

3.   Ճատ տաք է:

4.   Դուք ո՞ւր էք:

5.   Հայրը եւ մայրը հոն են:

6.   Տղան շատ բարի է:

7.   Ես շատ լաւ չեմ:

8.   Օրը ի՞նչպես է:

9.   Աննոք գեշ չեն:

10. Օրը անձրեւոտ չէ:

11. Բարեւ: Ի՞նչպես էք:

12. Ճնորհակալութիւն:

13. Թիւը ճիշդ է:

14. Մարդն ու տղան հոն են:

15. Մենք ադեկ ենք:

16. Հոն շատ պա՞ղ է:

17. Գիրքը լաւ չէ:

18. Օրը արեւոտ է:

19. Ան ադեկ չէ:

20. Դուն շատ ճիշդ ես:

21. Տղան եւ կատուն հոն են:

22. Անիկա հայ չէ՞:

23. Ո՞չ, ինքը հայ չէ:

24. Բարի լոյս: Օրը շատ լաւ է:

25. Ո՞չ, շատ ամպոտ է:

1. It is very rainy.

2. The book is good.

3. The night is cold.

4. He is correct.

5. The mother and father are not here.

6. How is the weather?

7. It is not very hot.

8. Thank you.

9. Hello! How are you?

10. We are well.

11. The number is not correct.

12. Where is the book?

13. Where are you (s.)?

14. I am here.

15. Is the book here?

16. He is well.

17. They are not well.

18. Is the man Armenian?

19. Where is he?

20. Good morning!

21. The weather is sunny.

22. It is cold.

23. Where are you (pl.)?

24. We are here.

25. They are not here.

1. The indefinite article is *մը* .

> E.g.   *գիրք մը*   a book
>
>   *տղայ մը*   a boy
>
>   *կատու մը*   a cat

Before a form of the present or imperfect of the verb "to be" (*եմ* etc.) and before *ալ* ("also"), the form *մըն* is used.

> E.g.   *Տղայ մըն է։*   He is a boy.

But   *տղայ մը ու աղջիկ մը*   a boy and a girl

2. *Adjectives*

a) Qualifying adjectives precede the noun (except for poetic emphasis):

>   *Հարուստ Հայ մըն է։*   He is a rich Armenian.
>
>   *Ան գեղեցիկ աղջիկ մըն է։*   She is a pretty girl.

b) Adjectives used as predicates remain in the singular. The usual word order is Subject, Predicate, Copula.

> E.g.   *Կատուն գեղեցիկ է։*   The cat is beautiful.
>
>   *Անոնք Հարուստ չեն։*   They are not rich.
>
>   *Հայրը աղքատ է։*   The father is poor.
>
>   *(Անոնք) առողջ են։*   They are well (healthy).

3. Predicative sentences with nouns follow a similar pattern.

> E.g.   *Անոնք Հա՞յ են։*   Are they Armenians?   (N.B.
>
>   singular predicate)
>
>   *Ան աշակերտ [մըն] է։*   He is a pupil.

18

When the subject belongs to a certain group or class, the indefinite article is not usually used.

4. *Negative* (cont.)

The simple verb plus negative cannot stand alone. E.g. "Are you an Armenian? No, I am not" must be rendered: *Հա՞յ էք: Ո՛չ, հա՛յ չեմ:* It is permissible to use *ոչ* alone.

Vocabulary: Lesson II

ազգ	nation	*ծաղիկ*	flower
աղջիկ	girl, daughter	*կամ; կամ...կամ*	or; either...or
աղքատ	poor	*կապոյտ*	blue
ամբողջ	complete, entire, whole	*հարուստ*	rich, wealthy
ամէն	each, every, all	*հին*	old, ancient
աշակերտ	pupil	*հիւանդ*	ill
աշխարհ	world	*մեծ*	great, big, large
առողջ	healthy	*նոր*	new; as adv.: recently
բայց	but	*շէնք*	building
բան	thing	*որդի*	son
բառ	word	*ուսանող*	student
բարեկամ	friend	*ուսուցիչ*	teacher (m.)
գեղեցիկ	beautiful, pretty	*ուսուցչուհի*	teacher (f.)
եկեղեցի	church	*պզտիկ*	little, small
եղբայր	brother	*սեւ*	black
երիտասարդ	young; young person	*տուն*	house, home
երկինք	sky, heaven	*քոյր*	sister
զաւակ	child	*օտար*	foreign (adj.);
ընկեր	friend, comrade		stranger, for-
ընտանիք	family		eigner (n.)
խելացի	intelligent, clever		

1. Աղջիկը հիւանդ է։

2. Եկեղեցին ո՞ւր է։

3. Տղան խելացի աշակերտ մըն է։

4. Ատիկա նոր շէնք մըն է։

5. Պզտիկ գաւակը ո՞ւր է։

6. Ուսուցիչը երիտասարդ է։

7. Երիտասարդը ուսուցիչ է։

8. Բան մը չէ։

9. Անոնք շատ աղքատ են։

10. Ամբողջ ազգը հարուստ է։

11. Երկինքը կապոյտ է։

12. Մենք աղողջ չենք։

13. Անոնք հա՞յ են։

14. Ո՛չ, օտար են։

15. Հոս ամէն տուն հին է։

16. Քոյրն ու եղբայրը ուսանող են։

17. Հին շէնքը սեւ է։

18. Սեւ կատուն հոս է։

19. Ան ալ ուսանող մըն է։

20. Կա՛մ հայ է, կա՛մ օտար։

21. Աշխարհը մեծ է։ Երկինքը շատ մեծ է։

22. Ամբողջ ընտանիքը հիւանդ է։

23. Ծաղիկը կապոյտ է։

24. Հայրը ծիշդ է։

25. Ան հարուստ է, բայց բարեկամը աղքատ է։

1. The big building is the church.

2. The church is the big building.

3. The whole family is here.

4. She is an intelligent girl.

5. The house is very small.

6. The old building is large.

7. The brother and sister are ill.

8. The friend is young.

9. The beautiful girl is the teacher.

10. The flower is blue.

11. They are well, but we (are) ill.

12. Are you ill? No, I am not.

13. They, too, are foreigners.

14. The father and the son are intelligent.

15. Are you (pl.) students?

16. That is a great task.

17. He is a good man.

18. The Armenian nation is very old.

19. Where is the church?

20. Are you the teacher?

21. The sky is blue.

22. Every word is correct.

23. The child is a good pupil.

24. The family is rich.

1. *Present Indicative of Verbs with Infinitives in* -ɨ ̣

In modern Armenian nearly all verbs fall into one of three categories which are distinguished by the vowel of the Infinitive and of the present indicative: -ɨ ̣ (-ɨʃ), -ʰ ̣ (-ʰʃ) or -ʍ ̣ (-ʍʃ).

With very few exceptions, the indeclinable prefix ʮ (ʮ' before vowels) precedes the conjugated form. [Before monosyllabic verbs the form is ʮʟ; see Lesson V.]

The endings for the present indicative of verbs with infinitives in -ɨ ̣ are the same as the forms of the verb "to be." Thus for the verb uʰɲɨʃ "to love" the paradigm is as follows:

	Singular	Plural
1st person	ʮ uʰɲɨʃ	ʮ uʰɲɨʮ ̣
2nd person	ʮ uʰɲɨu	ʮ uʰɲɨ ̣
3rd person	ʮ uʰɲɨ	ʮ uʰɲɨʮ

Note that the personal pronouns are primarily used for emphasis.

E.g.	ʮ uʰɲɨʮ ̣:	We love.
	Uɨʮ ̣ ʮ uʰɲɨʮ ̣:	We love.
	ʔʰ ̣ʮ ̣ ʮ uʰɲɨ ̣:	Do you love?

2. *The Object of Transitive Verbs*

For the moment, it is sufficient to note that with the majority of verbs the subject and object are not distinguished by any change in form but merely by their position in the sentence; i.e., the nominative and accusative cases are identical in form. (For the declension of nouns see Lesson VI ff.)

23

The word order of simple transitive sentences is usually Subject, Object, Verb.

E.g. *Տղան կատուն կը սիրէ:*   The boy loves the cat.

Հայրը նամակ մը կը գրէ: The father is writing a letter.

3. *Demonstratives*

A. Adjectives. In Armenian there is a threefold distinction for demonstrative adjectives.

այս   this (by me); also *աս, սա*

այդ   that (by you); also *ատ*

այն   that (over there); also *ան*

Note that the definite article must be used with demonstrative adjectives:

E.g. *այս գիրքը*   this book

այդ կատուն   that cat

There are some exceptions with expressions of time:

այս առտու   this morning

The form *այդ* is as usual for "that" as the form *այն*.

B. Pronouns. The forms *աս ի, ատ ի, ան ի* are widely used in conversation as demonstrative pronouns:

E.g. *Ասի լաւ մարդ մըն է:*   He is a good man.

Ատի գեղեցիկ է: She is pretty.

Անի ուսանող է: He/She is a student.

Note the extended forms: *ասիկա, ատիկա, անիկա.* They are used as pronouns with more nuance of reference than the simple *ան*. Plurals: *ասոնք, ատոնք, ան*

4. *Possessive Suffixes*

The suffixes *-ս* and *-դ* are used as possessives for the 1st and 2nd pers. singular, "my," "your (s.)." The use of *-ն* as a definite article has been noted in Lesson I 5.   (Cf. §3 above: *այ_ս_, այ_ղ_, այ_ն_.*)

E.g.   *գիրքս*   my book

գիրքղ   your (s.) book

but   *գիրքը, գիրքն ալ*   the book

5.   The definite article is used in several situations in Armenian where English
would have no article.

   a)   It is used with proper nouns: always for the object, and by some
speakers for the subject:

   E.g.   *Տիգրան Անին կը սիրէ:*   Dikran loves Ani.

               (but some would say *Տիգրանը Անին....*)

   b)   It is used in general expressions for the subject, but not the object.

   E.g.   *Մենք գինի կը խմենք:*   We drink wine.

      but   *Գ_ի_նին համով է:*   Wine (in general) is tasty.

26

Vocabulary: Lesson III

այդ; ատ, ատի	that	*խնծոր*	apple
այն; ան, անի	that	*կաթ*	milk
այս; աս, ասի, սա	this	*համ*	taste, flavor
Անահիտ	Anahid (fem. name)	*համով*	tasty
Անի	Ani (fem. name)	*Հայկ*	Hayg (male name)
անուն	name	*հաց*	bread
առտու	morning	*ճերմակ*	white
գարեջուր	beer	*նախընտրել*	to prefer
գինի	wine	*նամակ*	letter
գնել	to buy	*ուզել*	to want
գոյն	color	*ուտել*	to eat
գրել	to write	*ուրախ*	glad, happy
դասարան	class (room)	*ջուր*	water
դպրոց	school	*սիրել*	to love, like
դրամ	money	*Վաչէ*	Vache (male name)
ընտրել	to choose, select	*տեսնել*	to see
ի՞նչ	what?	*Տիգրան*	Dikran (male name)
խմել	to drink	*օր*	day
խնդրել	to ask, request	*այսօր*	today

1. Ձաւակը կաթ կը սիրէ:

2. Պաղ ջուր կ'ուզեմ:

3. Այս առու ՀագՀ կ'ունեմ:

4. Տիգրան կը նախընտրէ զարեջուր խմել:

5. Անահիտ նամակ մը կը գրէ:

6. Ուսուցիչը կը տեսնեմ:

7. Անունդ ի՞նչ է: Անունս Անի է:

8. Մայրն ալ գեղեցիկ է, աղջիկն ալ:

9. Այս ՀագԸ Համով չէ:

10. Աշակերտը դպրոցը շատ կը սիրէ:

11. Դասարանդ ու՞ր է:

12. Ի՞նչ կը գնես:

13. Այսոր Հայկ գինի կը խմէ:

14. Դպրոցը մեծ շէնք մըն է:

15. Այս գիշեր օրը շատ աղեկ է:

16. Կաթ ու Հագ կը գնես:

17. Այս գոյնը կը սիրե՞ս:

18. Ուսանողը դրամ կը խնդրէ:

19. Այո՛, դուք շատ ծիշդ էք:

20. Նոր տուն մը կը գնես:

21. Ուրա՞խ էք: Այո՛, շատ ուրախ ենք:

22. Այսոր Վաչէն Հոս չէ:

23. Համը ի՞նչպէս է:

24. Խնձոր կը սիրէ՞ք:

25. Հայկ Անին կը տեսնէ:

1. What are they eating? They are eating white bread.

2. I see a big building.

3. Where is your (s.) house? My house is there.

4. Would you like an apple?

5. The classroom is very small.

6. I drink milk every morning.

7. We are writing a letter.

8. The father and son are drinking beer.

9. They are very happy.

10. Vache is an intelligent student.

11. What are you (pl.) eating?

12. Do you (pl.) want water?

13. My name is not Ani, it's Anahid.

14. This apple is very tasty.

15. He is buying a book.

16. Does Dikran like my friend?

17. Your (s.) teacher is very young.

18. Do you (s.) like your job?

19. They want hot water.

20. I am selecting a book.

21. Do you see the church?

22. The cat prefers milk.

23. Hayg is ill today.

24. My school is that white building.

1. *Plurals of nouns*

A. Monosyllabic nouns add -եր to the singular form.

    E.g.   գիրքը   the book   գիրքերը   the books

              հայր մը   a father   հայրեր   fathers

              [ձի մը   a horse   ձիեր   horses]

B. Polysyllabic nouns add -ներ to the singular form.

    E.g.   բարեկամը   the friend   բարեկամներր   the friends

But note:

a) Polysyllabic nouns ending in -այ lose the յ before -ներ.

    E.g.   քահանայ   priest   քահանաներ   priests

(The plural of մղայ is usually մղաք, and of ծնող, ծնողք "parents.")*

    Monosyllabic հայ etc. are regular: հայեր etc.

b) Several nouns, monosyllabic but originally with a final -ն , have lost the ն in the singular but sometimes retain it in the plural.

    E.g.   լեռ   mountain (< լեռն) but լեռներ mountains - also լեռեր

          դուռ   door (< դուռն) but դռներ**, դուռեր.

c) Many compounds whose last component is monosyllabic have plurals in -եր :

    [E.g.   Ամերիկահայ (American-Armenian) - Ամերիկահայեր.]

2. *Numbers*

    The cardinal numbers from one to ten are:

* I.e. the two parents of a given child. If many parents are indicated, the forms ծնողներ or ծնողքներ are used. The -ք is the classical nom. pl. marker.

** For the reduction of -ու- see p. 241.

մէկ	one	*վեց*	six
երկու	two	*եօթը*	seven
երեք	three	*ութը*	eight
չորս	four	*ինը*	nine
հինգ	five	*տասը*	ten

3. In several respects Armenian differs from English in the use of singular nouns where plurals might be expected. See esp. 8b and d.

a) Qualifying adjectives remain in the singular.

E.g.   *այս հին գիրքերը*   these old books

       հայ հայրեր   Armenian fathers

b) After cardinal numbers indefinite nouns are singular:

E.g.   *Ես երկու աղջիկ կը սիրեմ:*   I love two girls.

But if the noun is emphsized or is definite, or if it is qualified by an adjective, it is usually put into the plural:

E.g.   *երկու նոր տուներ*   two new houses

       երեք զաւակները   the three children

If the noun is singular in form and the verb is transitive, the latter is put in the plural:

Երկու հոգի այդ աղջիկը կը սիրեն: Two people love that girl.

But if the verb is intransitive or passive, it is usually put in the singular. See further Lessons V 6 and XXV 6.

c) The same rule applies with the interrogative *քանի՞* "how many?" and with *շատ*, "many":

E.g.   *քանի՞ մարդ:*   how many people?

       շատ մարդ   many people

d) The singular is also used for general statements:

E.g. Խնձոր կը սիրեմ: I like apples.

      Խնձորը համով է: Apples are tasty.

(For use of the article see Lesson III 5b.)

      Հայրս նամակ կը գրէ: Father is writing letters.

4. Adjectives with the definite article or indefinite article can be used as substantives:

E.g. Հարուստները   the rich (i.e. rich people in

                                          general)

      Հարուստ մը   a rich person

      Հարուստը   the rich person

5. *There is, there are*

In modern Armenian the third person forms, singular and plural, of the verb կամ "I exist" are used to express the English "there is, there are": sing.: կայ; plural: կան .

The negatives are չկայ and չկան respectively (cf. I 4: չեմ etc.).

E.g. Եկեղեցին ո՞ւր է: Հոս   Where is the church? There is

      եկեղեցի չկայ: no church here.

      Հոն շատ հայ կայ: There are many Armenians there.

      (Note sing. verb with sing. subj.)

      Հոս հարուստ շատ հայեր   There are many rich Armenians

      կան: here.

      Հոս քանի՞ հոգի կայ: How many (people) are there

      Վեց (հոգի):   here? Six.

      Քանի՞ հոգի էք: How many are you?

N.b. *ինչ* "person" must be supplied; *քանի̂* cannot stand alone. Sometimes *ինչ*
is also used after numbers.

Note that for things (not persons) *հատ* is used in response.

> E.g. How many apples have you?   *Քանի̂ խնձոր ունիք:* *

> Six.   *Վեց:* or *Վեց հատ:* or *Վեց խնձոր:*

> But: I have six.   *Վեց հատ ունիմ:* *

6. *Expressions of measure and quantity*

In Armenian the complement to an expression of measure or quantity remains
in the absolute (= nominative).

> E.g.   a cup *of* tea   *գաւաթ մը թէյ*

> a glass *of* water   *բաժակ մը ջուր*

> three litres *of* milk   *երեք լիտր կաթ*

> two boxes *of* cigarettes   *երկու տուփ ծխախոտ*

Note that when such expressions are the subject of a verb the definite
article is used.

> E.g. A glass of milk is good (for you).   *Գաւաթ մը կաթ̲ը̲ լաւ է:*

> But: I am buying two glasses of beer.   *Երկու բաժակ գարեջուր*

>   *կը գնեմ:*

---

* For the verb *ունիմ* etc. see Lesson VIII 3.

Vocabulary: Lesson IV

ամերիկացի	American (person)	*ծառ*	tree
անգամ	time, occasion	*ծխախոտ*	tobacco
անգամ մը	once	*ծնողք*	parents
արժել	to be worth, cost	*կայ, կան*	there is, there are
բաժակ	drinking glass	*հատ*	see Lesson IV, 6.
բարձր	high; loud	*հինգ*	five
գաւաթ	cup	*հոգի*	person
գործաւոր	workman	*մատ (մատներ)*	finger
գոց	closed, shut	*մեծ հայր*	grandfather
գոցել	to close, shut	*մեծ մայր*	grandmother
դուռ	door	*մեթր*	meter
երեք	three	*մէկ*	one
երկար	long	*շաբաթ*	week
երկու	two	*շինել*	to make, build
երկուքն ալ	both	*ութը*	eight
եօթը	seven	*ուրիշ*	other
էջ	page	*չորս*	four
ընել	to do	*սուրճ*	coffee
ըսել	to say, tell	*վեց*	six
ըսել ուզել	to mean	*տասը*	ten
թէյ	tea	*տարբեր*	different
ժամ	hour	*տուփ*	box, pack (of
ինը	nine		cigarettes)
լեռ (լեռներ)	mountain	*քահանայ*	priest (married)
լիտր	litre	*քանի*	how many?

1. Աղջիկները լիար մը կաթ կը գնեն:

2. Ամէն շաբաթ գիրք մը կը գնեմ:

3. Ամերիկացիները գարեջուր շատ կը խմեն:

4. Հոս բարձր շէնքեր չկան:

5. Երեք տուփ ծխախոտը քանի՞ կ'արժէ:

6. Ինչ՞ ըսել կ'ուզէք:

7. Այսօր աշակերտներդ ինչ՞ կ'ընեն:

8. Եօթը գործաւոր նոր շէնք մը կը շինեն:

9. Այդ երկու լեռները շատ բարձր են:

10. Դուք քանի՞ ճաշի էք: Չորս ճաշի ենք:

11. Տիգրան տարբեր գիրքեր կ'ընտրէ:

12. Ամբողջ ընտանիքը քանի՞ ճաշի է:

13. Մատներդ երկար եւ գեղեցիկ են:

14. Բաժակ մը գինի կ'ուզե՞ս:

15. Ծնողքդ ինչ՞ գործ կ'ընեն:

16. Քանի՞ խնձոր կ'ուզէք: Վեց հատ:

17. Եղբայրներդ առո՞ղջ են:

18. Գաւաթ մը թէյ կը խմէ՞ք:

19. Այս հին տունը քանի՞ կ'արժէ:

20. Այս գիրքը կ'ուզէ՞ք: Ո՞չ, ուրիշ մը չկա՞յ:

21. Քանի՞ կատու կը տեսնես:

22. Անի դուռը կը գոցէ:

23. Հայկ մեծ տուփ մը կը շինէ:

24. Այդ ութը բարձր ծառերը կը տեսնե՞ս:

1. Are these young men Armenian?

2. How are your (s.) children? They are both ill.

3. Vache is buying four packs of cigarettes.

4. I'll do the job another time. (present tense)

5. I see my friends. What do you see?

6. There are three Armenian priests here.

7. Are the boys drinking coffee?

8. They are saying bad things.

9. The nights are very cold here.

10. Your friends are very good.

11. Where is the school? There is no school here.

12. How much do these glasses cost?

13. What do your parents mean?

14. There are ten people there.

15. How many workmen are there here? Seven.

16. The day is very long.

17. How many pages (long) is the letter? Nine.

18. Does your (s.) grandfather eat very much?

19. Both of them are healthy.

20. Would you like a cup of tea?

21. No, I prefer a glass of beer or wine.

22. Dikran drinks five glasses of milk every day.

23. My sister buys flowers every day.

1. *Present Indicative of verbs in* -ի լ, -ա լ

Verbs with infinitives in -ի լ and -ա լ have corresponding present indicatives in -իմ and -ամ . E.g. հասնի լ "to arrive," երթա լ "to go":

	Singular	Plural
1st person	կը հասնիմ, կ' երթամ	կը հասնինք, կ' երթանք
2nd person	կը հասնիս, կ' երթաս	կը հասնիք, կ' երթաք
3rd person	կը հասնի, կ' երթայ	կը հասնին, կ' երթան

Note that with the three monosyllabic verbs գա լ, լա լ, տա լ the կը is
replaced by կու . Thus the present indicative of տա լ "to give" is:
կու տամ, կու տաս, կու տայ, կու տանք, կու տաք, կու տան.

2. *Negative of the Present Indicative*

The negative of regular verbs in the -ե լ, -ի լ and -ա լ groups is formed
by combining the negative of the present tense of the verb "to be" with an
indeclinable participle. This participle consists of the present stem of the
verb plus an ending -եր (for verbs in -ե լ), -իր (for verbs in -ի լ), or -ար
(for verbs in -ա լ).

Note, however, that the 3.p.s. negative form is not չէ but չի (չ'
before vowels).

Thus for verbs in -ե լ :

	Singular	Plural
1st person	չեմ սիրեր	չենք սիրեր
2nd person	չես սիրեր	չէք սիրեր
3rd person	չի սիրեր	չեն սիրեր

(from ըսե լ: չ'ըսեր)

36

Likewise for verbs in $-hl$ and $-wl$:

	Singular	Plural
1st person	չեմ հասնիր, չեմ երթար	չենք հասնիր, չենք երթար
2nd person	չես հասնիր, չես երթար	չէք հասնիր, չէք երթար
3rd person	չի հասնիր, չ'երթար	չեն հասնիր, չեն երթար

3. *The Imperfect Indicative*

The imperfect indicative of the verb "to be" is formed as follows:

	Singular	Plural
1.	էի	էինք
2.	էիր	էիք
3.	էր	էին

The imperfect indicative of verbs in $-bl$ and $-hl$ is formed with these same
endings; as in the present indicative, the particle կը (or կ' before vowels)
precedes the conjugated form:

1.	կը սիրէի,	կը խօսէի	կը սիրէինք,	կը խօսէինք
2.	կը սիրէիր,	կը խօսէիր	կը սիրէիք,	կը խօսէիք
3.	կը սիրէր,	կը խօսէր	կը սիրէին,	կը խօսէին

The imperfect indicative of verbs in $-wl$ has the diphthong $-wj-$ in all forms
except the 3.p.s. As in the present indicative, monosyllabic verbs in $-wl$ have
the particle կու instead of կը. Thus from կարդալ ("to read"):

1.	կը կարդայի,	կու տայի,	կը կարդայինք,	կու տայինք
	կ'երթայի etc.			
2.	կը կարդայիր,	կու տայիր	կը կարդայիք,	կու տայիք
3.	կը կարդար,	կու տար	կը կարդային,	կու տային

4. *Negative of the Imperfect Indicative*

The negative of these imperfects is formed by combining the negative imperfect of the verb *եմ* with the same indeclinable participle as is used for the negative of the present indicative, EXCEPT that verbs in *-իլ* have *-եր* (NOT *-իր*) for the imperfect.

Singular

1.   չէի սիրեր, չէի խօսեր, չէի կարդար

2.   չէիր սիրեր, չէիր խօսեր, չէիր կարդար

3.   չէր սիրեր, չէր խօսեր, չէր կարդար

Plural

1.   չէինք սիրեր, չէինք խօսեր, չէինք կարդար

2.   չէիք սիրեր, չէիք խօսեր, չէիք կարդար

3.   չէին սիրեր, չէին խօսեր, չէին կարդար

Note, therefore, that in both the positive and negative imperfect indicative the forms for verbs in *-ել* and *-իլ* are similar.

Note that the imperfect negative of *կայ* is *չկար, չկային*.

5. Many verbs in *-իլ* are intransitive. In such cases, a subject which is logically plural but grammatically singular usually entails a singular verb.

E.g.   Երկու տարին շուտ կ՚անցնի: The two years (will) pass

quickly.

Vocabulary: Lesson V

ամիս	month	*հասնիլ*	to arrive, reach
անցնիլ	to pass, cross	*հիմա*	now; just (of time)
աշխատիլ	to work; try	*ճանչնալ*	to know (a person), recognize
բանալ	to open		
գալ	to come; as adj.: next	*մաքրել*	to clean
դաս	lesson, class	*միշտ*	always, ever
երթալ	to go	*յիշել*	to remember
զբաղած	busy	*շուտ*	quickly
ինչո՞ւ	why?	*պտուղ*	fruit
լալ	to cry, weep	*սորվիլ*	to learn
խոսիլ	to talk, speak to	*վստահ*	sure, certain
կայարան	station	*տալ*	to give
կարդալ	to read	*տարի*	year
համալսարան	university	*փողոց*	street
համրել	to count	*փորձել*	to try, attempt
հայկական	Armenian (adj.)	*քաղաք*	city, town
հանգստանալ	to rest	*օրաթերթ*	(daily) newspaper

1. Ուսանողները ամէն օր դաս կ՚ընեն։

2. Անունս չե՞ս յիշեր։

3. Այս ծառերը ամէն տարի պտուղ կու տան։

4. Թարեկամս շատ կը սիրեմ։

5. Ամէն շաբաթ փողոցները կը մաքրեն։

6. Ինչո՞ւ դասերդ չես կարդար։

7. Աշակերտները համբել կը սորվին։

8. Հայկական դպրոցը ու՞ր է։

9. Մայրդ ինչո՞ւ կու լար։

10. Աննռք շատ կը խոսին։

11. Այսօր գործաւորները չեն աշխատիր։

12. Ամէն առու այդ օրաթերթը կը կարդանք։

13. Հայրդ ու՞ր կ՚աշխատէր։

14. Երթայրները շատ հիւանդ էին բայց հիմա առողջ են։

15. Ուսուցիչը գիրքը կը թանայ։

16. Անահիտը կը ճանչնա՞նք։

17. Ամէն իրիկուն վաչէ Անին կը տեսնէր։

18. Ամէն մարդ հոն կ՚երթար։

19. Աշխատիլ կ՚ուզէին, բայց գործ չկար։

20. Հայկ այդ օրը շատ զբաղած էր։

21. Մայրս կ՚ուզէր պտուղ գնել։

22. Հիմա գործաւորները կը հանգստանան։

23. Վստա՞հ էք։ Այո՛, վստահ ենք։

24. Տղան դրամ կը խնդրէր, բայց աննք չէին տար։

1. The children are learning to read.

2. The fruit was very tasty.

3. I used to buy a newspaper every day.

4. Anahid was reading her lesson.

5. They are counting the books.

6. What was he saying?

7. They talk too much.

8. We didn't want to go.

9. I used to clean the house every month.

10. The teacher does not remember your name.

11. I am certain now.

12. Ani was resting this morning.

13. Intelligent students always try to do the lessons.

14. You are ill, why don't you rest?

15. Are you (pl.) busy this week?

16. The sick child was crying all night.

17. What were they doing? They were buying books.

18. I used to see my parents every week.

19. The rich used to give much money.

20. Why don't you learn to read?

21. What was Dikran drinking? He was drinking wine.

22. Were they very happy?

23. What did Ani want?

24. The weather was very cold.

25. The young man was opening the door.

1. *Declension of Nouns (Part A)*

In modern Western Armenian there are six cases for substantives (nouns, pronouns, adjectives, infinitives, some participles). However, only personal pronouns have different forms for each of the six cases; some pronouns have different forms for five cases. But in all other substantives there is no distinction between the Nominative and Accusative, or between the Genitive and Dative.

One of the major difficulties of Armenian is that there are numerous categories of nouns. In some respects the complexity of the classical declensions has been modified, but new groups have been formed, and sometimes old and new forms co-exist. With most nouns, however, if the nominative and genitive singular are known the other cases can be deduced.

Except for some fossilized classical endings, all plurals have the same endings. Problems arise only with the singular.

The largest category of nouns in modern Western Armenian has the following endings:

   -*ի*   for the Genitive and Dative,

   -*է*   for the Ablative,

   -*ով* for the Instrumental.

Thus for *գրիչ* "pen" and *լեզու* "language" we have the following paradigms:

42

	Singular		Plural	
Nom/Acc.	գրիչ	լեզու	գրիչներ	լեզուներ
Gen/Dat.	գրիչի	լեզուի	գրիչներու	լեզուներու
Ablative	գրիչէ	լեզուէ	գրիչներէ	լեզուներէ
Instrumental	գրիչով	լեզուով	գրիչներով	լեզուներով

Note the parallels between the endings for singular and plural EXCEPT IN THE GENITIVE/DATIVE.

2. The various cases are used to express different meanings or roles within a sentence. Many of the nuances will be introduced later; the basic distinctions are the following:

Nominative: used for the subject of all verbs and for the predicate with the verb "to be":

E.g. Այդ մարդը հարուստ/ուսուցիչ է: *That man is rich/a teacher.*

Այս տղան նամակ մը կը գրէ: This boy is writing a letter.

Accusative: used for the direct object of most active verbs:

Այս տղան նամակ մը կը գրէ: This boy is writing *a letter.*

Դուք հարցում մը կը հարցնէք: You are asking *a question.*

Տունս կը տեսնե՞ս: Do you see *my house?*

Հարուստները դրամը կը սիրեն: Rich men love *money.*

(Note the use of the definite article; cf. Lessons III, IV.)

Genitive: used to indicate possession:

Երեւանի փողոցները լայն են: The streets *of Erevan* are wide.

Այդ ուսանողին հայրը *That student's* father is a

    ուսուցիչ է: teacher.

Մենք ընկերներուդ ընկերները We do not love *your friends'*

    չենք սիրեր: friends.

Dative: used for the indirect object of transitive verbs, and for the direct object of a few verbs:

Ծնողքիս նամակ կը գրեմ:	I am writing a letter *to my parents.*
Ինչո՞ւ ամէն շաբաթ նամակ կը ղրկես ծնողքիդ:	Why do you send *your parents* a letter every week?
Ընկերներուս կը սպասեմ:	I am waiting *for my friends.*
Ան ուսուցիչին հարցում մը կը հարցնէ:	He is asking *the teacher* a question.

Ablative: used to indicate the place from which movement begins or something is taken:

Այդ խանութէն ծաղիկներ կը գնէ:	He is buying flowers *from* that shop.

Instrumental: used to indicate the means by which an action is accomplished:

Ես ծնողքիս կը խօսիմ հեռաձայնով:	I am speaking to my parents *by* telephone (*on* the telephone).
Ան միշտ ինքնաշարժով կը ճամբորդէ:	She always travels *by* car (train/ boat, etc.).

Note the use of genitive and ablative when describing part of a whole.

a) The genitive is used if the part is a noun.

E.g. the majority of the Armenians	հայերուն մեծ մասը
some of those girls	այդ աղջիկներուն մէկ մասը

b) The ablative is used if the part is described numerically.

E.g. five of these girls	այս աղջիկներէն հինգը*

Քանի մը (a few) and մաս մը (some) also fall into this category.

a few of these students	այս ուսանողներէն քանի մը հոգ

* Note the definite article if there is no qualifying noun: cf. մէկը, երկուքը, երեքը, etc.

Note the order in which plural suffixes, case endings and demonstrative suffixes occur:

E.g.   գիրք, գիրքը, գիրքս, գիրքդ.

գրքի, գրքին, գրքիս, գրքիդ.

գրքեր, գրքերը, գրքերս, գրքերդ.

գրքերէ, գրքերէն, գրքերէս, գրքերէդ.

3. *Diminutive suffix* -իկ

The suffix -իկ is widely used in Armenian to form diminutives. E.g.

հայր - հայրիկ	father
մայր - մայրիկ	mother
քոյր - քոյրիկ	sister

These are declined regularly (-ի, -է, ով) as opposed to հայր etc.; see Lesson XIV.

Vocabulary: Lesson VI

ազնիւ	kind	լայն	broad, wide
այդպիսի	such (like that)	լեզու, -ի	tongue, language
այժմ	now	լսել	to hear (dat. of pers.)
այնպիսի	such (like that)	խաղալ	to play
այսպիսի	such (like this)	խանութ, -ի	shop
այցելել	to visit (+ dat. for persons)	հարցնել	to ask, inquire
		հարցում, -ի	question
արագ	fast	հեռաձայն, -ի	telephone
բժիշկ, -ի	doctor, physician	որկել	to send
գին, -ի	price	ճամբորդել	to travel
գործածել	to use	մաս, -ի	part
գրիչ, -ի	pen	մատիտ, -ի	pencil
դժուար	hard, difficult	ներկայ	present (adj.)
դիւրին	easy	շոգեկառք, -ի	train
երբեմն	sometimes, occasionally	շուկայ, -ի	market
Երեւան	Erevan (capital of Armenian S.S.R.)	պատասխանել	to answer, reply
		պարտէզ, -ի	garden
երկայն	long	սպասել	to wait for, expect (+ dat. of person)
երջանիկ	happy		
ինքնաշարժ, -ի	car, automobile	օդանաւ, -ի	airplane

1. Բարեկամիդ մայրը շատ ազնիւ է։

2. Ամէն շաբաթ Անին կ՚այցելեմ։

3. Այդպիսի դժուար գործ մը չեմ ուզեր ընել։

4. Ինչո՞ւ ուսուցիչին չէք լսեր։

5. Աննա միշտ ինքնաշարժով կը ճամբորդեն։

6. Տիգրանին խանութէն կու գանք։

7. Աշակերտները ամբողջ դասը մատիտով կը գրեն։

8. Եղբայրներուս կը սպասեմ։

9. Ծնողքիս ինքնաշարժը կը գործածեմ։

10. Երջանիկ պզտիկները կը խաղային։

11. Վաչէ Անահիտին ծաղիկ կը որկէ։

12. Կը նախընտրենք շոգեկառքով ճամբորդել։

13. Աղջիկները շուկայէն կու գային։

14. Բժիշկը հիւանդներուն կ՚այցելէր։

15. Անին բարեկամներէն մէկը կը տեսնեմ։

16. Խելացի աշակերտները հարցումներ կը հարցնեն։

17. Շոգեկառքը շատ արագ կ՚երթայ։

18. Այդ դպրոցին դասարանները մեծ են։

19. Այս դիւրին լեզուն ինչո՞ւ չէք սորվիր։

20. Անահիտ նամակիս չի պատասխաներ։

21. Հեռաձայնով երկար չեմ ուզեր խօսիլ։

22. Գործաւորները ներկայ չէին։

23. Քոյրիկիս երբեմն դրամ կը որկեմ։

24. Բարեկամներուս կը սպասեմ։

25. Այս ինքնաշարժին գոյնը կը սիրեն։

1. She is sending a letter to her family.

2. My parents are coming from Erevan today by plane.

3. The majority of Erevan'a streets are very long.

4. Those happy children are playing now.

5. One of my friends is a physician.

6. Vache is talking to my friend.

7. They come home from the university every Saturday.

8. That wealthy man always gives money to the poor.

9. I visit my friends every evening.

10. Do you buy your books from that shop?

11. The students are cleaning the classroom.

12. The mother is giving an apple to the child.

13. They are going to town by train.

14. Hayg is sending flowers to Ani.

15. Are you going to market today?

16. I was speaking to my family on the telephone.

17. Are those flowers from Anahid's garden?

18. (For) how many hours were you waiting for the doctor?

19. Are those beautiful girls your sisters?

20. They do not speak that difficult language.

21. He is sending a pen and two pencils to Dikran.

22. She is always saying such things.

23. Where is your new car?

24. This station is very large.

25. What is the price of bread now?

1. *Prepositions and postpositions*

Most of the words called "*preposition*" in English *follow* the substantive in Armenian, so are usually called "*post*positions." Prepositions and postpositions govern different cases.

Two of the most common *prepositions* are:

դէպի + acc.: towards; դէպի քաղաք   towards the city

but + *dat.* with pronouns: դէպի ինծի * towards me

առանց + dat.: without;

թէյը առանց շաքարի կը խմեմ   I drink tea without sugar.

Some of the most common *post*positions are the following:

+ gen.: մասին about, concerning

     ուսուցչին մասին   (we are talking) about the teacher

մէջ in

     դասարանին մէջ   in the classroom

մօտ near

     եկեղեցիին մօտ   near the church

վրայ on, over, concerning

     սեղանին վրայ   on the table

տակ under

     աթոռին տակ   under the chair

քով beside, near

     ճաշարանին քով   near the restaurant

*See Lesson VIII for personal pronouns.

+ dat.:   *համար* for

        ծնողքիս համար   for my parents

        ինծի համար   for me

    հետ   with

        քեզի հետ   with you

+ abl.:   *դուրս* outside (of)

        պանդոկէն դուրս   out of the hotel; outside the

                                 hotel

    ներս inside

        սենեակէն ներս   inside the room

Note that the compound prepositions (e.g. "from under") are rendered by a declined form of the postposition. See further Lesson XVII.

2. *Expression of motion*

The use of the various cases for motion to or from a place, or for rest in a place, is complicated.

a) *Motion to a place:* The Accusative is used:

    (Մենք) Երեւան կ՚երթանք։   We are going to Erevan.

    Անոնք Երեւան կը մեկնին։   They are leaving for Erevan.

    Տուն կ՚երթաս։   Are you going home?

    Դպրոց կ՚երթամ։   I am going to school.

    (Անոնք) երբ կը հասնին Պոսթըն։ When do they arrive in Boston?

    Ան նոր ճաշարանը կ՚երթայ։   She is going to the new restauran

Note that no article is used when the place is unspecified:

    Շուկայ կ՚երթամ։   I am going to (the) market.

Note also that when physical space is not intended the *dative* is used:

Դասի կ՚երթամ։ I am going to class.

Ժողովի կ՚երթամ։ I am going to a (the) meeting.

Բժիշկի կ՚երթամ։ I am going to the doctor.

b) *Motion from a place:* The Ablative is used, plus the definite article:

Պոսթընէն Երեւան կը մեկնինք։ We are leaving Boston for Erevan.

Պանդոկէն ճաշարան կ՚երթան։ They are going from the hotel
to the restaurant.

Ամէն օր Երեւանէն հինգ oդանաւ Every day five planes leave

կը մեկնի Մոսկուա։ Erevan for Moscow.

c) *Rest in a place:* The Accusative or a postposition is used:

Մենք Պոսթըն կ՚ապրինք։ We live in Boston (or *Պոսթընի*
մէջ).

Հարվըրտ Համալսարանը You work at Harvard University.

կ՚աշխատիս։

Անոնք տունը կը հանգստանան։ They are resting at home.

Note that in this construction the definite article is used - unlike §a
above. Distinguish therefore between:

Երախաները դուրսը կը խաղան։ The children are playing outside.

Երախաները դուրս կ՚երթան։ The children are going outside.*

3. *The genitive of complement*

In English two nouns may be set in apposition to each other, the first
modifying the second: e.g. "cigarette-box," "tea-cup," "watch factory." In
such cases the first noun in Armenian is put into the genitive case: *ծխախոտի*
տուփ, թէյի գաւաթ, ժամացոյցի գործարան.
[But if the first noun indicates the material *out of which* something is made,
then it is put into the ablative: e.g. *երկաթէ գործիքներ* iron tools.]

* See further XVII 2 for the article with postpositions.

Vocabulary: Lesson VII

աթոռ, -ի	chair	հագուստ, -ի	clothes, dress, suit
անցեալ	last, past	համար	for (postposition + dat.)
անցեալ օր	the other day		
ապրիլ	to live	Հարվըրտ	Harvard
առանց	without (preposition + dat.)	հետ	with (postposition + dat.)
բնակիլ	to live, reside, dwell	ճաշարան, -ի	restaurant
գործարան, -ի	factory	մասին	about, concerning (postposit. + gen.)
գործիք, -ի	tool		
դէպի	towards (preposition + acc., + dat. of pronouns)	մեկնիլ	to go away, leave, depart
		մէջ	in, at (postposition + gen.)
դուրս	out of (postposition + abl.)		
		միասին	together
դուրսը	outside	միս, -ի	meat
երախայ, -ի	child	Մոսկուա	Moscow
երէկ	yesterday	մտնել	to enter
երէկ գիշեր	last night	մօտ	near, close to (postposition + gen.)
երկաթ, -ի	iron		
երկիր, երկրի	country	նամակատուն	post-office
թուղթ, -ի	paper	ներս	(motion) into (postposition + abl.)
ժամացոյց, -ի	clock, watch		
ժողով, -ի	meeting	ներսը	inside, indoors
հագնիլ	to wear, put on	Նիւ Եորք	New York

շաքար, -ի	sugar	*վրայ*	on, above (post-
ուրկէ	whence (interrogative		position + gen.)
	and relative)	*տակ*	under, beneath (post-
պանդոկ, -ի	hotel		position + gen.)
Պոսթըն	Boston	*տանիլ*	to take, carry, bear
սեղան, -ի	table	*փայտ, -ի*	wood
սենեակ, -ի	room, chamber	*քով*	beside (postposition
վաղը	tomorrow		+ gen.)

1. Ծնողքիս տունը եկեղեցիին քովն* է:

2. Հարվըրտ Համալսարանին մօտ ճաշարան կա՞յ:

3. Թէյը առանց շաքարի կը խմեմ:

4. Այս ժամացոյցը բարեկամիս համար կը գնեմ:

5. Այդ աշակերտները առանց գիրքի դպրոց կ'երթան:

6. Մարդը առանց ջուրի չ'ապրիր:

7. Դուք ո՞ւր կը բնակիք: Ժամացոյցի գործարանին մօտ կը բնակինք:

8. Թուղթերն ու մատիաները սեղանին վրայ են:

9. Այդ մեծ պանդոկէն կու գանք:

10. Պոսթոնի մէջ քանի՞ դպրոց կայ:

11. Դեպի ո՞ւր կ'երթաք:

12. Այս դասարանին մէջ տասը փայտէ աթոռ կայ:

13. Անցեալ շաբաթ եկեղեցին շատ մարդ կար:

14. Երեկ գիշեր ո՞ւր էիք: Տիգրանին տունն էինք:

15. Այդ տղաքը ամէն իրիկուն դուրս կ'երթան:

16. Կատուն աթոռին տակն է:

17. Վաղը օդանաւը Երեւանէն Պոսթոն կը հասնի:

18. Այդ երկրին մէջ մարդ ի՞նչպէս կ'ապրի:

19. Պզտիկ երախան մայրիկէն բաժակ մը ջուր կը խնդրէ:

20. Այս գործը բարեկամիս համար կ'ընեմ:

21. Աղջիկները հին հագուստները ո՞ւր կը տանին:

22. Խանութին մօտ նամակատուն մը կայ:

23. Միսը Տիգրանին խանութէն կը գնեմ:

24. Թէյի գաւաթները պզտիկ սեղանի մը վրայ են:

25. Շատ պաղ է: Ինչո՞ւ երախաները ներս չեն գար:

*Before the verb "to be," many postpositions take –ն ; see further Lesson XVII 3.

1. Yesterday evening they were talking about the meeting.

2. Tomorrow I am going to Boston with my friends.

3. My parents' house is near the university.

4. The pupil is giving the newspaper to the teacher.

5. We eat at that restaurant.

6. My brothers are not going to Erevan together.

7. It is very hot inside the factory.

8. The workmen are making small chairs for the children.

9. The train arrives at the station tonight.

10. How many people live in this house (acc.)?

11. The students are entering the classroom.

12. The girls are wearing long dresses.

13. Every day I go to the city by train.

14. Do you drink tea without milk?

15. The cat is in my room under the chair.

16. The plane leaves for Boston tomorrow morning.

17. Are you going to market today?

18. The books are on the table.

19. Vache is making an iron box with my tools.

20. They were talking about my friend the other day.

21. Where do your children live? They live in Boston.

22. Where is the plane arriving from? It's arriving from New York.

23. In that country the poor do not live long.

24. Where are the boys going today?

25. The children were playing outdoors, but now they are coming inside.

26. How many nations are there in the world?

1. *Personal Pronouns*

a) 1st and 2nd persons; all six cases are distinguished:

	Singular		Plural	
Nom.	ես	դուն	մենք	դուք
Acc.	զիս	քեզ	մեզ	ձեզ
Gen.	իմ	քու	մեր	ձեր
Dat.	ինծի	քեզի	մեզի	ձեզի
Abl.	ինծմէ	քեզմէ	մեզմէ	ձեզմէ
Instr.	ինծմով	քեզմով	մեզմով	ձեզմով

b) 3rd person; only ինք distinguishes all six cases:

Nom.	ան, անիկա	ինք	անոնք	իրենք
Acc.	զայն, անիկա	զինք (ը)	(զ) անոնք	զիրենք
Gen.	անոր	իր	անոնց	իրենց
Dat.	անոր	իրեն	անոնց	իրենց
Abl.	անկէ	իրմէ	անոնցմէ	իրենցմէ
Instr.	անով	իրմով	անոնցմով	իրենցմով

Similarly: ասոր, ատոր; ասկէ, ատկէ; ասով, ատով; ասոնք, ատոնք etc.

c) With some verbs the dative case is used for the direct object. E.g.

հաւատալ (to believe)

I believe him.   Անոր կը հաւատամ:

I believe in his ideas.   Իր գաղափարներուն կը հաւատամ:

56

սպասել (to wait)

Are you waiting for me? *ինծի՞ կը սպասես։*

I am waiting for your letter. *Քու նամակիդ կը սպասեմ։*

(Such verbs are so indicated in the vocabularies.)

A few verbs distinguish the accusative for things and the dative for

persons. E.g.

այցելել (to visit)

They are visiting Erevan. *Երեւան կ՚այցելեն։*

The doctor is visiting his *Բժիշկը իր հիւանդներուն*

    patients. *կ՚այցելէ։*

d) With personal pronouns sometimes the dative is used instead of the accusative

to render the direct object. E.g.

Do you love her? *Անոր (զայն, զինք) կը սիրե՞ս։*

We see you. *Քեզի (ձեզ) կը տեսնենք։*

e) The genitive of the pronoun is used to indicate possession. But, as with

demonstrative adjectives, the article must then be used:

        իրենց մայրը   their mother

        մեր նոր տունը   our new house

With *իմ* and *քու* the following noun generally takes the possessive

suffix, *-ս* or *-դ*, instead of the article. Thus

        իմ հայրս   my father

        քու մայրդ   your (s.) mother

A similar construction is found with some postpositions (cf. Lesson XVII):

        իմ քովս   beside me

But: *իր քովը*   beside her

2. *Possessive pronouns*

The possessive pronouns "mine," "ours," "yours," etc. are rendered by forms based on the genitive of the personal pronouns:

Singular

1.   *իմս, իմինս* (mine)   *մերը, մերինը* (ours)

2.   *քուկդ, քուկինդ* (yours)   *ձերը, ձերինը* (yours)

3.   *անորը, անորինը* (his,hers,its) *անոնցը, անոնցինը* (theirs)

      իրը, իրենը,   *իրենցը, իրենցինը*

The forms in -*ին*- are generally used when the nouns they qualify are not expressed in the clause. These are declined regularly (-*ի*, -*է*, -*ով*).

Thus: *իմինիս, իմինէս, իմինովս*

           քուկինիդ   etc.

           անորինին

           իրենինին

           մերինին

           ձերինին

           անոնցինին

           իրենցինին.

Plural

1.   *իմիններս (իմիններուս* etc.)   *մերիններ*

2.   *քուկիններդ*   *ձերիններ*

3.   *անորիններ*   *անոնցիններ*

      իրենիններ   *իրենցիններ*

E.g.   That book is mine.   *Այդ գիրքը իմս է:*

      This book is yours.   Where is   *Այս գիրքը քուկդ (ձերն) է:*

         mine (his)?   *իմինս (անորինը) ո՞ւր է:*

Their house is next to ours.	*իրենց տունը մերինին քովն է։*
I am waiting for your group	*Ձերիններուն կը սպասեմ։*
(family, friends, etc.).	

3. *Verbs without կը*

A very few (but common) verbs in modern Western Armenian do not have կը in the present or imperfect indicative:

ես	*եմ*	I am	(*էի*)
կայ,	*կան*	there is, are	(*կար,* *կային*)
գիտեմ		I know	(*գիտէի*)
ունիմ		I have	(*ունէի*)
կրնամ		I can, am able	(*կրնայի*)
կարծեմ		I think (1 p.s. only)	(*կը* *կարծէի*)

But with *կարծեմ* a form with *կը* means "I definitely think," while the form without *կը* is less emphatic "I think (perhaps)."

The above verbs are conjugated in the regular fashion for the appropriate group. The negatives are also regular EXCEPT for *եմ, կայ, ունիմ.*

Thus	*չեմ գիտեր, չէի գիտեր*	etc.
	չես կրնար, չէիր կրնար	etc.
	չի կարծեր, չէր կարծեր	etc.
But	*չեմ, չէի*	etc.
	չկայ, չկար	
	չկան, չկային	
	չունիմ, չունէի	etc.

4. *Verbs with more than one subject*

If the speaker is included, the verb is always in the 1st pl.

E.g.   Neither my brother nor I like

       apples.

(Note that the order of persons is variable: *Ո̂չ եղբայրս, Ո̂չ ալ ես...*)

       Sentences with a 2nd and 3rd pers. take 2nd pl.

       She and you both live in

         Erevan.

Ո̂չ ես, ո̂չ (ալ) եղբայրս խնծոր

կը սիրենք:

Դուն եւ ան երկուքդ ալ Երեւան

(Ե.-ի մէջ) կ'ապրիք:

Vocabulary: Lesson VIII

անշուշտ	of course, certainly	ծանր	heavy; grave, serious
աշխատանք, -ի	work	ծեր	old (person)
աչք, -ի	eye	ծovեզերք, -ի	seashore
առջև	before, in front of (postposition + gen.)	կամաց	slow; slowly
		կարծել	to think, reckon
արդիւնք, -ի	result,effect,product	կարմիր	red
արհեստ, -ի	profession, trade	կրնամ	I can
բաց	open	հաւատալ	to believe ("in" = dat.)
բաւական	enough (adj., adv.), quite; considerably		
		հեռու	far, distant (adj.) far from, away from (postposition + abl.)
գաղափար, -ի	idea		
գիտեմ	I know		
դեռ	still, yet	միայն	only (adv.)
դիմաց	across,opposite,facing (postposit. + gen.)	յաճախ	often
		նպատակ, -ի	purpose, aim, goal
եզերք, -ի	coast, shore, edge	նպատակ ունիմ	I intend
ընտիր	choice, fine, superb	նստիլ	to sit, sit down; ride (in a car)
թերթ, -ի	newspaper		
ժողովուրդ, -ի	people	ոչ...ոչ (ալ)	neither...nor
լեցուն	full	ունիմ	I have
լուր, -ի	news	պատկեր, -ի	picture, painting
խնդալ	to laugh ("at"= վրայ)	ցած	low; soft (not loud)
խնդիր, -ի	matter,problem,question	քիչ	little, somewhat
խնդրի		քիչ մը	a little
ծախել	to sell		

1. Այս արդիւնքներուն մասին ի՞նչ կը կարծէք։

2. Անշուշտ կրնաք մեզի հետ երթալ։

3. Հիւանդ տղան դեռ չի կրնար դասի երթալ։

4. Անոր մայրը յամախ կ՚այցելէ մեզի։

5. Մեր տունը ծովեզերքէն բաւական հեռու է։

6. Այդ խանութը ընտիր հագուստներ կը ծախեն։

7. Ինչո՞ւ վրաս կը խնդաք։

8. Այս ամիս աննից եղբայրը համալսարանէն տուն չի կրնար գալ։

9. Վախէ միշտ անոր քովը կը նստի դասարանին մէջ։

10. Ինչո՞ւ գած չես կրնար խօսիլ։

11. Այդ երկրին մէջ ամէն մարդ արհեստ մը ունի՞։

12. Անոր նպատակները գէշ են։

13. Այդ քաղաքին մէջ շատ բարեկամ ունէի, բայց հոս միայն երկու հոգի
    կը ճանչնամ։

14. Այդ ծեր մարդը կամաց կը խօսի։

15. Դեռ լուր չունինք աննից մէ։

16. Կրնա՞մ ձեզի հարցում մը հարցնել։

17. Իր պզտիկ եղբայրը օրաթերթ կը ծախէ դպրոցին առջեւը։

18. վաղը դաս ունի՞ք։ Ո՛չ, համալսարանը բաց չէ։

19. Այս իրիկուն ուսուցիչներս ժողով ունին։

20. Երախային գաւաթը կաթով լեցուն է։

21. Աղջիկները իրենց սենեակը կը մաքրեն։

22. Իմ ընկերներս Տիգրանին համար կ՚աշխատին։

23. Ձեր անունը հիմա կը յիշեմ։

24. Ծեր մարդուն աչքերը լաւ չեն տեսներ։

25. Այս սենեակէն ձեզի չեմ կրնար լսել։

1. I am going to their house.

2. The people of that country do not believe in such ideas.

3. What do your friends think about this serious matter?

4. How many houses are there on your street? Eight.

5. Can you give me a little money?

6. Ani is not coming with us this evening.

7. Do you like them?

8. Anahid's brother is choosing a car for her.

9. There's still no work for them.

10. That old man does not know (how) to read, but he's very intelligent.

11. The post-office is opposite our store.

12. The Armenians are quite an old people.

13. The child is sitting on a little red chair.

14. We have many paintings at our house.

15. That was not my purpose.

16. We were expecting a letter from him.

17. What is your friend's profession?

18. Can you hear me? No, you are speaking too softly.

19. They live very far from us.

20. Of course you know him, he used to work with you.

21. Those girls always laugh at their friends.

22. Why don't you go to that good restaurant?

23. Every day Vache takes his father home from work.

24. This newspaper gives the news of the entire world.

25. Can you take this heavy box to the post-office for me?

1. *The Future Indicative*

The future indicative of all verbs is formed by combining the conjugated forms of the present indicative with the indeclinable particle պիտի (cf. պէտք է "it is necessary"); the կը is dropped.

Singular

1. պիտի սիրեմ, պիտի խօսիմ, պիտի կարդամ

2. պիտի սիրես, պիտի խօսիս, պիտի կարդաս

3. պիտի սիրէ, պիտի խօսի, պիտի կարդայ

Plural

1. պիտի սիրենք, պիտի խօսինք, պիտի կարդանք

2. պիտի սիրէք, պիտի խօսիք, պիտի կարդաք

3. պիտի սիրեն, պիտի խօսին, պիտի կարդան

Note that there is no future with the form եմ; the infinitive ըլլալ ("to become, occur," կ՚ըլլամ, կ՚ըլլաս, etc.) supplies all forms except the indicative and imperfect (եմ, էի).

Thus:

1. պիտի ըլլամ   պիտի ըլլանք

2. պիտի ըլլաս   պիտի ըլլաք

3. պիտի ըլլայ   պիտի ըլլան

The negative for all future indicatives is formed by prefixing the negative particle չ- to the conjugated forms: E.g.

1. պիտի չսիրեմ   պիտի չըլլանք

2. պիտի չխօսիս   պիտի չսիրէք

3. պիտի չկարդայ   պիտի չկրնան

64

(Avoid the colloquial *չպիտի սիրեմ* etc.)

Usage

As in English, the present indicative is often used with a future sense:

I shall go home tomorrow.	*Վաղը տուն պիտի երթամ:*
I am going home tomorrow.	*Վաղը տուն կ'երթամ:*
When will you leave for Erevan?	*Ե՞րբ պիտի մեկնիս Երեւան:*
When do you leave for Erevan?	*Ե՞րբ կը մեկնիս Երեւան:*

Note: In a very few verbs in modern Western Armenian the stems of the present indicative and of the future are different. The future (and subjunctive) usually derive from an expanded stem, while the imperfect is based on the present. See further Lesson XXIII.

E.g.   *գիտեմ,*   Inf. *գիտնալ*   Future *պիտի գիտնամ*

   ունիմ,   *ունենալ*   *պիտի ունենամ*

   կրնամ,   *կրնալ* or *կարենալ*   *պիտի կրնամ*

   or *պիտի կարենամ*

Future negative: *պիտի չունենամ* etc.

The two present tenses *կ'ունենամ* and *ունիմ* may be distinguished:

   Հաց ունի՞ք: Do you have bread? (in the shop *now*)

   Հաց կ'ունենա՞ք: Do you have bread? (generally = do you stock ?)

2.   *Declension of Nouns with Gen./Dat. in* -*ու*

Many nouns (mostly, but not exclusively, monosyllabic) have a Gen./Dat. in -*ու* instead of the more usual -*ի* . Other cases are declined regularly.

E.g.

	Singular			*Plural*
N/A	ծով (sea)	տղայ (boy)		ծովեր
G/D	ծովու	տղու		ծովերու
Abl.	ծովէ	տղայէ		ծովերէ
Instr.	ծովով	տղայով		ծովերով

Like ծով are declined, e.g.: մարդ (man), կով (cow), հայ (Armenian), գլուխ (head, գլխու). Like տղայ are declined, e.g.: ճամբայ (but not monosyllabic nouns). Pl.: ճամբաներ (regular). However, genitives in -ի are sometimes found, e.g.: ծով, ծովու or ծովի.

Note: Several nouns have irregular plurals (based on classical forms):

մարդ but մարդիկ, G/D մարդոց, Abl. մարդոցմէ. But մարդեր etc. are also found.

տղայ but տղաք, տղոց, տղոցմէ, տղոցմով. But տղաներ and տղաքներ (!) are also found.

[հայ, հայեր, հայերու etc.; but the classical gen. pl. հայոց is found in a few expressions, e.g. Հայոց Պատմութիւն Armenian history.]

3. *Expressions of time*

The Accusative case is used to indicate duration or frequency; note the use of the definite article for general statements as opposed to a specific occasion.

	once a week	շաբաթը մէկ անգամ (անգամ մը)
	all day	ամբողջ օրը
	in the evening(s)	իրիկունը (իրիկուններր)
But:	this evening	այս իրիկուն
	every day (week, year)	ամէն օր (շաբաթ, տարի)

The Ablative case is used to denote time within which an action occurs; note the use of the definite article.

E.g.   He will be arriving in a week.   *Մէկ շաբաթէն կը գանի:*

Note the use of the present tense to indicate a state that has existed (and still exists). *ի վեր* + Abl. renders "since":

They have been living in Erevan   *Հինգ տարիէ ի վեր Երեւան*

for five years.   *կ'ապրին:*

Note that *ի վեր* is not always necessary:

I have been waiting for you for   *Երկու ժամ* է քեզի կը սպասեմ:*

two hours.

*N.B.   Nominative.

Vocabulary: Lesson IX

առաւօտ	morning	նաւ, նաւու	ship, vessel
գիտնալ (գիտեմ)	to know	շաբաթ օր	Saturday
գլուխ, -ի, գլխու	head	շահ, շահու	profit
դար, դարու	century	շահիլ	to earn
երբ	when (interrogative and relative)	շնորհակալ ըլլալ	to thank
երեքշաբթի	Tuesday	ունենալ (ունիմ)	to have
երկուշաբթի	Monday	ուշ	late, tardy
էշ, էշու	donkey, ass	ուրբաթ	Friday
ըլլալ	to be, become	չորեքշաբթի	Wednesday
ծով, ծովու	sea	պահ, պահու	moment, while
կանուխ	early	այս պահուս	at the moment
կարենալ (կրնամ)	to be able (+ inf.)	պարոն, -ի	gentleman, sir, Mr.
կիրակի	Sunday	պէտք ունենալ	to need, require (+ dat.)
կով, կովու	cow		
կովու միս	beef	սկսիլ	to begin, start
հաւ, հաւու	chicken, hen	ստանալ	to get, receive
հաւու միս	chicken (dish)	վազել	to run
հինգշաբթի	Thursday	վախնալ	to be afraid (of), fear (+ abl. or dat.)
ձի, ձիու	horse		
ճամբայ, ճամբու	road, way	ի վեր	since (time) (postposition + abl.)
մահ	death		
մանչ, մանչու	boy	վիճակ, -ի	state, condition
մարդիկ, մարդոց	men, people	տեղի ունենալ	to take place

տեսակ, -ի	kind, type, sort	փոքր	little
տիկին	lady, Mrs.; wife	oգնել	to help, aid, assist
տխուր	sad		(+ dat.)
ցավ, -ի	pain	oրինակ, -ի	example, copy
գլխու ցավ	headache	oրինակի համար	for example
փափաքիլ	to desire, want, wish	oրիորդ, -ի	young lady, Miss

1. Կիրակի առաւօտ կանուխ ձեզի հետ եկեղեցի պիտի երթամ:

2. Ուսուցիչներուն ժողովը երբ պիտի սկսի:

3. Ամէն շաբաթ իրմէ նամակ կը ստանամ:

4. Պզտիկները դպրոցէն տուն կը վազեին:

5. Այդ գործաւորները շատ դրամ կը շահին:

6. Ժողովը մեր դասարանին մէջ տեղի պիտի ունենայ:

7. Պարոն Հայկը ձի մը պիտի գնէ իր տղուն համար:

8. Այդ տղոցմէ մէկը քեզի պիտի օգնէ:

9. Վաղը դուք պիտի աշխատիք:

10. Հինգշաբթի իրիկուն միասին պիտի երթանք Տիկին Անահիտին տունը:

11. Երկար պիտի չսպասենք անոնց:

12. Այս ծամբուն վրայ շատ ծառ կայ:

13. Վաղը ամբողջ օրը գբաղած պիտի ըլլանք:

14. Տիգրան իր հին ընկնաշարժը ինծի պիտի ծախէ:

15. Այդ տեսակ մարդոց պէտք չունինք:

16. Բժիշկը ի՞նչ կ'ըսէ անոր վիճակին մասին:

17. Երկու տարի է եղբայրս համալսարան կ'երթայ:

18. Քոյրդ քանի՞ զաւակ ունի: Երկու մանչ, մէկ աղջիկ ունի:

19. Չորեքշաբթի (օր) շոգեկառքը ուշ պիտի հասնի Պոսթոն: Պիտի կարենա՞ք զիս կայարանէն տուն տանիլ:

20. Օրը շատ լաւ է: Կ'ուզէ՞ք մեզի հետ ծով երթալ:

21. Մենք շատ շնորհակալ ենք:

22. Կովու միս կը սիրես:

23. Կը փափաքիմ անոնց տունը երթալ այս իրիկուն:

24. Իր տղուն մահէն ի վեր միշտ տխուր է:

25. Տղուն վիճակը լաւ չէ, ՞րբ բժիշկն պիտի տանիս զինքը:

1. That intelligent young lady is going to be a doctor.

2. On Monday I will speak to my friend on the telephone.

3. Will you write me a letter?

4. We are going to sell our house to them.

5. All men (= every man) fear death.

6. When will he arrive? I do not know.

7. Do you need a little money?

8. Every morning Vache drinks a full glass of milk.

9. Where do you buy your clothes from?

10. The meeting will take place in that small room.

11. What kind (of) work do you want? For example, do you want to work in a factory?

12. We make a large profit from our store.

13. He will speak to his parents about that matter.

14. I am very busy at the moment.

15. The children will be playing outside today.

16. On Tuesday Vache will receive money from his parents by mail (letter).

17. When will you be able to visit us?

18. Both of them will be present at the meeting.

19. Do you often eat chicken at home?

20. Early Friday morning the teacher will speak to Ani about her lessons.

21. Tomorrow I will take flowers to my sick friend. She has been ill for seven weeks.

22. In this century people do not travel by donkey or horse.

23. Of course I will not go to the city without you.

24. They prefer to go by ship.

25. He will send a copy of his book (abl.) to his parents.

26. Yesterday evening I had a headache.

LESSON X

1. *The Aorist Indicative (Part I)*

Verbs in Armenian have a present stem (the infinitive without the ending
-ել/իլ/ալ) and an aorist stem. These may differ in various ways. But in
all cases the endings for the aorist indicative belong to one of two groups:

Either:	Sing.	Pl.	or	Sing.	Pl.
1.	ի	ինք		այ	անք
2.	իր	իք		ար	աք
3.	zero in some categories,	ին		ալ	ան
	ալ in others				

Here we shall study the most numerous group of verbs, those which form
the aorist by adding a suffix to the present stem.

   a) Verbs in -ել have aorists in -եցի .

       E.g. սիրել (to love)

	Sing.	Pl.
1.	սիրեցի	սիրեցինք
2.	սիրեցիր	սիրեցիք
3.	սիրեց	սիրեցին

   b) Verbs in -իլ have aorists in -եցայ .

       E.g. խոսիլ (to speak)

1.	խոսեցայ	խոսեցանք
2.	խոսեցար	խոսեցաք
3.	խոսեցալ	խոսեցան

72

c) Verbs in *-ալ* have aorists in *-ացի*.

E.g. *կարդալ* (to read)

1.   *կարդացի*   *կարդացինք*

2.   *կարդացիր*   *կարդացիք*

3.   *կարդաց*   *կարդացին*

The negative is formed by prefixing the negative particle *չ-*.to the

verbal form:

E.g.   *չսիրեցի*,   *չխոսեցաւ*,   *չկարդացինք*.

2. *Abstract nouns in* *-ություն*

An unlimited number of abstract nouns may be formed in Armenian by adding

the ending *-ություն* to a stem. The stems are usually either adjectives or

verbal stems. Such nouns are declined as follows:

E.g. *ճշմարտություն* truth   (cf. *ճշմարիտ* true)

	Sing.	Pl.
N/A	(*ճշմարտ*)*ություն*	*-ություններ*
G/D	(*ճշմարտ*)*ություն*	*-ություններու*
Abl.	(*ճշմարտ*)*ությենէ*	*-ություններէ*
Instr.	(*ճշմարտ*)*ությամբ*	*-ություններով*

Note that genitives in *-եան* do not usually take a definite article:

E.g.   Patience is a good thing.   *Համբերությունը լաւ բան է:*

But: the end of his patience   *իր Համբերության վերջը*

From adjectives are derived, for example:

դժուար   difficult; *դժուարություն*   difficulty

չար   wicked, evil; *չարություն*   wickedness, evil (as a noun)

ազնիւ   kind, decent;   *ազնուություն* honesty (also written:

ազնվություն)

From verbal stems (without the infinitive ending), for example:

[ՀամբԵրԵլ   to endure] Համբերու թիւն endurance, patience

[մատնԵլ   to betray; մատնու թիւն betrayal]

Note that a form -ու թիւնով is often used for the Instr. sing. instead of the classical -ու թեամբ. Conversely, the classical pl. G/D -ու թեանg is sometimes found instead of the modern -ու թիւննԵրու.

75

Vocabulary: Lesson X

ազնութիւն,   honesty

  -եան

ակնկալել   to expect

անկեղծունիւն, sincerity

  -եան

անձրեւ, -ի   rain

ատեն   time

բերել   to bring

բնակչունիւն, population

  -եան

բնաւ   at all

գեղեցկունիւն, beauty

  -եան

գիտունիւն,   science, knowledge

  -եան

գրենէ   almost

դժուարունիւն, difficulty

  -եան

երբեք   ever

ընկերուհի, -ի friend (female)

խնամել   to take care of

հաճելի   pleasant

համբերունիւն, patience

  -եան

հասկնալ   to understand

հետաքրքրական   interesting

հետեւիլ   to follow, pursue (+

      dat.)

հսկայ   giant, enormous

ճիւղ, -ի   branch

ճշմարիտ   true

ճշմարտունիւն, truth

  -եան

յաճախել   to attend, frequent

շնորհիւ   thanks to (postposi-

      tion + gen.)

որովհետեւ   because

չար   bad, evil, wicked

չարաճճի   naughty

չարունիւն,   wickedness, evil

  -եան

պատճառաւ   because of, on account

      of (postposit. + gen.)

պատմել   to tell, relate

պատմունիւն,   story, history

  -եան

պատուհան, -ի window

պարզ   simple, plain

պարզութիւն, *–եան*	simplicity	*սխալ,* *–ի*	mistake; wrong (adj.), wrongly
պարկեշտ	decent, honest	*քալել*	to walk
պոռալ	to shout (at: *վրայ*)	*օգնութիւն,* *–եան*	help, aid

1. Երեք իրիկուն Տիգրան մեզի այցելեց։

2. Այս գիրքը մեծ դժուարութեամբ կարդացի։

3. Ամբողջ ծամբան աննոց հետեւեցանք։

4. Իրմէ ազնուութիւն բնաւ չենք ակնկալեր։

5. Ամէն առտու մեծ մայրս պատուհանին աղջել կը նստի։

6. Անցեալ տարի գրեթէ չորս ամիս չաշխատեցայ։

7. Հայկ մեզի հետաքրքրական պատմութիւն մը պատմեց։

8. Քոյրս շատ համբերութիւն չունի։

9. Եղբայրս ուզեց ծխախոտ գնել, բայց մեր փողոցի խանութները գոց էին։

10. Այդ մարդը գիտութեամբ եւ գիտութեան համար կ՚ապրի։

11. Ամէն մարդ անոր կը սիրէ իր գեղեցկութեան համար։

12. Երեք ժամ սպասեցինք մեր բարեկամներուն։

13. Ձեր մարդը անկեղծութեամբ խոսեցաւ մեր երկրի դժուարութիւններուն
    մասին։

14. Պատուհանները ինչու՞ գոցեցիր, ներսը շատ տաք է։

15. Շոգեկառքը երբ մեկնեցաւ Պոսթոն։

16. Աղջիկները երկայն հագուստ մը գնեցին իրենց ընկերուհիին համար։

17. Ինչու՞ ձեր ինքնաշարժը իրեն ծախեցիք։

18. Այս ծշմարիտ պատմութիւնը երբ լսեցիր։
    Այս առտու։ Անահիտ ամբողջ պատմութիւնը պատմեց ինծի։

19. Անցեալ շաբաթ բարեկամիս երկու նամակ գրեցի։

20. Կիրակի առտուները Տիկին Անին իր պարտէզէն ծաղիկ կը բերէ մեզի։

21. Անահիտին հագուստներուն պարզութիւնը կը սիրեմ։

22. Մեր դժուարութիւններուն մասին չեք ուզեր լսել։

23. Այս առտու գրեթէ հինգ ժամ քալեցինք։ Հիմա պիտի հանգստանանք։

24. Երկար ատենէ ի վեր ընկերուհիիս զաւակը կը խնամեմ, որովհետեւ
    ընկերուհիս ծանր հիւանդ է։

25. Համալսարանին մօտ հսկայ նամակատուն մը շինեցին։

1. Did you send copies of your book to your brothers?

2. I helped my friends yesterday.

3. When did you learn that trade?

4. He never answered my letter.

5. Ani's mother bought her a beautiful dress.

6. Decent men don't believe in such wicked ideas.

7. I was sitting right in front of her.

8. He is pursuing this branch of science because he wishes to become a doctor.

9. On Saturday they cleaned the classroom windows.

10. Did you attend school last year?

11. Why didn't you sell your old books to me?

12. Anahid took care of her grandfather for seven years.

13. We will go home by car because of the rain.

14. The naughty children did not like their teacher.

15. Did you visit my parents last night?

16. I was resting all day yesterday.

17. They were trying to read, but they were not able to understand the foreign words.

18. Don't you remember your mistakes?

19. I don't like him because he is not a pleasant man.

20. Thank you very much. You helped me considerably.

21. Our teacher told us an interesting story.

22. Thanks to their assistance we will be able to attend the university.

23. The mother was shouting at her little boy because he was not drinking his milk.

24. The population of our town is not very great.

1. *Relative Pronoun*

In modern Western Armenian the relative pronoun *որ* is used for both persons and things. It is declined as follows:

	Singular	Plural	
Nom.	որ	որոնք	
Acc.	որ (զոր)*	(զ)որոնք	զորս, written only; in conversation (զ) որ
G/D	որու(ն)	որոնց	
Abl.	որմէ	որոնցմէ	
Instr.	որով	որոնցմով	

Note that in English the relative pronoun is not always used, but it is obligatory in Armenian:

E.g. the girl who loves me   (այն) աղջիկը որ զիս կը սիրէ

the girl I love   (այն) աղջիկը (զ)որ կը սիրեմ

the children to whom she is   երախաները, որոնց համար** ան

    reading a story   պատմութիւն մը կը կարդայ

the man you met yesterday   (այն) մարդը որուն երէկ հանդիպեցար

the pen with which I write   (այն) գրիչը որով նամակներս կը

    my letters   գրեմ

the window from which you can   այն պատուհանը որմէ կրնաս

    see the church   եկեղեցին տեսնել

Note the rendering of the English "whose" in a relative sense:

the man whose daughter I love   այն մարդը որուն աղջիկը կը սիրեմ

*The prefixed *զ-* is the classical definite accusative marker.
**Note the idiom with *համար*.

our old friends by whose help...   մեր հին ընկերները որոնց

oզնութեամբ...

the students in whose school...   այն ուսանողները, որոնց

դպրոցին մէջ...

2. *The Imperative of "regular" verbs*

In modern Western Armenian there are special forms for the second person imperatives, positive and prohibitive. [For the first and third persons ("let us, let them," etc.) the subjunctive is used - see Lesson XXIII.] The sing. is based on the present stem, the pl. on the aorist.

The imperative forms of regular verbs follow this pattern:

	սիրել	խօսիլ	կարդալ
Sing.	սիրէ	խօսէ	կարդա
Pl.	սիրեցէք	խօսեցէք	կարդացէք

Note: 1. The forms for verbs in -ել and -իլ are identical.

2. The sing. ending for verbs in -ալ is ա , not այ.

The prohibitive forms are introduced by the particle մի (not ոչ). For the singular the form is derived from the present stem plus the characteristic vowel of the infinitive plus -ր. For the plural the form is identical with the 2pl. present indicative. Thus:

Sing.	մի սիրեր	մի խօսիր	մի կարդար
Pl.	մի սիրէք	մի խօսիք	մի կարդաք

Vocabulary: Lesson XI

բարձրաձայն	aloud; loudly	ձեռք, -ի	hand
բացատրել	to explain	ձեռք ձեռքի	hand in hand
բացի	except, besides	ճաշ, -ի	meal; dish
	(preposition or	մազ, -ի	hair (often in pl.)
	postposit. + abl.)	մինչև	until
բոլոր	all	միջև	between (postposition
բոլորն ալ	all of them		+ gen.)
գետին, գետնի	ground, floor, earth	յայտնել	to express; reveal
դասախոս, -ի	lecturer	յայտնի	evident; well-known,
զգալ	to feel		famous
ընդունիլ	to receive, admit,	նայիլ	to look at (+ dat.)
	accept	նշանաւոր	famous
թեթև	light (not heavy)	նոյն	same
ժամանակ, -ի	time	շարունակել	to continue
ժամանակին	on time	ճ̂ր, որ	which (interrogative
խոստանալ	to promise		and relative)
խոսակցիլ	to talk, converse	չափ, -ի	measure, quantity
խոսակցություն,	conversation		(+ dat. = as)
-եան		չափազանց	extremely
կրկին	again; a second time	պատճառ, -ի	cause, reason
կրկնել	to repeat	պատրաստ	ready
հանդիպիլ	to meet (+ dat.)	պատրաստել	to prepare
հնչել	to pronounce; ring	սակայն	but
հնչում	pronunciation	սիրուն	pretty
ձայն, -ի	voice, sound	սիրտ, -ի	heart
			(or սրտի)

uխալիլ	to err, be wrong	_վեր_	above, overhead (adv., postposition + abl.)
վար	down (adv., postposition + abl.)	_տխրություն,_	sadness
		−եան	

1. Կրկնեցէ՛ք այն պատմութիւնը, որ երէկ Տիգրան պատմեց ձեզի:

2. Այդ խանութէն գնեցի այն մատիտները, որոնցմով հիմա դուք կը գրէք:

3. Այն մարդը, որուն քով կ'աշխատիմ՝ շատ բարի սիրտ մը ունի:

4. Գետինը մի՛ նստիք, շատ պաղ է:

5. Այն տղան, որուն դաս կու տաս, խելացի՞ է:

6. Վաղը պիտի գնեմ այն գիրքը, որուն պէտք ունիս:

7. Կը խոստանամ՝ հին գիրքերս ձեզի տալ:

8. Կը ճանչնա՞ս այդ երկար մազերով աղջիկը:

9. Այն երիտասարդները, որոնց հետ խօսեցանք՝ համալսարանի ուսանողներ են:

10. Շնորհակալութիւն բոլոր անոնց՝ որոնք օգնեցին մեզի:

11. Վաղը ճաշարանին առջեւ ինծի հանդիպեցէ՛ք:

12. Ձեր երախանները շատ խելացի՝ բայց չարաճճի են:

13. Այն մարդը, որ ձեր քով կը բնակի, շատ դրամ կը շահի:

14. Ուսուցիչը, որուն հետ հանդիպեցանք երկուշաբթի իրիկուն, շատ նշանաւոր մարդ մըն է:

15. Իմ սխալներս կ'ընդունիմ, դուք ալ ձեր սխալները ընդունեցէ՛ք:

16. Ճաշը շՈ՛րը պիտի պատրաստէք, անոնք հիմա պիտի գան:

17. Մեզի սպասեցէ՛ք մինչեւ իրիկուն:

18. Տասը անգամ բացատրեց ինծի իր տխրութեան պատճառները:

19. Շարունակեցէ՛ք, մենք բոլորս ալ կը լսենք ձեր խօսակցութիւնը:

20. Լաւ պատրաստեցէ՛ք ձեր դասերը:

21. Երիտասարդները ձեռք ձեռքի կը քալէին:

22. Անոնց խօսակցութեան ձայնը հեռուէն կը լսէի:

23. Վեր վար մի՛ նայիր, գործիդ նայէ՛:

24. Բացի ինձմէ, բոլոր ուսանողները սխալ հնչեցին այդ դժուար բառը:

25. Ի՞նչ են այդ սեղանին չափերը:

1. Read these two pages aloud.

2. The pretty girl who was crying is my little sister.

3. The lecturer you were talking to is one of the famous teachers of our university.

4. Did you earn much money last year?

5. This is the same man whom we used to see every day on the train.

6. The book which I read last night was light but interesting.

7. The clothes you wanted aren't ready yet.

8. Look at the little boy who is playing outside in the cold!

9. How do you feel today? I feel exceedingly happy.

10. Explain to me again the ideas you expressed at the meeting.

11. My brother doesn't like the man with whom I used to go to work.

12. Do you know the girl who was sitting between us at church?

13. The family we shall visit this evening is an Armenian family.

14. The plane by which my parents are coming is arriving exactly on time.

15. Do you know Ani's parents? We are now living in their old house (acc.).

16. Tell her the same interesting story you told me last week.

17. The people in front of whom we were sitting were speaking very loudly.

18. Are those the flowers Vache sent to you?

19. Do not sit there.

20. Did you hear the man who was shouting outside?

21. Answer my letter! I've been expecting a letter from you for two weeks.

22. The man from whom I bought my car is an honest man.

23. Don't look at her, look at me, I'm talking to you!

24. That road is closed now.

Numbers

1. The cardinal numbers 1-10 were given in Lesson IV. The remaining numbers are as follows:

Numbers: 11 - 1,000,000

Տասնըմէկ	11	Քսան	20	Քսանմէկ	21
Տասներկու	12	Երեսուն	30	Քսաներկու	22
Տասներեք	13	Քառասուն	40	Քսաներեք	23
Տասնըչորս	14	Յիսուն	50	Քսանչորս ...	24...
Տասըհինգ	15	Վաթսուն	60		
Տասըվեց	16	Եօթանասուն	70		
Տասնեօթը	17	Ութսուն	80	Հազար	1,000
Տասնութը	18	իննսուն	90	Միլիոն	1,000,000
Տասնինը	19	Հարիւր	100	Զէրօ	0

Note that the spelling of the numbers 11-19 varies:

E.g.   տասնըերկու.

These cardinal numbers may be declined (-ի, -է, -ով).

E.g.   They all played well except no. 11.   Բացի թիւ տասնըմէկկէն, բոլորն

աւ լաւ կը խաղային:

Compound numbers

112   Հարիւր տասներկու

1,525   Հազար հինգ հարիւր քսանհինգ

(Note that in Armenian one does not say "fifteen hundred" or "fifteen, twenty-five," for example; nor does one say *one* hundred, *one* thousand.)

5,807 հինգ հազար ութը հարիւր եօթը.

Note that nouns following numbers are singular, with the exceptions noted in Lesson IV 3b.

E.g. 5,000 dollars հինգ հազար տոլար.

2. The ordinal numbers are formed by adding -երորդ to the nominative of the cardinal numbers. But note that "first" to "fourth" are irregular, that the final ը of 7 to 10 drops, and that "ninth" shows an earlier form of ինը.

first	առաջին	11th	տասնըմէկերորդ
second	երկրորդ	12th*	տասնըերկուերորդ
third	երրորդ	13th*	տասնըերեքերորդ
fourth	չորրորդ	14th*	տասնըչորսերորդ
fifth	հինգերորդ	15th	տասնը հինգերորդ
sixth	վեցերորդ	16th	տասնըվեցերորդ
seventh	եօթ(ն)երորդ	17th	տասներօթերորդ
eighth	ութերորդ	18th	տասնութերորդ
ninth	իններորդ	19th	տասնիններորդ
tenth	տաս(ն) երորդ	20th	քսաներորդ

21st քսանմէկերորդ (not *քսանառաջին !)

All other forms are regular.

քանիերորդ = how many-eth?

In compound numbers only the last one takes the ordinal suffix:

355th երեք հարիւր յիսունհինգերորդ

Ordinal numbers are declined in regular fashion.

E.g. I shall go by the first train, Ես առաջին շոգեկառքով պիտի

you by the second. ճամբորդեմ, դուն՝ երկրորդով:

*Also found are տասնըերկրորդ, տասնըերրորդ, տասնըչորրորդ.

3. *Fractions*

   Half: կէս

         (three and a half: երեք ու կէս [*not* * կէս մը])

   Quarter: քառորդ

         (seven and a quarter: եօթը եւ քառորդ)

For other fractions the ordinals are used:

       a third   մէկ երրորդ

       two-fifths   երկու հինգերորդ

       three-tenths   երեք տասներորդ

Note that with expressions such as "half of," "a third of," "part of" (մէկ մասը),
the genitive is usually used rather than the ablative (cf. Lesson VI).

E.g. He sold half of his books.   իր գիրքերուն կէսը ծախեց:

4. The repetition of a cardinal number indicates a grouping.

       E.g.   երկու- երկու   two by two, in two's

           (ուսանողները երկու- երկու նստեցան դասարանին մէջ)

       Speak in turn (one by one), said   Մէկ-մէկ խoսեցէք, ըսաւ ուսուցիչը

           the teacher to his pupils.   իր աշակերտաներուն:

See further Lesson XVIII-4.

5. The letters of the alphabet have numerical value:

       E.g. Գիրք Ա Book I; գլուխ ԺԲ chapter 12. Cf. the alphabet, pp. 5-6.

6. *Price*

   "For" is indicated by the dative case.

E.g. I bought this book for three   Այս գիրքը երեք տոլարի գնեցի:

       dollars.

He sold me a pen for fifty cents.

(Անիկա) ինծի յիսուն սենթի գրիչ մը ծախեց:

But:

Apples are ten cents a kilo.

Խնձորի (gen.) քիլոն տասը սենթ է (or կ՚արժէ):

Note also the use of the ending *-ung* to render value or an actual denomination of money:

E.g.   I bought a dress worth 500 dollars.

Հինգ հարիւր տոլարնոց հազուստ մը գնեցի:

Will you give me a 5 (dollar bill)?

ինծի հինգնոց մը կու՞ տաք:

7.   The date in years is expressed by թուական in the dative, or by the dative of the last number in the date.

E.g.   in 1066:   հազար վաթսունվեց թուականին

or   հազար վաթսունվեցին

թուական with the adjectival form of numbers is also used in the following sense: ութսունական թուականներ "the eighties." For the adjectival form in *-ական* see further Lesson XVIII 5.

Vocabulary: Lesson XII

Learn the cardinal and ordinal numbers 0 to 1,000,000

գրականութիւն, -եան	literature
թուական, -ի	year, date
ժամանել	to arrive
խօսք, -ի	word, phrase, speech
կարեւոր	important
կէս, -ի	half
Հայաստան, -ի	Armenia
հայերէն, -ի	Armenian (language)
յարկ, -ի	floor, storey
Յարութիւն Շմաւոնեան	Harutiun Shmavonian
շիշ, -ի	bottle
սենթ, -ի	cent
վէպ, -ի	novel
տեղաւորել	to place
տոլար, -ի	dollar
տպել	to print
քառորդ, -ի	quarter

1. Հինգ – տասնչորս – երեսունչորս – հարիւր քսանեօթը – հազար
հարիւր վեց – երեք հազար տասնըմէկ : քսան հազար քսաներկու –
երեսունինը հազար եօթը հարիւր իննսունինը – հարիւր հազար
հինգ – երկու հարիւր հազար տասնըհինգ – չորս հարիւր հազար
հինգ հարիւր քսան – չորս հարիւր քսանմէկ հազար եօթը հարիւր
վաթսունչորս – քսանմէկ միլիոն վեց հարիւր եօթանասունհինգ
հազար չորս հարիւր քառասունմէկ:

2. Տղաս իր դասարանին առաջինն է:

3. Այս շիշը քանի՞ լիթր կ՚առնէ:

4. Այս սենեակին մէջ կրնա՞նք տասնչորս հոգի տեղաւորել:

5. Երկու հարիւր քառասունեօթը հոգիէն հարիւր քսանհինգ հոգի՝
նաւով, հարիւր վեց հոգի՝ օդանաւով, եւ տասնըվեց հոգի ալ՝
ինքնաշարժով ժամանեցին:

6. Այս քանի՞երորդ անգամն է, որ նոյն խօսքերը կը կրկնէ:

7. Մեր հեռաձայնի թիւն է ութը, եօթը, վեց, չորս, զէրօ, ինը, հինգ:

8. Հինգերորդ դարը շատ կարեւոր է հայ գրականութեան պատմութեան
մէջ:

9. "Հազար ինը հարիւր ութսունչորս" վէպը ե՞րբ կարդացիք:

10. Մէկ տուփ ծխախոտը քառասուն սենթ կ՚արժէ:

11. Քանի՞ գնեցիք ձեր նոր ինքնաշարժը:

12. Աղջիկները չորս-չորս տուն մեկնեցան:

1. 17; 29; 48; 52; 85; 96; 131; 263; 777; 1,001; 6,908; 8,749; 68,467; 319,526; 123,456,789.

2. 2nd; 3rd; 7th; 11th; 13th; 21st; 1st.

3. He bought his house last year for 25,000 dollars, but today it is worth 28,000.

4. How many hairs do you have on your head?

5. They were conversing in groups of three.

6. Our house has two doors, four large rooms on the first floor, six small rooms on the second, and sixteen windows.

7. A year has twelve or thirteen months, fifty-two weeks, and 365 or 366 days.

8. Next year nearly 9000 students will attend Erevan University, of which one-tenth will be foreigners.

9. My grandfather lived in the second half of the nineteenth century.

10. Three-quarters of the books in the shop are about Armenia.

11. In the market only one shop sells fifty or sixty different kinds of flowers.

12. Harutiun Shmavonian printed the first Armenian newspaper in 1794.

1. *Interrogative pronouns and adjectives*

In modern Western Armenian the interrogative pronoun for persons is ո՛վ
(who?) and for things ի՞նչ (what?). They are declined as follows:

	Sing.	Pl.	Sing.	Pl.
Nom.	ո՛վ	որո՛նք	ի՞նչ	ինչե՛ր
Acc.	ո՛վ (զո՛վ)*	որո՛նք (զորո՛նք)*	ի՞նչ	ինչե՛ր
Gen.	որո՛ւ(ն)	} որո՛նց	} ինչի՛	} ինչերո՛ւ
Dat.	որո՛ւ(ն)			
Abl.	որմէ՛(ն)	որոնցմէ՛	ինչէ՛	ինչերէ՛
Instr.	որո՛վ	որոնցմո՛վ	ինչո՛վ	ինչերո՛վ

E.g.   Who is it? It is I.   Ո՛վ է։ Ես եմ։

Whom do you see?   (զ)Ո՛վ կը տեսնես։ (or Որո՛ւն,

cf. Lesson VIII 1d)

From whom did you buy that book?   Որմէ՛ գնեցիր այդ գիրքը։

What do you mean?   Ի՞նչ ըսել կ՚ուզես։

What do you write with?   Ինչո՞վ կը գրես։

The interrogative adjective for persons and things is ո՛ր (note use of the
article except with the instrumental case):

Which students will not be present   Ո՛ր ուսանողները ներկայ պիտի

tomorrow?   չըլլան վաղը։

From which tree did you pick that   Ո՛ր ծառէն քաղեցիր այդ խնձորը։

apple?

*The forms with the classical prefix q- are not common in spoken Armenian.

With which pen will you write the   *Ո՞ր գրիչով պիտի գրես նամակը:*

letter?

However, *ի՞նչ* is used in certain expressions (corresponding to "what" rather

than "which"):

with what aim/purpose...   *ի՞նչ նպատակով ...*

What kind of fruit is it?   *ի՞նչ տեսակ պտուղ է:*

Note the rendering of the interrogative "which?" as a pronoun:

Which of you waited for me?   *Զեզմէ ո՞վ սպասեց ինծի:*

2. *Noun clauses*

Subordinate noun clauses in modern Western Armenian are introduced by the

particles *թէ* or more usually *որ* . The particle cannot be omitted, as "that"

often is in English.

E.g. I know that I am right.   *(Ես) գիտեմ, որ ճիշտ եմ:*

You say you are wrong.   *(Դուն) կ՚ըսես թէ դուն սխալ ես:*

The tense in the subordinate clause is generally that of the original statement.

Thus:

He wrote: "I shall come."   *Գրեց. "Պիտի գամ:"*

in oblique speech:

He wrote he would come.   *Գրեց, որ պիտի գայ:*

If the noun clause is interrogative, the particle *թէ*, not *որ*, is used in

addition to the interrogative word:

Do you know where we are going?   *Գիտէ՞ք, թէ ո՞ւր կ՚երթանք:*

I do not know who has that much   *Ես չեմ գիտեր, թէ ո՞վ այդքան*

money.   *դրամ ունի:*

3. In interrogative sentences *Թէ* (not *կամ*) is used to render "or".

    E.g. Do you write with a pen   *Գրիչո՞վ կը գրէք թէ մատիտով:*

        or a pencil?

    But: We shall drink either wine   *Կամ գինի պիտի խմենք կամ*

        or beer.   *գարեջուր:*

Vocabulary: Lesson XIII

այղքան, այնքան	so (much),that much	կախել	to hang, suspend (tr.)
այսքան	so (much),this much	կատարել	to perform, carry
աջ, -ի	right (hand)		out, execute
առաջ	ago; before (post-	կեանք, -ի	life
	position + abl.)	կողմ, -ի	side; direction; pl.:
արդի	modern		area, region
բանակ, -ի	army	հեռաձայնել	to telephone
դասախousntլթիւն,	lecture	հրաման, -ի	order, command
-եան		ձախ	left (adj. & adv.)
երգ, -ի	song	ձգել	to drop; leave; allow
երգել	to sing	մտածել	to think, contemplate,
երգիչ, -ի	singer (male)		consider
երգչուհի, -ի	singer (female)	Յակոբեան	Hagopian
զինուոր, -ի	soldier	յոգնիլ	to get tired ("of":
զօրավար, -ի	general		abl.)
ընթացք, -ի	course, conduct	յոյս, -ի	hope
ընթացքին	during (postposi-	յուսալ	to hope
	tion + gen.)	նկար, -ի	picture, image
թէ	that; whether; or	շուտով	soon, quickly
թշնամի, -ի	enemy (adj. & noun)	ով	who?
թուիլ	to appear,look,seem	որքան	how much?
ինչքան	how much?	ուրախութիւն,	joy, gladness
խորհիլ	to think, ponder,	-եան	
	reflect upon	պատ, -ի	wall

պատերազմ, -ի   war   ցաւիլ   to hurt (= be painful)

պատճառել   to cause   be sorry

սպայ, -ի   officer   փնտռել   to look for, search

սպաննել   to kill   քաղել   to pick

տեղ, -ի   place, site, loca-   քաջութիւն,   courage

                tion; in place of   -եան

1. Շատ գեղեցիկ ձայն է։ Ո՞վ է երգիչը։

2. Ինծի կը թուի, որ դուք այս տեսակ ճաշեր չէք սիրեր։

3. Ի՞նչ նպատակով կը հարցնես այդ հարցումները։

4. Պարոն Հայկ Յակոբեան դասախօսութիւն մը պիտի տայ արդի հայ
    գրականութեան մասին։

5. Որո՞նց հետ եկեղեցի պիտի երթաք։

6. Որո՞ւ մասին կը մտածէք։

7. Բանակը դէպի ո՞ւր կը քալէ։

8. Այդ նկարը ի՞նչ ո՞վ կախեցիր պատէն։

9. Աշակերտը գետին ձգեց իր մատիտը։

10. Անի, որո՞ւն պարտէզէն քաղեցիր այդ սիրուն ծաղիկները։

11. Մի՛ կարծեր, թէ միայն քու կեանքդ դժուարութիւններով լեցուն է։

12. Անոնցմէ ո՞վ է բժիշկը։ Ան, որ սենեակէն դուրս կու գայ հիմա։

13. Յոյս ունիմ, որ ընկերս շուտով պիտի այցելէ ինծի։

14. Առանց դրամի ինչպէ՞ս պիտի ապրիս։

15. Պատերազմի ընթացքին, սպաները քաջութեամբ կատարեցին իրենց
    զօրավարին հրամանները։

16. Որո՞ւ կը հետամտյնես։

17. Տիգրան որմէ՞ գնեց այդ աթոռները։

18. Որո՞ւն ինքնաշարժով պիտի երթանք։ Ծնողքիս ինքնաշարժը պիտի
    գործածենք։

19. Ձեր մայրը ի՞նչ ո՞վ զբաղած է այսօր։

20. Դպրոցին առջեւ որո՞ւն կը սպասես ամէն առտու։

21. Ո՞ւր էիր ժամ մը առաջ։

22. Ձեր նամակը մեծ ուրախութիւն պատճառեց ինծի։

23. Այս գիշեր տեղ մը պիտի երթա՞ք։

1. Which of you left his books in the classroom last Friday?

2. What type of literature do you prefer to read?

3. Whose house are you coming from?

4. What are you going to open the window with?

5. For whom does your father work?

6. What do you think about this idea?

7. During the war the enemy army killed 1,036 of our soldiers.

8. On which side of the room does grandmother sit? On the right hand side or the left?

9. With whose help did you prepare your lesson?

10. Who are these children you are taking care of?

11. Which of these students attend Harvard University?

12. He says that you were wrong, but I do not believe him.

13. You are hanging the picture wrongly.

14. I think that your pupils are all very clever.

15. In whose room will the meeting take place?

16. Whom are you looking for? I'm looking for my little boy.

17. You are so pretty in that picture.

18. Sing a song for me. You have such a sweet voice. Which songs do you want to hear?

19. To whom are you writing this letter?

20. What did you make this box out of?

21. To whom is Vache speaking? He is speaking to his teacher.

22. The young soldiers tired very quickly.

23. I am very sorry that you will not be able to help us.

1. *The Perfect and Pluperfect*

The perfect and pluperfect tenses of verbs are formed by combining the past participle and the present or imperfect tenses of the verb "to be." The past participle is formed by adding *-ած* or *-եր* to the present stem of "regular" verbs in *-ել* and *-իլ*, and to the aorist stem of "regular" verbs in *-ալ*. (In all verbs except those with the suffix *-ցg* in the aorist, it is the aorist stem that provides the past participle.) Thus for the verbs *սիրել*, *խոսիլ*, *կարդալ* the following paradigms are formed:

1.	*սիրած* (*սիրեր*)	*եմ*,	*էի*	*խոսած* (*խոսեր*)	*կարդացած* (*կարդացեր*)
2.	*սիրած* (*սիրեր*)	*ես*,	*էիր*	*եմ*, *էի* etc.	*եմ*, *էի* etc.
3.	*սիրած* (*սիրեր*)	*է*,	*էր*		
4.	*սիրած* (*սիրեր*)	*ենք*,	*էինք*		
5.	*սիրած* (*սիրեր*)	*էք*,	*էիք*		
6.	*սիրած* (*սիրեր*)	*են*,	*էին*		

2. The negative is formed with the participle in *-ած* and the negative form of the verb "to be": *սիրած չեմ*, *խոսած չէի* etc.

or *չեմ սիրած*, *չէի խոսած* etc.

The form in *-եր* preceded by the negative *չեմ* etc. is sometimes found when there would be no confusion with the present or imperfect. Thus *չեն մնացեր* but not *չեն սիրեր* (= present, not perfect). But never *մնացեր չեն* etc.

Examples:

Have you read this book?   *Այս գիրքը կարդացած էք:*

99

They have never visited Erevan.	Թնաւ չեն այցելած Երևան:
When I met your friend he had already had breakfast.	Երբ ընկերոջդ հանդիպեցայ, ան արդէն նախամօշ2ած էր:
The students could not answer the questions because they had not read their books.	Ուսանողները չէին կրնար պատասխ հարցումներուն, որով ետեւ իրենց գիրքերը կարդացած չէի

Note: When the English perfect expresses a continuous state that still pertains then the present is used in Armenian (cf. Lesson IX 4).

| E.g. How long have you been living here? | Քանի՞ տարիէ ի վեր հոս կ՚ապրիք: |
| But: How often have you spoken to your parents lately? | Քանի՞ անգամ ծնողքիդ հետ խօսած ես վերջերս: |

A distinction is sometimes made between the participles in —ած and —եր :

| I have read that book. | Կարդացած եմ այդ գիրքը: |
| He has read the book (at least, he says so). | Անիկա կարդացեր է գիրքը: |

| My friend has left Boston. | Ընկերս մեկնած է Պոսթընէն: |
| My friend has left (so people say). | Ընկերս մեկներ է: |

3. The future perfect is formed with ըլլալ:

Սիրած պիտի ըլլամ: I will have loved.

4. *Nouns of kinship*

Such nouns in Armenian are mostly irregular; they fall into two main groups: a) those with G/D in օր , and b) those with G/D in ոջ .

a) Only the words for "father, mother, brother" fall into this group:

N/A	հայր	(father)	մայր	(mother)	եղբայր	(brother)
G/D	հօր		մօր		եղբօր	
Abl.	հօրմէ		մօրմէ		եղբօրմէ	
Instr.	հօրմով		մօրմով		եղբօրմով	

The plurals are regular: հայրեր, մայրերու, եղբայրներով etc.
The compounds հօրեղբայր, մօրեղբայր (uncle) follow the same pattern.

b) To this group belong կին (wife), քոյր (sister), տէր (lord), տիկին (Mrs., wife), ընկեր (friend, companion), and several less common words of kinship: կեսուր (mother-in-law), տագր (husband's brother), տալ (husband's sister), ներ (wife of husband's brother), աներ (wife's father). These are declined as follows:

N/A	կին	քոյր	տէր	կեսուր
G/D	կնոջ	քրոջ	տիրոջ	կեսրոջ
Abl.	կնոջմէ	քրոջմէ	տիրոջմէ	կեսրոջմէ*
Instr.	կնոջմով	քրոջմով	տիրոջմով	կեսրոջմով*

The plurals are regular: կիներ, քոյրերու, տէրեր. The classical տեարք "gentlemen" and տիկնայք "ladies" are used in formal address. But կեսրայր, father-in-law, has gen. կեսրայրի.

*The declension of such nouns is sometimes assimilated to the regular pattern in -ի, -է, -ով. E.g. կեսուրէ, կեսուրով; ընկերէ, ընկերով.

Vocabulary: Lesson XIV

ազգական, -ի	relative	*կին, կնոջ*	woman, wife
ախորժակ, -ի	appetite	*հեծանիւ, -ի*	bicycle
ամուսին, -ի	husband	*հորեղբայր, -որ*	uncle (paternal)
or *ամուսնի*		*մասնակցիլ*	to take part in, participate in (+ dat.)
աներ, աներոջ	wife's father		
անկողին, -ի	bed	*մալ*	to remain, stay
or *անկողնի*		*մտահոգութիւն,*	worry, concern
արդէն	already	*-եան*	
բարեւել	to greet, salute (+ dat.)	*մորեղբայր, -որ*	uncle (maternal)
		նախաճաշ, -ի	breakfast
գրադարան, -ի	library	*նախաճաշել*	to have breakfast
ենթադրել	to suppose, assume	*ներ, ներոջ*	wife of husband's brother
երեւիլ	to appear, seem		
ընթրիք, -ի	supper	*որոշել*	to decide, determine
թատրոն, -ի	theater	*պահել*	to keep
լուռ	silent	*պաղպաղակ, -ի*	ice cream
խաղ, -ի	game	*պատկանիլ*	to belong to (+ dat.)
ծախք, -ի	cost, expense	*սէր, սէրի*	love
կազմակերպութիւն,	organization	or *սիրոյ*	
-եան		*սիրելի*	dear, beloved
կացութիւն,	situation, state	*վերջերս*	lately
-եան		*վերջին*	last, final
կեսուր, կեսրոջ	husband's mother	*վճարել*	to pay, settle
կեսրայր, -ի	husband's father	*տագր, տագրոջ*	husband's brother

տալ, տալոջ   husband's sister   ցուցարար, -ի   demonstrator

տէր, տիրոջ   master, lord, owner;   փափաք, -ի   desire, wish

          Mr. (only in con-   քանի (որ)   as long as, since

          junction with տիկին

1. Ամուսինս իր մօրը համար նոր տուն մը գներ է:

2. Մենք արդէն որոշած էինք թատրոն երթալ այս իրիկուն:

3. Այս տեսակ խաղի մը մասնակցած ես վերջերս:

4. Այսպիսի խօսքեր երբեք չեմ լսած:

5. Ուսանողը չէր կրնար հասկնալ դասախօսութիւնը՝ քանի որ չէր կարդացած իր դասերը:

6. Ան շատ գրած է հայ ժողովուրդի ներկայ կացութեան մասին:

7. Կը կարծէի, որ անոնք նիւ եորքէն մեկնած էին արդէն: Բայց երեկ լսեցի, որ մինչեւ զալ շաբաթ հոն պիտի մնան:

8. Քանի որ դեռ չէք նախաճաշած, մեզի սպասեցէք:

9. Երկու ժամէ ի վեր կեսուրս կը փնտռեմ այս շուկային մէջ:

10. Ինչո՞ւ անկողինս չէք պատրաստած մինչեւ հիմա:

11. Վաչէ իր պզտիկ եղբօր համար հեծանիւ մը բերեր է Պոսթընէն:

12. Կը ցաւինք՝ որ երկար սպասեր էք մեզի:

13. Իր մտահոգութեան պատճառաւ ապուրժակ չունի եւ քան մը չի կրնար ուտել:

14. Երբ վերջին անգամ հանդիպեցայ Անահիտին՝ ան գրադարանը նստած էր իր ընկերոջ հետ:

15. Բոլոր ծախքերը մէկ անգամէն վճարեցին:

16. Ժամանակ մը կը հաւատայի անոր զաղափարներուն, բայց հիմա՝ ես իմ զաղափարներս ունիմ:

17. Այս գեղեցիկ նկարը ինչո՞ւ չէք կախած պատէն:

18. Տալոչս աղջիկը, որուն երկու շաբաթ խնամեցի, վաղը տուն պիտի մեկնի:

19. Որոշած ես, թէ ո՞ր համալսարանը պիտի յաճախես:

20. Երախան ինչո՞ւ չէ խմած իր կաթը:

21. Լուռ ցուցարարները ո՞ր կազմակերպութեան կը պատկանէին։

22. Սիրելիս, ի՞նչ է փափաքդ։

23. Ո՞վ է այս ինքնաշարժին տէրը։ Ինչո՞ւ լուռ կը մնաք։ Պատասխանեցէ՛ք։

1. Haig had already spoken to me about the same matter.

2. Have you ever heard her voice?

3. Vache has explained the entire situation to you, hasn't he?

4. I have never travelled by train.

5. Have you decided what you are going to prepare for supper?

6. Anahid has already sent three letters to her sister this week.

7. It seems that they had never heard such an interesting story.

8. I suppose your father is going to pay for (the price of) this bicycle?

9. That student won't be able to prepare his lessons this evening because he has left his books at his brother's house.

10. Anahid has chosen a beautiful dress for her mother-in-law.

11. We are very tired (perf.). We hope we can go soon.

12. She had never worked before her husband's death.

13. When you greeted us, we were coming from the theatre.

14. They have closed the schools today (so people say).

15. I haven't yet read the newspaper.

16. He had written to my parents about his wife's condition.

17. I hear they've built a new library on your street.

18. The young man repeated to his father the story which his friend had told him.

19. I am sure they have made a mistake.

20. Will you have read the book by tomorrow?

21. In our letter we have answered all your questions.

22. How many times have you visited New York? I have only visited New York once or twice in my life.

23. Why haven't you sent us the book we had requested?

24. She has always helped her sister-in-law.

1. *Comparison*

There are no comparative or superlative forms of adjectives corresponding to the English "long, longer, longest." For the comparative the adverb *աւելի* ("more") may be used with the simple adjective; for the superlative, various constructions are possible.

A. The object of comparison, if a substantive other than the subject, may be put into the ablative, or into the nominative preceded by *քան* (*թէ*).

E.g. I am bigger than you.　　　　　*Ես քեզմէ աւելի մեծ եմ:*

　　　　　　　　　　　　　　　　　(or merely *քեզմէ մեծ եմ*)

　　It is better to work than play.　*Աւելի լաւ է աշխատիլ քան* (*թէ*)

　　　　　　　　　　　　　　　　　խաղալ:

If the comparison refers back to the subject, only the second construction is possible:

E.g. She is more beautiful than in-　*Ան աւելի գեղեցիկ է քան* (*թէ*)

　　　telligent.　　　　　　　　　*խելացի:*

　　Food was cheaper then than now.　*Այն ատեն սնունդը աւելի աժան էր*
　　　　　　　　　　　　　　　　　քան (*թէ*) *հիմա:*

B. The superlative is generally introduced by the adverb *ամենէն* :

E.g. He is the biggest in the class　*Ան դասարանի ամենէն մեծ_ է:*

　　　(Armenian "of").

The prefix *ամենա-* and the suffix *-ագոյն* are also common:

E.g. That is the best plan (of all).　(*Այդ*) *ամենալաւ ծրագարն է:*

　　What is his best book?　　　　*Ո՞րն է իր լաւագոյն գիրքը:*

107

(Note that the adverbs շատ, խիստ (very) are not strictly superlative.)

In general, Armenian does not render literally such English expressions as "less (intelligent) than," "the least (intelligent) of." Such expressions are usually reversed.

E.g. "He is less intelligent than his sister" becomes "His sister is more intelligent than he."

"This is the least expensive dress in the shop" becomes "This is the cheapest dress in the shop."

However, the adverbs աւելի պակաս, աւելի քիչ (less) are sometimes used.

E.g. I bought it for less   Աւելի պակաս (or ավանի) գնեցի:

Note that the expression "as...as" is rendered by չափ with the dative case.

E.g. I am as clever as you.   Ես քեզի չափ խելացի եմ:

2. *Indefinite pronouns*

	Singular		Plural
N/A	մէկը	(someone)	ոմանք
G/D	մէկուն, մէկու մը		ոմանg
Abl.	մէկէն, մէկէ մը		ոմանgմէ
Instr.	մէկով		ոմանgմով

Note the following points:

Nom.s. A form ոմն is also found; rare and literary.

G/D s. մէկուն is used after a preceding noun or pronoun. E.g.

I shall give this book to one   իմ ընկերներէս մէկուն պիտի

of my friends.   տամ այս գիրքը:

But: I shall give my book to some-one.   *Գիրքս մէկու մը պիտի տամ:*

Do not confuse with *մէկի*, G/D of the numeral "one."

Abl.   Do not confuse with the adverb *մէկէն* "suddenly."

Instr.   Extremely rare.

Something: *բան մը* (gen. *բանի մը* etc.)

Whoever: *ով որ*)   The *որ* is not declined; for the declension of
)
Whatever: *ինչ որ*)   *ով* and *ինչ* see Lesson XIII.

Negatives: No one *ո՛չ որ* (declined regularly) or *ո՛չ մէկը* (declined as above)

Nothing *ո՛չ ինչ* (*ո՛չ ինչի* etc.)

or *ո՛չ մէկ բան* (*ո՛չ մէկ բանի* etc.)

3. *Indefinite adjectives*

For persons: *ոեւէ*
                        (both undeclined)
For things: *որեւէ*

4. From *ոեւէ* and *որեւէ* indefinite pronouns "anyone" and "anything" can be

formed:

Anyone: *ոեւէ մէկը*

Anything: *որեւէ բան*

E.g. Do not tell this to anyone.   *Այս պատմութիւնը ոեւէ մէկու մը մի՛*

պատմեր:

110

Vocabulary: Lesson XV

ամժան	cheap	հանգիստ	quiet, comfortable; rest
ամենալալ	best		
ամենավերջին	latest	հիւանդութիւն, -եան	illness
ամենատկար	weakest		
ամենէն	superlative adverb	մէկէն	suddenly
անցընել	to pass (tr.)	մէկը	somebody
առանձին	alone	միւս	other
աւելի	more	նման	like, alike (+ dat.)
գոհ (often with մնալ)	satisfied (+ abl.)	նմանիլ	to look like, resemble (+ dat.)
դժգոհ	dissatisfied (+ abl.)	նշանակել	to mean, signify, appoint
երազ, -ի	dream		
թարմ	fresh	նեւէ	whoever
թերեւս	perhaps	նմ	someone
լաւագոյն	better, best	նչ ինչ	nothing
խաբել	to trick, deceive	նչ ոք	no one, nobody
խաղաղութիւն, -եան	peace	որեւէ	any, whatever
		ուսանիլ	to study
խիստ	severe; very	պակաս	less
ծրագիր, ծրագրի	plan	պատասխան, -ի	answer, reply
կատարեալ	perfect	սնունդ, -ի	food
կարծիք, -ի	opinion	սուտ	false, untrue
կարող	able, capable	տկար	weak
հայրենիք, -ի	fatherland, country	քան	than

1. Ոչ որ կատարեալ է:
2. Այս գործը միւսէն աւելի կարեւոր է:
3. Իմ կարծիքովս անոնց ծրագիրը ամենալաւն է:
4. Մէկը թարմ ծաղիկներ ղրկեր է Անահիտին:
5. "Պատերազմ եւ խաղաղութիւն"ը ամենէն հետաքրքրական գիրքն է որ կարդացած եմ:
6. Ատիկա Պոսթոնի ամենաբարձր շէնքն է:
7. Մէկէ մը լսեցինք, թէ դուն ծանր հիւանդ ես: Ուրախ ենք որ լուրը ճիշդ չէ:
8. Ներսը դուրսէն պաղ է:
9. Ոեւէ մէկու մը խօսա՞ծ ես մեր վերջին ծրագիրներուն մասին:
10. Մեզի համար վերջին դասերը առաջիններէն աւելի դիւրին են:
11. Պարոն Յակոբեանին տունը մեր քաղաքի ամենամեծ տունն է:
12. Ձեր կարծիքով Վաչէ իր քրոջմէն աւելի խելացի՞ է:
13. Աւելի կարեւոր է խելացի ըլլալ՝ քան թէ հարուստ:
14. Անոնցմէ ոեւէ մէկուն չեմ հաւատար: Բոլորն ալ սուտ կը խօսին:
15. Մայրս իր ամենէն հին հագուստները աղքատներուն կու տայ:
16. Ոմանք կ'ուզեն իրենց ամբողջ կեանքը առանձին անցընել:
17. Ոմանք երազներու կը հաւատան, ոմանք ալ չեն հաւատար:
18. Չեմ հասկնար, թէ ան ինչո՞ւ իր հիւանդութեան մասին բան մը ըսած չէ ինծի:
19. Ամէն շաբաթ առտու, Տիկին Անահիտը ամենատկար աշակերտներուն կ'օգնէ:
20. Այդ տեսակ բանի մը համար այսքան դրամ չեն տար:
21. Շատ մը աղքատներ չեն կրնար ուսանիլ:
22. Մեր ուսուցիչը ձեր ուսուցիչէն կարող է:
23. Այս գիրքը ինչո՞վ նման է միւսին:

1. The story which Dikran told us was the most interesting of all.

2. He speaks our language better now than he did a year ago.

3. Perhaps you are wealthier than your brother, but that does not mean that you are as intelligent as he is.

4. You can ask us for anything you like.

5. The baby will be more comfortable here than in your room.

6. For some of my friends, I would do (*կ'ընեմ*) anything.

7. Which is the latest of Mr. Haig's books?

8. I am not very satisfied with your answers.

9. Who is your dearest friend?

10. Some deceive their friends more readily (*աւելի*) than strangers.

11. Just at that moment someone shouted that the enemy was coming.

12. Is Ani older (*մեծ*) than you? No, I am two years older than she is.

13. Vache has heard from someone that one of our country's most famous doctors will visit our school.

14. Your oldest boy looks exactly like his father.

15. Dikran's father is always talking about his children.

16. Perhaps your brother's plan is the best of all.

17. My friend walks much faster than I do.

18. When was the last time I met you?

19. It seems that their train will arrive very late this evening.

20. At the meeting all the young people were talking about their country's difficulties.

21. For a long time we have been dissatisfied with your conduct.

I. *The Aorist (Part II). "Irregular" verbs, A*

As noted in Lesson X there are several categories of verbs where the aorist is not formed by adding a suffix $-bg$ or $-wg$ to the present stem. Eight general categories may be distinguished:

1. Verbs with identical stems for present and aorist ($-b\iota$ and $-h\iota$ verbs only).

2. Verbs with suffix $-\check{u}$ in the present stem which drops in the aorist ($-b\iota$, $-h\iota$ and $-w\iota$ verbs).

3. Verbs with suffix $-w\check{u}$ in the present stem which drops in the aorist ($-w\iota$ verbs only).

4. Verbs with suffix $-b\check{u}$ in the present stem which drops in the aorist ($-w\iota$ verbs only).

5. Verbs with suffix $-\zeta$ in the present stem which drops in the aorist ($-h\iota$ verbs only).

6. Verbs with suffix $-g\check{u}b\iota$ in the present stem which becomes $-gn\iota g-$ in the aorist.

7. Irregular verbs that follow no general pattern.

8. Verbs which use different roots for the present and aorist stems.

In this lesson we shall deal with categories 1, 2 and 8.

Although most verbs in $-b\iota$ have aorist endings in $-h$ etc., and most verbs in $-h\iota$ and $-w\iota$ have aorist endings in $-wj$ etc., there is no absolute rule. Special attention must be paid to the endings of the 3p.s.

---

1. a) բերել (to carry, bring), ըսել (to say):

    e.g. բերի, բերիր, բեր֊ա֊լ; բերինք, բերիք, բերին.

  b) ծնիլ (to be born), նստիլ (to sit), սկսիլ (to begin):

    e.g. նստայ, նստար, նստաւ; նստանք, նստաք, նստան.

2. a) առնել (to take): առի, առիր, առաւ; առինք, առիք, առին.

  b) գտնել (to find), իջնել (to descend), հեծնել (to ride, usually animals),
    մտնել (to enter), տեսնել (to see):

    N.B. e.g. տեսա֊յ, տեսար, տեսաւ; տեսանք, տեսաք, տեսան.

  c) անցնիլ (to pass), հագնիլ (to wear), հասնիլ (to arrive), մեռնիլ
    (to die):

    e.g. հասայ, հասար, հասաւ; հասանք, հասաք, հասան.

  d) գիտնալ (to know), կրնալ (to be able), մոռնալ (to forget), հասկնալ
    (to understand), etc. Note here the -g-; this category is a variant
    of cat. 3, see Lesson XIX.

    e.g. մոռցայ, մոռցար, մոռցաւ, մոռցանք, մոռցաք, մոռցան;
    գիտցայ, etc.; կրցայ, etc.

8. գալ (to come) - եկայ (regularly conjugated)

  ըլլալ (to become) - եղայ (regularly conjugated)

  ուտել (to eat) - կերայ (regularly conjugated)

  երթալ (to go) - գացի, գացիր, գ֊նաց, գացինք, գացիք, գացին.

II. *The Perfect and Pluperfect of "irregular" verbs (A)*

    It is important to note that the past participles of the preceding verbs
are always formed from the aorist stem.   Thus the forms are:

1. a) բերած եմ, բերած էի   etc. (or բերեր եմ)

  b) նստած եմ, նստած էի   etc.

2. a) առած եմ, առած էի   etc.

  b) տեսած եմ, տեսած էի   etc.

c) *Հասած եմ, Հասած էի* etc.

d) *մոռցած եմ, մոռցած էիetc.*

8. *եկած եմ, եկած էի*   etc.

եղած եմ, եղած էի   etc.

կերած եմ, կերած էի   etc.

գացած եմ, գացած էի   etc.

III. The common English possessive (e.g.) Anahid's, meaning "Anahid's house,

family, etc." is rendered in Armenian by the old Genitive plural in *-ենց*.

Thus: *Անահիտենց.*

For family names the modern Gen/Dat. pl. is used.

E.g. We went to the Hagopians'.   *Յակոբեաններուն գացինք:*

Vocabulary: Lesson XVI

անմիջապէս	at once, immediately	կասկած, -ի	doubt
անցնիլ	to pass, go past,	Կարապետ	Garabed (male name)
	cross (+ abl.)	կարճ	short, brief
առթիւ	on the occasion of	համբուրել	to kiss
	(postpos. + gen.)	Հայկազեան	Haygazian (family name)
առնել	to take, get, receive	հայհոյել	to curse
բաւել	to be enough, suffice	հեծնել	to mount, ride
գտնել (+ abl.	to find	մեռնիլ	to die
of place found)		մոռնալ	to forget
դէմ	against (postpos.	մուտք, -ի	entrance
	+ dat.)	յետոյ	then, afterwards
դէպք, -ի	event, occasion	նոյնիսկ	even
դրացի, -ի	neighbor	նուէր, -ի	gift
ետ	back (adv.)	պատահիլ	to happen
երկրաշարժ, -ի	earthquake	պէս	as, like (postpos.
թէեւ...բայց	although...yet		+ dat.)
ժպտիլ	to smile	պէտք, -ի	need, want
իջնել	to descend	սովորական	usual, customary,
լուրջ	serious		ordinary
ծերութիւն,	old age	վերջ, -ի	end, ending
-եան		վերջ	after (postpos. + abl
ծնիլ	to be born	վերջը	later
		տարեդարձ, -ի	birthday, anniversary

1. Ժողովէն վերջ Անահիտենց գացինք:

2. Շողեկաթքէն իշանք եւ տեսանք, որ ոչ մէկը կը սպասէր մեզի:

3. Իր երկու տղաքն ալ նոյն հիւանդութենէն մեռած են:

4. Տիգրանին ծնողքը Երեւան ծնած են:

5. Մոգսայ որ տեղ մը պիտի երթաք այսօր: Վաղը ետ կու գամ:

6. Ուսուցիչը պիտի չկրնայ դասը գալ՝ որովհետեւ պաղ առած է:

7. Մեծ մայրիկը ամբողջ օրը բան մը չէ կերած: Կարծեմ հիւանդ է:

8. Իր մօրը տարեդարձին առթիւ՝ Վաչէ քանի մը ծաղիկ բերաւ անոր:

9. Սովորականին պէ՛ս ան ուշ եկաւ ուրբաթ իրիկուն:

10. Հայրս ալ Տիգրանին քով գործ մը գտաւ: Բայց շաբաթը երեք օր
    պիտի աշխատի միայն:

11. Երբ եղբօրդ հանդիպեցանք՝ օրանաւէն նոր իշած էինք:

12. Չէի գիտեր, որ դուք ալ մեր կազմակերպութեան կը պատկանիք: Ասկէ
    առաջ մեր ժողովներուն մէջ բնաւ չեմ տեսած ձեզ:

13. Տէր եւ Տիկին Հայկազեաններր երեք իրիկուն մեզի եկան, բայց
    չկրցան երկար մնալ:

14. Երբեք չեմ մոռցած այդ դէպքերը:

15. Քանի՞ հոգի մեռաւ երկրաշարժէն:

16. Երիտասարդը իր նոր հագուստը հագաւ եւ քաղաք գնաց:

17. Երեք դպրոց չեկաք: Ո՞ւր գացած էիք:

18. Այս ճամբան ձեր քաղաքէն կ՚անցնի:

19. Կասկած չունիմ, որ իր հիւանդութիւնը ծերութեան արդիւնք է:

20. Թէեւ լուրջ դժուարութիւններ ունէր, բայց կ՚աշխատէր միշտ ժպտիլ:

21. Ամենակարճ ճամբայէն պիտի երթանք տուն:

22. Ձեր դրամին պէտք չունիք: Մեր դրամը մեզի կը բաւէ հիմա:

23. Թատրոնի մուտքին առջեւ ինծի սպասեցէ՛ք:

24. Ժողովուրդին մեծ մասը ձեր կարծիքներուն դէմ է:

25. Իր կնոջ տարեդարձին առթիւ՝ Հայկ երկու անգամ համբուրեց անոր: Յետոյ միասին ճաշարան մը գացին:

1. He was already dead when the doctor arrived.

2. Since we didn't have any money, we ate at home.

3. Have you seen the history book which I took from the library yesterday?

4. Did you see what happened?

5. What did you buy your mother for her birthday?

6. Your brother forgot his books at school.

7. She couldn't take her sister to the theater because she was busy.

8. We went to New York by train, but we came back by plane.

9. My sister's first baby was born seven months ago.

10. When did you begin to study history?

11. We found these old clothes on the street.

12. Is this money sufficient for you?

13. Didn't you see her at church yesterday?

14. Garabed entered the room and immediately began cursing.

15. Her grandfather died six years ago.

16. How did you find our house?

17. What did the children eat this morning?

18. On Sunday morning the girls put on their newest dresses and went to church.

19. Even your neighbors came to the meeting.

20. I couldn't stay any longer because my sister was waiting for me at home.

21. Dikran's brother brought him a gift from Erevan.

22. Where was your teacher born?

23. Last night Anahid prepared a delicious dinner for her friends.

1. *Uses of the participle in* -ած

The participle in -ած (*not* that in -եր) has a wide use in modern Armenian as verb, adjective and substantive.

a) with the auxilliary ըլլալով it may render a subordinate clause of time:

> Arriving (having arrived) in Erevan, Երեւան հասած ըլլալով,
>
> we went immediately to our անմիջապէս մեր պանդոկը
>
> hotel. գացինք:

Note that the participle is not declined in such clauses, and that the subject of both clauses must be identical.

The negative without ըլլալով has a special meaning:

> Before arriving in Erevan... Երեւան չ հասած...

Note also:

> Scarcely had we/you/etc. arrived... Հազիւ հասած...

b) The participle in -ած may render relative clauses, with the subject in the genitive case. Note the use of the suffixes:

E.g. the book you bought yesterday երէկ գնած գիրքդ

> at the time of my arrival իմ հասած ատենս

> the city where you were born ծնած քաղաքդ

> Did they find what they were իրենց փնտռածը գտա՞ն:
>
> looking for?

c) The participle in -ած may be used adjectivally:

E.g. The tired children were sleeping. Յոգնած երախաները կը քնանային:

> The frightened man could not speak. Սարսափած մարդը չէր կրնար խօսիլ:

119

(For the passive form in −ուած see below, Lesson XXV.)

d) As with ordinary adjectives, the participle in −ած may be used as a substantive, in which case it takes the definite article and may be declined:

E.g. Speak no evil about the dead.   Մեռածներուն մասին գէշ մի խօսիք:

as much as you want   ուզածիդ չափ

2. *The declension of postpositions*

a) Postpositions must be put into the appropriate case when governed by a verb. [ի, է, ով as nouns in Lesson VI.]

E.g. անցնիլ "to pass by" takes the ablative.

The bus passes in front of the   Հանրակառքը դպրոցին առջեւէն

school.   կ՚անցնի:

Such compound prepositions as "from under" are rendered in Armenian by the ablative:

E.g. I took the book from under the   Գիրքը սեղանին տակէն առի:

table.

b) Postpositions are also declined when governed by nouns:

E.g. the book in front of her   իր առջեւի գիրքը

c) From the genitive of postpositions substantives may be formed by the addition of −ն− plus the definite article.

E.g.   ետեւ   behind   ետեւինը   that which is behind

տակ   under   տակինը   the one underneath

3. *Postpositions with articles*

We have already noted (VII 2c) the differences between դուրս and դուրսը: motion towards, position in. But such a distinction is not made with many postpositions; they can take the definite article with no change in meaning. The definite article is always used before the verb "to be," and usually when the

postposition comes at the end of a sentence.

E.g.   There is a book under the table.   *Սեղանին տակ(ը) գիրք մը կայ:*

But: Where is the book? Under the   *Ո͞ւր է գիրքը: Սեղանին տակը:*

       table.   *[...տակն է]** *

     When pronouns of the first or second person (singular) are involved, the

suffixes −*u* or −*η* may be used.   Cf. Lesson VIII le.

E.g.   beside me   *քովս*   behind you (s.)   *ետևդ*

    A pretty girl is sitting next to me.   *Քովս գեղեցիկ աղջիկ մը նստած** է:*

*Note change of *ը* > *ն* before *է*.

**Note the continuous sense of the participle: "has taken her seat."

122

Vocabulary: Lesson XVII

ազատ	free	*յաղթել*	to win, beat (in a game)
անտառ, -ի	forest, wood		
անօթի	hungry	*յուսահատիլ*	to despair, give up hope
ապահով	safe, secure		
աստիճան, -ի	degree, grade	*նախկին*	former
աստիճաններ	stairs	*նայուածք, -ի*	look, glance
արդար	fair, just	*նետել*	to throw
գող, -ի	thief	*շունչ, -ի*	breath
ելլել	to go up, out; to rise	*շուրջ*	round (postposition + gen.)
ճամբայ ելլել	to set out		
ետեւ	behind (postposition + gen.)	*ոտք, -ի*	foot
		պահանջել	to demand
ետք	after (postposition + abl.)	*պաշտպանել*	to protect, defend
		սարսափիլ	to be frightened
իրաւունք, -ի	right, justice	*սքանչելի*	wonderful, splendid
իրաւունք ունենալ	to be right	*վախ, -ի*	fear, dread
		տեսարան, -ի	view, panorama
ծայր, -ի	tip, end	*փախչիլ*	to escape, flee
կտոր, -ի	piece	(or *փախիլ*)	
հազիւ	hardly, scarcely	*քնանալ*	to sleep, fall asleep
հանրակառք, -ի	bus, tram		
հասցէ, -ի	address		

1. Անոր դրկած նամակին պիտի չպատասխանեմ:

2. Մենք անտառին ծայրը կը բնակինք:

3. Հանրակառքէն իջած ատենս՝ եղբայրդ առջեւս անցաւ:

4. Հազիւ տուն մտած, մարդը սկսաւ իր կնոջ վրայ պոռալ:

5. Կարապետին նստած տեղէն տեսարանը շատ գեղեցիկ է:

6. Ձեր քովի տունը որո՞ւ կը պատկանի:

7. Անոթի պզտիկը հաց կը պահանջէր:

8. Կարդացած գիրքերդ ինչո՞ւ չես պահեր:

9. Անահիտ ճաշը հազիւ պատրաստած՝ իր ընկերները եկան:

10. Իրենց շահած դրամով տուն մը պիտի գնեն:

11. Անոր նոր գնած խանութը ճիշդ մեր նախկին դպրոցին դիմացն է:

12. Ասպիծաններէն ինչ ատենս եղբորս հանդիպեցայ:

13. Ո՞վ յաղթեց, ծերմակնե՞րը թէ սեւերը:

14. Անիին ճագածը չափազանց գեղեցիկ է:

15. Ձեր նախընտրած ճաշարանի ճասցէն ի՞նչ էր:

16. Ժողովի ընթացքին իր ամբողջ լսածները Արամ պատմեց մեզի:

17. Մեր առջեւինը շատ նշանաւոր մարդ մըն է:

18. Անոթի մարդը միսի մնացած կտորները ախորժակով կերաւ:

19. Լուրը լսած ըլլալով, անմիջապէս ձեզի եկայ:

20. Այսօր սորվածը վաղը պիտի մոռնայ:

21. Գողը նայուածք մը նետեց իր շուրջը եւ անմիջապէս վազեց:

22. Ամենէն նախընտրած գոյնդ ո՞րն է:

23. Տիգրան որո՞ւ ճետ զացած էր ճամերգին:

24. Արամի ծնած ատենը մենք նիւ եօրք կը բնակէինք:

1. Is the street on which you live safe?

2. We were in Boston at the time of his arrival in America.

3. Who wrote the book you read last week?

4. Do not repeat what I have just said.

5. The letter he wrote yesterday has not yet arrived.

6. The bus on which we travelled was very fast.

7. Don't we have what he wants?

8. Not having heard the question, I cannot answer you.

9. The flowers I brought from the garden are on the table.

10. It was very cold the day we went to New York.

11. He set out immediately on hearing the news of his father's illness.

12. The adjacent building is a post office.

13. I'll give you (s.) as much as you want.

14. Next month I shall visit my grandfather's birthplace.

15. Who lives in the room opposite us?

16. The frightened cat ran under the chair.

17. All the places we visited were very interesting.

18. The soldiers defended the city to (մինչեւ) the last man.

19. Do not listen to them.

20. Where is the newspaper the boy brought this morning?

21. The book I found is Anahid's.

22. Having heard her sad story, I shall try to help her.

23. The pictures you sent us were splendid!

24. Don't despair.

LESSON XVIII

1. *Reciprocal pronouns*

There are two different ways of rendering "each other" in modern Western Armenian. These pronouns do not occur in the nominative case.

	a	*b*
Acc.	(q)իրար	մէկզմէկ
	(the standard form)	(written as one word; literary only)
G/D	իրարու	մէկմէկու
Abl.	իրարմէ	մէկմէկէ
Instr.	իրարմով	մէկմէկով

2. *Reflexive pronouns*

These pronouns do not occur in the nominative case.

1st person sing.

A	ես զիս
G	ես իմ
D	ես ինծի
Abl.	ես ինծմէ
Instr.	ես ինծմով

1st person pl.

A	մենք մեզ
G	մենք մեր
D	մենք մեզի
Abl.	մենք մեզմէ
Instr.	մենք մեզմով

125

2nd person sing.

A	դու՛ն քեզ
G	դու՛ն քու
D	դու՛ն քեզի
Abl.	դու՛ն քեզմէ
Instr.	դու՛ն քեզմով

2nd person pl.

A	դուք ձեզ
G	դուք ձեր
D	դուք ձեզի
Abl.	դուք ձեզմէ
Instr.	դուք ձեզմով

3rd person sing.

A	ինքզինք
G	ինքնիր
D	ինքնիրեն (also: "on his own" and "by himself" in certain idioms)
Abl.	ինքնիրմէ
Instr.	ինքնիրմով

3rd person pl.

A	իրենք զիրենք
G	իրենք իրենց
D	իրենք իրենց
Abl.	իրենք իրենցմէ
Instr.	իրենք իրենցմով

Sometimes the form ինքզինք (regularly declined) plus the suffix -ս, -դ or -ն is found for the singular, and ինքզինքնի for the plural.

3. *Distributive pronouns*

Each one: ամէն մէկը or իւրաքանչիւրը

N/A	ամէն մէկը	իւրաքանչիւրը
G/D	ամէն մէկուն	իւրաքանչիւրին
Abl.	ամէն մէկէն	իւրաքանչիւրէն
Instr.	ամէն մէկով	իւրաքանչիւրով

4. *Distributive adjectives*

Each: ամէն or իւրաքանչիւր (both undeclined)

5. *Distributive numbers*

These are formed by adding the suffix -ական to the cardinal numeral.

E.g. He bought them each four   Չորսական խնծոր գնեց

apples.   իւրաքանչիւրին։

Note also the following adjectives which are often used substantively and de-

clined:

միւս	other: միւսը, միւսները the other(s)
ուրիշ	other: ուրիշը
բոլոր	whole: բոլորը (cf. բոլորս ալ all of us)
ամբողջ	entire: ամբողջը
շատ	much, many: շատեր(ը) many (people)
շատ մը	much, many
ամէն	all, each: ամէնը or classical pl. ամէնքը all
քանի մը	a few, some BUT քանիներ how many! (exclamation)

Vocabulary: Lesson XVIII

ամէն, ամէնը	each one, everyone, all	*կրակ, -ի*	fire
այցելութիւն, -եան	visit	*հակառակ*	contrary to, despite (prepos. and postpos. + dat.)
անդամ, -ի	member	*հաճոյք, -ի*	pleasure
արտասանել	to pronounce, recite	*համաձայն*	in agreement with (prepos. and postpos. + dat.)
բնաւորութիւն, -եան	nature, character		
բռնել	to catch, hold	*հանդէպ*	with regard to, for (postpos. + dat.)
գնդակ, -ի	ball		
գովել	to praise	*մօտենալ*	to approach, come near (+ dat.)
զգուշանալ	to be careful, beware of (+ abl.)	*մօտիկ*	close, intimate
ըմբռնել	to grasp, comprehend	*յարգանք, -ի*	respect
ընկերանալ	to go with, accompany	*նախադասութիւն, -եան*	sentence
իրար, իրարու	each other		
իւրաքանչիւր	each (adj. and pron.)	*նեղ*	narrow
խեղճ	miserable, poor	*նշանակութիւն, -եան*	meaning
խրատ, -ի	advice, counsel		
ծանօթանալ	to know, be acquainted with (+ dat.)	*շատ մը* (+ pl.)	many
		որոշում, -ի	decision
ծեծել	to beat	*չանալ*	to try, attempt
կորուստ, -ի	loss	*սխալմամբ*	by mistake, wrongly
կուսակցութիւն, -եան	party (political)	*տեղեկութիւն, -եան*	information

1. Ջանացէ՛ք գիրար աւելի լաւ ճանչնալ, որովհետեւ միասին պիտի աշխատիք:

2. Տիգրան միշտ ինքնիրեն կը խոսի:

3. Ինչո՞ւ ամէն մարդու խրատ կուտաս: Առաջ դուն քեզի նայէ՛:

4. Հակառակ իր բնաւորութեան, շատ լուրջ է այսոր:

5. Պարոն Հայկ իր իրաքանչիւր զաւակին երկու հազար տոլար պիտի տայ:

6. Իրարու նայեցանք եւ սկսանք բարձրաձայն խնդալ:

7. Երախան պարտէզը ինքնիրեն կը խաղար:

8. Անցեալ շաբաթ Արամ իր կնոջ համար ինքնաշարժ մը գնեց:

9. Մենք որոշեցինք որ մը երեւան երթալ:

10. Խեղճ մարդը ինքզինքը սպաննեց:

11. Իրենք գիրենք շատ կը գովեն առանց պատճառի:

12. Ինքզինքդ կը խաբես այս տեսակ զաղափարներով:

13. Չեն կրնար իրարու մօտենալ, որովհետեւ իրարմէ կը վախնան:

14. Ամբողջ օրը նոյն նախադասութիւնը կը կրկնէր:

15. Չար տղաքը գիրար կը ծեծէին:

16. Իր բնաւորութեան մասին զաղափար չունիմ:

17. Ուրիշներու մի՛ ըսէք ձեր լաձծները:

18. Կուսակցութեան թլոր անդամներն ալ համաձայն էին մեր որոշումներուն:

19. Մեր դպրոցի ուսանողները յարգանք ունին իրենց ուսուցիչներուն հանդէպ:

20. Այս հին քաղաքին մէջ շատ մը նեղ փողոցներ կան:

21. Ձեզի ընկերանալը՝ մեծ հաձոյք մըն է ինծի համար:

22. Ամէնքն ալ ներկա՛յ էին ժողովին:

23. Երախաները կրակէն կը վախնան:

1. Can I accompany you home (*մի՞նչև առւն*)?

2. My older brothers are very close to each other.

3. They are very wary of each other.

4. He tried to prepare his lessons by himself, but he later asked his sister for help.

5. After his serious illness, his wife took care of him.

6. She considers herself beautiful.

7. Can't you grasp the meaning of this sentence?

8. Don't think so badly of yourself. All of us make mistakes.

9. They are not against our plans.

10. Your gain is my loss.

11. Having taken a new job, Dikran hoped to buy a new car.

12. They looked at each other and smiled.

13. Each one recited a sentence from the book.

14. The advice of his elders has no meaning for him.

15. Young people get acquainted with each other more quickly than old people do.

16. These opinions are contrary to your character.

17. In which room did the fire begin?

18. Aram caught the ball in his hands.

19. From whom do they get such information? From each other.

20. Most members of that Armenian party were students until recently.

21. Do you consider yourselves intelligent?

22. My grandfather gives me the same advice every Sunday.

1. *The Aorist Indicative (Part III): "Irregular" verbs, B*

As noted in Lesson XVI, there are numerous categories of verbs where the aorist stem is not formed by the simple addition of the suffix *-եց-* or *-աց-* to the present stem. In this Lesson we shall study categories 3, 4, 5, 6, 7.

cat. 3. Verbs which have a suffix *-ան-* in the present stem form the aorist by dropping *-ան-* and adding *-ացայ* etc. [*-ալ* verbs only].

e.g. *բարկանալ* (to get angry):

բարկացայ, բարկացար, բարկացաւ; բարկացանք, բարկացաք, բարկացան.

This is a very productive category of verbs that describe a state and are derived from nouns:

e.g. *ամուսին* husband: *ամուսնանալ* to get married (either sex)

վերջ end, finish: *վերջանալ* to come to an end

There is one exception to this category: *բանալ* (to open) has aorist endings in *-ի*, not *-այ*.

բացի, բացիր, բացաւ; բացինք, բացիք, բացին.

cat. 4. Verbs which have a suffix *-են-* in the present stem form the aorist by dropping *-են-* and adding *-եցայ* etc. [*-ալ* verbs only].

e.g. *կենալ* (to stop)

կեցայ, կեցար, կեցաւ; կեցանք, կեցաք, կեցան.

ունենալ (to have) *ունեցայ* etc. (I had, I acquired)

131

cat. 5. Verbs which have a suffix -չ- in the present stem form the aorist by
dropping -չ- and adding the ending -այ etc. [-իլ verbs only].

> e.g. փախչիլ (to flee) [but փախիլ is also found]
>
> փախայ, փախար, փախաւ; փախանք, փախաք, փախան.

EXCEPT հանգչիլ (to rest): հանգչեցայ

cat. 6. Verbs which have a suffix -gն- in the present stem form aorists in
-gուցի. These are in origin factitives (see further Lesson XXX); but հարցնե
(to ask - from հարg, not հար-gնել) has been assimilated to this category.
[-ել verbs only]. Note the 3 p.s.

> e.g. կորսնցնել   (to lose)
>
> կորսնցուցի, կորսնցուցիր, կորսնցուց; կորսնցուցինք,
>
> կորսնցուցիք, կորսնցուցին.
>
> հարցուցի, հարցուցիր, հարցուց; հարցուցինք, հարցուցիք,
>
> հարցուցին.

Note also ցուցընել (to indicate), aor. ցուցուցի etc.

cat. 7. Several verbs are quite irregular. E.g.,

դնել	(to place, set, put) - դրի	(-իր, -աւ, -ինք, -իք, -ին)
ելլել	(to go up) - ելայ	(-ար, -աւ, -անք, -աք, -ան)
ընել	(to do) - ըրի	(-իր, -աւ, -ինք, -իք, -ին)
զարնել	(to hit) - զարկի	(-իր, -աւ, ինք, -իք, -ին)
տանիլ	(to take, bring) - տարի	(-իր, -աւ, -ինք, -իք, -ին)
տալ	(to give) - տուի	(-իր, -աւ, -ինք, -իք, -ին)
դառնալ	(to turn, become) - դարձայ	(-ար, -աւ, -անք, -աք, -ան)
իյնալ	(to fall) - ինկայ	(-ար, -աւ, -անք, -աք, -ան)

2. *The Perfect and Pluperfect of "irregular" verbs, B*

As noted in Lesson XVI B, it is important to remember that the past participles of the preceding verbs are formed from the aorist stem. Thus the forms are:

cat. 3   բարկացած եմ, էի

           ամուսնացած եմ, էի

           վերջացած եմ, էի

           բացած եմ, էի

cat. 4   կեցած եմ, էի

           ունեցած եմ, էի

cat. 5   փախած եմ, էի

     (but   հանգչած եմ, էի)

cat. 6   կորսնցուցած եմ, էի

           հարցուցած եմ, էի

cat. 7   դնել - դրած եմ, էի

           ելլել - ելած եմ, էի

           ընել - ըրած եմ, էի

           զարնել - զարկած եմ, էի

           տանիլ - տարած եմ, էի

           տալ - տուած եմ, էի

           դառնալ - դարձած եմ, էի

           իյնալ - ինկած եմ, էի

Vocabulary: Lesson XIX

ամուսնանալ	to marry (+ *հետ* and dat.)	*լմնցնել*	to complete
անհետանալ	to disappear, vanish	*լուսանկար, -ի*	photograph
առաջնորդ, -ի	leader; prelate	*կարօտնալ*	to long for, miss (+ dat.)
առաջնորդել	to lead, guide	*կենալ*	to stop; stand
Արարատ (Մասիս)	Ararat	*կորսնցնել*	to lose (tr.)
արուեստագէտ, -ի	artist	*հանգչիլ*	to rest
բարեբախտաբար	fortunately, luckily	*մասնագէտ, -ի*	specialist
բարկանալ	to become angry	*մաքուր*	clean, pure
բարձրանալ	to rise, go up, climb	*մեծութիւն, -եան*	greatness; size
գագաթ, -ի	summit, peak		
գլխարկ, -ի	hat	*մէջտեղ, -ի*	middle, space between
գողնալ	to steal	*յարմար*	suitable, fitting
դառնալ	to turn; become		(adj. and postpos. + dat.)
դարձեալ	again		
դնել	to put, place	*ներքին*	inner, internal
զարմանալ	to be surprised, astonished at	*նիւթ, -ի*	matter; subject, topic
զարնել	to hit, strike, knock	*վերջանալ*	to come to an end
իյնալ	to fall	*վերջապէս*	finally
լաւանալ	to get better, improve (intrs.)	*վերջացնել*	to finish, bring to an end
լեցնել	to fill; pour into	*տարիք, -ի*	age (years old)
		ցուցնել	to show, indicate (tr

1. Վերջերս, Անահիտ օտար տղու մը հետ ամուսնացեր է:

2. Բարկացած առենը, երբայրս ռեւէ մեկուն չի խօսիր:

3. Արարատի զագաթը առաջին անգամ ո՞վ բարձրացաւ:

4. Տիգրան չէր յիշեր, թէ ուր դրած էր իր գիրքերը:

5. Արուեստագէտին պատրաստած նոր գործը երբ պիտի կարենանք տեսնել:

6. Երկար ժամանակէ ի վեր գիրար տեսած չենք: Շատ կարօտցեր եմ իրեն:

7. Շողեկաթի վերջին կայարանը ո՞րն է:

8. Երգիչը ի՞նչպէս կորսնցուց իր ձայնը:

9. Քիչ մը գինի կը լեցնե՞ք բաժակիս մէջ:

10. Աննոյ խօսած հայերէնը շատ մաքուր է:

11. Դասերը անցեալ ամիս վերջացան:

12. Ուսուցիչը իր աշակերտները դեպի դիմացի անտառը կ'առաջնորդեր:

13. Սխալմամբ կարծեցինք թէ այդ գիրքը մեզի կը պատկանի:

14. Անոր դասախօսութենէն քան մը հասկցած չեմ:

15. Երբայրս ներքին հիւանդութիւններու նշանաւոր մասնագէտ է:

16. Վերջին անգամ այս նիւթին մասին չխօսեցանք:

17. Մեր քաղաքը մի՞շտ մաքուր կը պահեն:

18. Պարոն Հայկ իր նոր գրած գիրքը ուսանողներուն ցուցուց:

19. Անի իր հին հագուստները ինծի տուաւ:

20. Ամբողջ դրամս հանրակառքին մէջ կորսնցուցի:

21. Գողերը իրենց գողցած ինքնաշարժով անհետացան:

22. Ո՞վ է ձեր առաջնորդը:

23. Բարեխառար հանրակառքը ժամանակին կեցաւ եւ պզտիկին չզարկաւ:

1. Have you finished your dinner?

2. How did they lose so much money?

3. We stayed in New York for ten days.

4. Hearing a noise, Dikran climbed the stairs, but no one was there.

5. Do you understand what I have just said?

6. The book she wrote is about women's rights.

7. We bought that house because its size was suitable for our family.

8. Have you seen the box I put on the table?

9. Aren't they married yet?

10. Since they were going to Boston, they took my daughter with them.

11. What was the subject of your long conversation on the telephone?

12. Where did you put Father's tools?

13. I turned around and saw that he was no longer (w_l) following me.

14. Have you completed your work?

15. Foreigners are always surprised at the size of New York.

16. We are very grateful for what we have.

17. Your brother and my sister are the same age.

18. The workmen have finally completed our house.

19. I miss you very much. When will you be able to return home?

20. He's turned into an intelligent young man.

21. What have you done with all the photographs of your family?

22. Last week my little brother fell from the window again; the doctors think that he will be better in a few days.

23. Have a rest now; tell us the end of the story later.

1. *Formation of adverbs*

a) Most *adjectives* may be used without change as adverbs:

    E.g. Speak (more) loudly.   (Աւելի) բարձր խօսեցէ՛ք:

           I worked hard.   Լուրջ աշխատեցայ:

           Certainly! By all means. Անպատճառ:

Note also reduplication for emphasis:

    E.g. (very) quickly   արագ արագ

           (very) slowly   կամաց կամաց (for կամաց see below, §5)

b) Many nouns in the instrumental case function as adverbs:

    E.g. gladly, willingly   սիրով

           He came quickly.   Շուտով եկաւ:

           We listened attentively. Ուշադրութեամբ լսեցինք:

(See further under the instrumental of infinitives, Lesson XXIV.)

c) Various suffixes may be added to adjectives:

    1)   *-աբար*: դժբախտաբար   unfortunately

    2)   *-ապէս*: պարզապէս   simply*

    3)   *-ովին*: բոլորովին   entirely

    4)   *-օրէն*: արագօրէն   quickly (cf. արագ above)

d) For languages the suffix is *-երէն* or sometimes *-արէն*. Cf. the Appendix
on Geographical Names.

    E.g. Հայերէն Armenian; ռուսերէն Russian; անգլերէն English; ինչերէ՞ն
in what language? (or ի՞նչ լեզուով).

*Note, however, that այսպէս, այդպէս, որպէս do not have *-ա-* before the ending.

These may be declined:

> E.g. He speaks five languages   *Հայերէնէն բացի (or զատ)*
>
>   apart from Armenian.   *Հինգ լեզու կը խօսի:*

e) There are numerous individual forms:

> E.g. *ակամայ*   unwillingly
>
>   *կամաց*   slowly
>
>   *թերեւս*   perhaps
>
>   *ուրեմն*   so, well then

f) The following have already been introduced:

>   *հոս, հոն*   here, there
>
>   *ուր, ո՞ւր*   where (rel.), where?
>
>   *հիմա, այն ատեն*   now, then
>
>   *երբեմն; երբեք* + negative   sometimes, never
>
>   *բնաւ* + negative   never, not at all
>
>   *երբ, ե՞րբ*   when (rel.), when?

2. *Imperatives of "irregular" verbs, A*

     The same categories will be used as in Lesson XVI.

1. *Verbs with identical stems in present and aorist*

-ել verbs. *բերել: բե՛ր, բերէ՛ք; ըսել: ըսէ՛, ըսէ՛ք*

Note that verbs in *-իլ* have been assimilated to the "regular" pattern:

> *նստիլ: նստէ՛, նստեցէ՛ք; սկսիլ: սկսէ՛, սկսեցէ՛ք*

     Prohibitives are formed regularly from the present stem:

>   *մի՛ բերեր, մի՛ բերէք*
>
>   *մի՛ նստիր, մի՛ նստիք*

2. *Verbs with infixed -ն- in the present stem*

Sections (a) and (b) of category 2 in Lesson XVI do not here coincide. առնել, տեսնել, and a few other verbs, have simple aorist stems for the singular imperative and a plural in -էք.

Thus: ա́ռ, առէ́ք

        տե́ս, տեսէ́ք

On the other hand, գտնել, իջնել, հեծնել and մտնել add the suffix -իր for the singular; the plural is in -էք.

Thus: գտի́ր, գտէ́ք

        իջի́ր, իջէ́ք

        հեծի́ր, հեծէ́ք

        մտի́ր, մտէ́ք

Prohibitives are all regular, based on the present stem:

        մի́ առնե́ր,   մի́ առնէք

        մի́ գտնե́ր,   մի́ գտնէք   etc.

8. *Verbs with different roots for the present and aorist stems:*

        գալ: եկո́ւր, եկէ́ք

        բլլալ: եղի́ր, եղէ́ք

        ունել: կե́ր, կերէ́ք

        երթալ: գնա́, գացէ́ք

Prohibitives are all regular, based on the present stem:

        մի́ գար,   մի́ գաք

        մի́ բլլար,   մի́ բլլաք

        մի́ ուներ,   մի́ ունէք

        մի́ երթար,   մի́ երթաք

Vocabulary: Lesson XX

ակամայ	involuntarily	*զարմանալի*	surprising, amazing
աղմուկ, -ի	noise	*զարմանալիորէն*	surprisingly, amazingly
անգլերէն	English (language)		
անկասկած	without doubt, doubtless	*զբաղիլ*	to be engaged in, busy with (+ instr.)
անկասկածորէն	undoubtedly	*ընդ հանրապէս*	in general, generally
անպատճառ	certainly, by all means		
անսխալ	right, correct	*խելօք*	well behaved
անտարբեր	indifferent	*համաձայնիլ*	to agree to, with (+ dat.)
առաջարկ, -ի	proposal, suggestion		
առաջարկել	to propose, suggest	*հանդարտ*	quiet, still
առեւտուր, -ի	trade, commerce	*մեղմորէն*	softly
առնուազն	at least	*նկատմամբ*	regarding, towards (postpos. + gen.)
աստիճանաբար	gradually		
արագօրէն	quickly, fast (adv.)	*ուշադրութիւն, -եան*	attention
բաժնել	to divide, distribute		
բացատրութիւն, -եան	explanation	*ուշադրութիւն ընել*	to be careful, look out
բոլորովին	entirely, totally	*ուրեմն*	so, well then
դժբախտ	unfortunate	*պարզապէս*	simply
դժբախտաբար	unfortunately	*ռուսերէն*	Russian (language)
դիրք, -ի	position	*սիրով*	gladly, willingly
երեւակայել	to imagine		

1. Վա՛շէ, Տիկին Անահիտին աթոռ մը բեր։

2. Բուլորովին անտարբեր մի՛ ըլլաք այդ խնդրին նկատմամբ։

3. Ուշադրութեամբ հետեւեցէ՛ք Պարոն Յակոբեանի դասախօսութեան։

4. Բժիշկը ըսաւ, որ հորս վիՃակը աստիՃանաբար պիտի լաւանայ։

5. Դժբախտաբար ձեր լեզուով դեռ չեմ կրնար լաւ խօսիլ, թէեւ կրնամ
   անսխալ գրել եւ կարդալ։

6. Տիգրանին խանութէն հայկական գինի գնեցէ՛ք։

7. Եւեւի կողմէն մտէ՛ք, որովհետեւ առՃելի դուռը գոց է։

8. Երախային սենեակը մի՛ մտնէք, դեռ նոր* ըսացաւ։

9. ՎաՃէին բրած առաՃարկին ակամայ համաձայնեցայ։

10. Երկու կուսակցութիւններն ալ մեզի անպատՃառ պիտի յայտնեն իրենց
    դիրքերը՝ այս խնդրին նկատմամբ։

11. Ժողովէն վերՃ գրադարան եկէ՛ք, ես հոն կ՚ըլլամ։

12. ԱստիՃաններէն կամաց իՃի՛ր։

13. Գնա՛, տես թէ ինչ գեղեցիկ եւ համելի է Անահիտէն պարտէզը։

14. Եկո՛ւր, ըսէ՛ ինծի թէ ինՃ կ՚ուզես։

15. Եթէ պաղ առած էք, տունը մնացէք եւ հանգստացէ՛ք։

16. Զգուշութեամբ քալեցէ՛ք, ծամբան նեղ է։

17. Այդ Ճաշարանը մի՛ երթաք, մաքուր չէ։

18. Ձեր բուլոր բարեկամները հանձյքով պիտի օգնեն ձեզի։

19. Վաղը առտու կայարանը եղէ՛ք։

20. Ինքնաշարժներու ադմուկէն՝ գիշերները չենք կրնար քնանալ։

21. Զարմանալի է, բայց անոնք պարզապէս չկրցան հասկնալ ձեր տուած
    բացատրութիւնները։

*դեռ նոր or դեռ հիմա: "just, just now."

1. Speak softly, everyone is sleeping.

2. Go and see the new library; it is a very beautiful building.

3. Unfortunately, this is not a quiet place. We'll go somewhere else.

4. Generally, Armenians engage in trade.

5. Follow attentively your teacher's explanations.

6. Enter the room from the other side!

7. I will gladly do that for you.

8. She is totally indifferent with regard to the unfortunate.

9. You cannot imagine what things he said!

10. Go and get a pencil for your little sister.

11. Eat this Armenian dish; it's very delicious.

12. Don't be so naughty.

13. Doubtless, Dikran was there too last night.

14. At least seven people agreed to our proposals.

15. Generally (speaking), everything she says is correct.

16. The well-behaved child sat quietly at his mother's side.

17. Bring your friend with you tomorrow evening.

18. Don't eat too much!

19. Be here early tomorrow morning.

20. Don't go too far away, we'll be leaving within an hour.

21. Take one of these.

22. You learned Armenian surprisingly quickly.

23. Come home now, it's time for supper (gen.).

24. He willingly accepted the money his grandfather offered him.

LESSON XXI

Nouns with Gen/Dat in -ան

There are four main categories of nouns with genitive/dative in -ան.

A. Nouns with nominatives in -ն , where - w- is inserted to form the genitive:

E.g. *անուն* (name) *անուան; անունէ, անունով*

Vowel changes frequently occur:

    արիւն (blood) *արեան ; արիւնէ, արիւնով*

    տուն (house) *տան ; տունէ, տունով*

B. Nouns originally ending in consonant plus -ն have frequently lost the final -ն in the modern nominative, but retain a genitive in -ան: The -ում, -ման category is very productive for abstract nouns:

լուծում (solution), *լուծման; լուծումէ, լուծումով*

բացում (opening), *բացման; բացումէ, բացումով*

լեռ (mountain), *լերան* ⎫ Note that an original ռ became ն before ն
                            ⎪ and remained when the ն dropped. For the

դուռ (door), *դրան* ⎭ plurals *լեռներ* etc. see Lesson IV 1 note b.

ձուկ (fish), *ձկան*

C. Some nouns without -ն in the nominative have genitives in -ան:

    աղջիկ (girl), *աղջկան; աղջիկէ, աղջիկով*

    կնիկ (woman, wife), *կնկան; կնիկէ, կնիկով*

D. Most nouns expressing concepts of time have genitives in -ուան. For these see Lesson XXVII.

Note, however, that in categories A, B and C a genitive in -ի is often found

143

rather than the classicizing *- wն*. E.g. * անւն - անււնի; ււււււ* (study) - *ււււււմի; արիւնի; դււի; կիիկի*, etc.

The ablative and instrumental cases are generally formed from the nominative. Thus: *անւն - անււէ, անււնվ; ււււււմէ, ււււււմնվ; տււէ, տււնվ* etc. In a few nouns, forms derived from the *-ն* form of the nominative are also found: E.g. *դււ(ն), դնէն* or *դււէն*.

The plurals are formed regularly from the nom. sing. Thus *անււններ; տււներ*, etc.

Note that nouns in *-ան* do not take a definite article in the genitive case:

    E.g.   the top of the tree   *ծառին qադաթը*

     But: the top of the mountain   *լեռան qադաթը*

Cf. Lesson X 2.

Vocabulary: Lesson XXI

ազատութիւն,	liberty, freedom	*ձեւել*	to form, shape
-եան		*ձուկ, -ի,*	fish
անձ, -ի	person; self	*ձկան*	
առողջութիւն,	health	*մեծնալ*	to grow, increase
-եան			in size, age
արիւն, -ի,	blood	*Յակոբ*	James
արեան		*յարմարիլ*	to adjust (oneself;
բարեկամուհի, -ի	(girl) friend		+ dat.)
բարձրահասակ	tall (people)	*յիշատակ, -ի*	souvenir, memory
բացում, -ի,	opening	*նիւթական*	material, financial
բացման		*շուն, -ի, շան*	dog
լուծում, -ի,	solution	*որպէս*	as
լուծման		*ուսում, -ի,*	study
կամք, -ի	will	*ուսման*	
կենդանի, -ի	animal; living (adj.)	*պայման, -ի*	condition, circum-
կնիկ, կնկան	woman		stance
կոտրել	to break	*սուղ*	expensive, dear
կրթութիւն,	education	*սուրբ*	holy; saint
-եան		*ստիպել*	to force, compel,
հանդէս, -ի	celebration, party;		insist
	review	*վտանգաւոր*	dangerous
հարց, -ի	question, matter	*տեւել*	to last, continue
հեղինակ, -ի	author	*տօն, -ի*	festival, feast
հիանալի	wonderful	*քաղաքական*	political

1. Արեան հիւանդութիւնը վտանգաւոր է:

2. Մեր ընտանիքին հագուստները կինս կը ձևէ:

3. Հայկական հանդէսներու ներկայ եղՁր նիւ եօրք եղած ատենդ:

4. Անոնց տուած գինները մեզի յարմար չեն:

5. Երբ երախաները չեն ուզեր ուտել, մի՛ ստիպեր:

6. Յակոբ պիտի չկարենայ իր կրթութիւնը շարունակել՝ առանց մեր նիւթական օգնութեան:

7. Դժբախտաբար դեռ յարմար լուծում մը չենք գտած այդ հարցին:

8. Բոլոր խելացի աշակերտները առանձին դասարանի մը մէջ տեղաւորեցին:

9. Ձեր քոյրը այնքան մեծցած էՐ որ հազիւ կրցայ ծանչնալ գինք:

10. Մեծ հայրիկին առողջութեան համարՐ որոշեցինք ֆլորիտա երթալ:

11. Առաջնորդը կատարեց հանդէսին բացումը:

12. Այս իրիկուն մեզի ճաշի եկէ՛ք:

13. Սուրբ Յակոբի տօնին առթիւ, անցեալ Կիրակի շատ մարդ կար մեր եկեղեցին:

14. Մայրիկս իր հին բարեկամուհիին այցելութենէն գոհ մնաց:

15. Մեր նոր տան տեղը աւելի յարմար է, քան նախկին տան տեղը:

16. Պէտք է կեանքի պայմաններուն յարմարիլ:

17. Ո՞վ էր այն անձը՝ որուն հետ երէկ գիշեր կը խօսէիք:

18. Հայրս կամքի տէր մարդ է:

19. Քաղաքական հարցերով չեմ զբաղիր:

20. Ժամանակս սուղ է, չեմ կրնար բոլոր հայկական հանդէսներուն ներկայ ըլլալ:

21. Այդ մարդը շատ վտանգաւոր է, հեռու գործ մի՛ ունենաք:

22. Ձեր առաջարկած պայմանները չենք կրնար ընդունիլ:

1. How long will the lecture last?

2. Do you prefer fish or meat?

3. Don't despair, I have found the solution to your difficulty.

4. Unfortunately, the glass your daughter broke was very expensive.

5. Many people attended the opening of the new library.

6. We are not satisfied with the explanation he gave.

7. The author of this book died young.

8. They keep the animals in a big field behind their house.

9. He stood in front of the door until they opened the shop.

10. Keep these photographs as a souvenir of our visit.

11. The view from the top of the mountain is marvellous.

12. Who broke the car window?

13. What is your wife's name?

14. I shall pay for the cost of my education within ten years.

15. Vache is going to marry the priest's daughter.

16. Besides your studies, what else are you engaged in?

17. Freedom has always been the most important political problem.

18. That child's mother does not allow him to go far away from his house.

19. He's grown so much that now he's even taller than his father.

20. Many people adjust to the circumstances of life without difficulty.

21. Did you know that Anahid's photograph was in the Armenian papers?

22. My little sisters love horses, dogs and almost every other kind of animal.

1. *Imperatives of "irregular" verbs, B.*

   Here categories 3-7 will be discussed (cf. Lesson XIX).

Cat. 3. Verbs with a suffix *-ան-* in the present stem and with aorists in *-ացայ* form imperatives in *-ացիր*, *-ացէք* (*-ալ* verbs only):

   E.g. բարկանալ (to get angry): բարկացիր, բարկացէք

However, բանալ (to open) with aorist in *-ացի* has բաց, բացէք.

The prohibitives are formed in a regular fashion from the present stem:

   մի բարկանար, մի բարկանաք

   մի բանար, մի բանաք

Cat. 4. Verbs which have a suffix *-են-* in the present stem and an aorist in *-եցայ* form imperatives in *-եցիր*, *-եցէք* (*-ալ* verbs only):

   E.g. կենալ (to stop): կեցիր, կեցէք

The prohibitives are formed regularly from the present stem:

   մի կենար, մի կենաք

Cat. 5. Verbs which have a suffix *-չ-* in the present stem and aorists in *-այ* form imperatives in *-իր*, *-էք* (*-իլ* verbs only):

   E.g. փախ (չ) իլ (to flee): փախիր, փախէք

However, հանգչիլ with aorist in *-չեցայ* has:

   հանգչէ, հանգչեցէք   (cf. խոսիլ : խոսէ etc.)

The prohibitives are formed regularly from the present stems:

   մի փախիր, մի փախիք   (or մի փախչիր, մի փախչիք)

   մի հանգչիր, մի հանգչիք

148

Cat. 6. Verbs with a suffix -*gʋ*- in the present stem and aorists in -*gnɩgh*
have imperatives in -*gnɩp*, *gnɩgէp* :

E.g.   կորսանցնել (to lose): կորսանցնո՛ւր, կորսանցուցէ՛ք

      հարցնել   (to ask): հարցնո՛ւր, հարցուցէ՛ք

      ցուցրնել (to indicate): ցուցնո՛ւր, ցուցուցէ՛ք

The prohibitives are formed regularly from the present stem:

մի՛ կորսանցներ, մի՛ կորսանցէք

մի՛ հարցներ, մի՛ հարցնէք

Cat. 7. Several verbs are quite irregular:

դնել   (to place): դի՛ր, դրէ՛ք

ելլել   (to rise): ե՛լ, ելէ՛ք

ընել   (to do): ըրէ՛, ըրէ՛ք

զարնել   (to hit): զա՛րկ, զարկէ՛ք

տանիլ   (to lead): տա՛ր, տարէ՛ք

տալ   (to give): տո՛ւր, տուէ՛ք

լալ   (to weep): լա՛ց, լացէ՛ք   (the pl. is regular)

դառնալ   (to turn, become): դարձի՛ր, դարձէ՛ք

իյնալ   (to fall): ինկի՛ր, ինկէ՛ք

The prohibitives are all formed regularly from the present stems:

մի՛ դներ, մի՛ դնէք	մի՛ տար, մի՛ տաք
մի՛ ելլեր, մի՛ ելլէք	մի՛ լար, մի՛ լաք
մի՛ ըներ, մի՛ ընէք	մի՛ դառնար, մի՛ դառնաք
մի՛ զարներ, մի՛ զարնէք	մի՛ իյնար, մի՛ իյնաք
մի՛ տանիր, մի՛ տանիք	

2. *"To wear"*

   The usual verb for "wearing" or "putting on" is *հագնիլ* (aor. *հագայ* ; imperative *հագիր, հագէք*).

E.g. On Sunday I shall wear my   Կիրակի նոր հագուստս պիտի

      new suit.   հագնիմ:

      Yesterday they put on their   Երէկ իրենց հին կօշիկները

      old shoes.   հագան:

However, with *hats, gloves, ties, glasses, rings,* etc. the verb *դնել* is used:

E.g. Put on your gloves.   Ձեռնոցներդ դիր:

      My wife is wearing her new ring.   Կինս իր նոր մատանին դրած է:

(Note the use of the *perfect*.)

Vocabulary: Lesson XXII

ակնոց, -ի	(eye) glasses
արեւի ակնոց	sun-glasses
ահա,	here (it) is; *voici*
ահաւասիկ	
այլապէս	otherwise
այլեւս with	no longer; not any
neg. verb (ալ	more
is also used	
in this sense)	
անգլիացի, -ի	Englishman
արեւելեան	eastern; oriental
արեւմտեան	western
արծաթ, -ի	silver
բարակ	thin, fine
բաց	light (in color)
գիւղ, -ի	village
գոց	dark (in color)
գումար, -ի	amount, sum
դպչիլ (դպնալ	to touch (+ dat.)
or դպիլ); դպայ	
եղանակ, -ի	season, weather;
	tune, melody
թանգարան, -ի	museum
խնամք, -ի	care, solicitude

խնամք տանիլ	to care for (+ dat.)
ծախսել	to spend
ծոյլ	lazy
կարօտ	lacking, in need of
	(+ dat.).
կռուիլ	to fight, quarrel
կօշիկ, -ի	shoe
հազուագիւտ	rare, scarce
հաշիւ, -ի	account, bill
հաշիւ մաքրել	to settle an account
հետեւեալ	following
ձեռնոց, -ի	glove
մատանի, -ի	ring
յաջորդ	next
նեղութիւն,-եան	trouble, difficulty
նկարագիր,	character (moral)
նկարագրի	
շիտակ	right, correct;
	straight ahead
ոտքի կենալ	to stand up
պարտք, -ի	debt
պարտքի առնել	to borrow money
սովորաբար	usually
վերադառնալ	to return

1. ԱՀաւասիկ ձեր փնտռած գիրքը:

2. Այլեւս չեմ կրնար ապրիլ այդպիսի աղջկան մը Հետ:

3. Մեծ Հօրս արձաթէ ժամացոյցը մինչեւ Հիմա կը պաՀեմ:

4. Մայրս բաց գոյնի Հագուստներ չի սիրեր, միշտ գոց գոյնի Հագուստներ կը Հագնի:

5. Այդ մեծ գումարը իր եղբօրմէն պարտքի առած է:

6. Արեւելեան եղանակներ չեն սիրեր, արեւմտեան եղանակներ կընախընտրեն:

7. Այս պզտիկները խնամքի կարօտ են:

8. Մեր դրացիները միշտ կը կռուին եւ իրարու վրայ կը պոռան:

9. Մեր Համալսարանի գրադարանը շատ մը Հագուագիւտ գիրքեր ունի Հայաստանի եւ Հայերու մասին:

10. Մենք մեր Հաշիւները արդէն մաքրած ենք:

11. Հետեւեալ Հեղինակներուն գիրքերը բաժնեցէք ուսանողներուն:

12. Հայրս ձեռնց երբեք չի դներ:

13. Սովորաբար անգլիացիները ամուսնութեան մատանի չեն դներ:

14. Շատ ազնիւ մարդ մըն է, ոչ մէկուն նեղութիւն կը պատճառէ:

15. Երբ պիտի վերադառնաք Հայաստանէն:

16. Շատ յոգնած էք, քիչ մը Հանգչեցէք:

17. Իմ տունէս անմիջապէս դուրս ելէք:

18. Ձեր Հին Հագուստներն ու կօշիկները աղքատներուն տուէք:

19. ձոյլերուն մի օգնէք:

20. Նամակին կէսը գրած եմ, միւս կէսը վաղը պիտի գրեմ:

21. Ազնիւ նկարագրի տէր մարդիկ այդպիսի բաներ չեն ընև ր:

22. Շատ մը երախաներ տկար աչքերով կը ծնին:

23. Ինչո՞ւ ոտքի կը կենաք: Նստեցէք, ազատ տեղեր շատ կան:

1. Last night thieves stole several rare paintings from the museum.

2. Here is the house where they live.

3. Get dressed, put on your shoes, gloves and hat, then follow us.

4. Don't be angry; I did not intend to deceive you.

5. I have never seen a book with such thin pages.

6. Stop in the next village and buy some bread and wine.

7. Our house has a very fine position in the forest outside Erevan.

8. Do not touch the pictures in the museum.

9. Turn back, the road is usually dangerous in this season.

10. She has already spent half of her money.

11. Put on your new clothes tomorrow. Grandfather will be visiting us.

12. The next three lessons are the most difficult in the book.

13. Take care of your mother; she is seriously ill.

14. Put on your sun-glasses today, otherwise your eyes will hurt.

15. Go straight on, then turn right at the next street (abl.)

16. Stand up when the teacher comes into the classroom.

17. Open the door. We have been waiting here for at least an hour.

18. Show us all the new books on Armenian history that you have bought this year.

19. Don't ask so many questions.

20. Put the wine glasses on the small table.

21. After the fourth century Eastern Armenia was larger than Western Armenia.

22. Do you know when and where you lost your gloves?

The Subjunctive

In addition to the indicative mood, modern Armenian also has a subjunctive; it is widely used in subordinate clauses, and also as a main verb in certain circumstances. There are subjunctive forms for the present and imperfect, the perfect and pluperfect.

In most verbs the present and imperfect subjunctives are formed by dropping the կը or կու from the present and imperfect indicative: E.g.

կը սիրեմ - սիրեմ, սիրէի   etc.

կու տամ - տամ, տայի   etc.

The present and imperfect subjunctives of a few verbs, where the present indicative and the infinitive have different stems, are based on the infinitive. Thus:

Pres. Indic.		Infinitive		Subjunctive
գիտեմ	(I know)	գիտնալ		գիտնամ, գիտնայի
ունիմ	(I have)	ունենալ		ունենամ, ունենայի
կրնամ	(I can)	կարենալ	(or կրնալ)	կարենամ, կարենայի
եմ	(I am)	ըլլալ		ըլլամ, ըլլայի

(For these verbs cf. Lesson IX.)

The perfect and pluperfect subjunctives are formed with the past participle and the auxiliary ըլլալ:

սիրած ըլլամ   (may) I have loved

սիրած ըլլայի had I loved

Such forms are frequently found in conditional sentences; see further Lesson XXVI.

154

Some uses of the subjunctive

A. As the main verb in a sentence, the subjunctive expresses a wish, exhorta-

tion or command. (In the 3 p.sing. and pl. *թող* is added to express the English "let.")

    Let us go.   *Երթանք:*

    Let them remain here.   *Հոս թող մնան:*

Note that wishes may be introduced with the indeclinable *երանի (թէ)*:

    I wish I were dead.   *(Երանի թէ) մեռած ըլլայի:*

Երանի + dat. renders "lucky, fortunate are..."

    E.g.   Lucky those who (will) see   *Երանի անոնց որ այդ օրը պիտի*

             that day.   *տեսնեն* (or *կը տեսնեն*):

The subjunctive also expresses doubt:

    What are we to do?   *Ի՞նչ ընենք:*

Cf. also: Why don't we go?   *ինչո՞ւ չերթանք:*

B. The subjunctive has a wide variety of uses in subordinate clauses. Two

categories will be discussed in this lesson:

    1. For requests and commands (with *որ*)

    2. For purpose clauses (with *որպէսզի*, sometimes *որ*)

1.   He asked us to do him a favor.   *Մեզմէ խնդրեց որ իրեն լաւութիւն*

                                            մը ընենք:

    Our teachers demand that we   *Մեր ուսուցիչները կը պահանջեն*

        not talk in class.   *որ դասարանին մէջ չխօսինք:*

    Do you want us to come to   *Կ՚ուզես որ ընթրիքի գանք*

        dinner tomorrow?   *վաղը:*

2.   We are going to Erevan to see the   *Մենք Երեւան կ՚երթանք, որպէսզի*

        famous Armenian churches   *հայկական նշանաւոր եկեղեցիները*

        and museums.   *եւ թանգարանները այցելենք:*

He works very hard that his family   Ան չարաչար կ'աշխատի որպէսզի

     may live well.   իր ընտանիքը լաւ ապրի:

He used to work very hard that his   Ան չարաչար կ'աշխատէր որպէսզի

     family might live well.   իր ընտանիքը լաւ ապրէր:

They used to visit us twice a   Շաբաթը երկու անգամ կ'այցելէին

     week so that we were not   մեզի որպէսզի առանձին

     left all alone.   չմնայինք:

With negative = "lest."

E.g.   Do not drink to excess lest you   Շատ մի խմեր, որպէսզի

     become ill.   չ հիւանդանաս:

Note: This construction with   որպէսզի and the subjunctive *must* be used if the subjects of the main and subordinate clauses are different. If the subjects are the same, the dative of the infinitive may be used. See further Lesson XXIV 2b.

Note the duplication of subjunctives, the second being negative.

E.g.:

     Հաւնին չ Հաւնին   whether they like it or not

     Ուզեմ չուզեմ: I have no choice.

Vocabulary: Lesson XXIII

ազգային	national	*կառավարութիւն,*	government
աճապարել	to hurry	*-եան*	
Հրաչեայ	H. Ajarian (famous	*կարծես թէ*	it looks as though;
Աճառեան	Armenian scholar)		one would think
ամուսնութիւն,	marriage	*հաւասարապէս*	equally
-եան		*հաւնիլ*	to like
անձրեւել	to rain	*յօդուած, -ի*	article
ապագայ, -ի	future	*նահանգ, -ի*	state
ապագային	in the future	*ներկել*	to paint
արժէք, -ի	value, worth	*նկատել*	to notice
աւելնալ	to increase (intr.),	*շատունց*	for a long time
	be left over		now; long ago
դանդաղ	slow (adj. & adv.)	*որպէսզի*	so that, in order
դեր, -ի	part, role		that
երանի (թէ)	I wish; would that	*չարաչար*	excessively, extremely
ընդհանուր	general (adj.)	*պաշտոն, -ի*	office, position
թող	"let" (with subjunc.)	*պարտականութիւն,*	duty, obligation
իմաստութիւն,	wisdom	*-եան*	
-եան		*պէտք է (որ)*	it is necessary that;
իրականութիւն,	reality, fact	*+ subj.*	"must"
-եան		*վերսկսիլ*	to resume, begin
լաւութիւն,	favor		again
-եան		*վերցնել*	to remove, lift
կայան, -ի	stop (for bus, etc.)	*տառապիլ*	to suffer
կառավարել	to govern	*օդակայան, -ի*	airport

1. Անապարեցէ՛ք, որպէսզի ժամանակին հասնինք օրակայան:

2. Մեր մեծ տղան կը յուսայ սպազային հայոց պատմութեան դասխոս ըլլալ:

3. Երանի դուք ալ մեր աղջկան ամուսնութեան ներկայ եղած ըլլայիք:

4. Իրականութիւնը այդպէս չէ, ձեզ խաբեր են:

5. Կը խնդրեմ որ, այդ լաւութիւնը ընէք ինծի:

6. Հօրեղբօրս աղջիկը Երեւանի համալսարանին մէջ՝ ընդհանուր պատմութեա կը հետեւի:

7. Երկու քոյրերս ալ հաւասարապէս կը սիրեմ:

8. Հաւնին չ՝հաւնին՝ այս հագուստը պիտի հագնիմ:

9. Մասնագէտները յաճախ յօդուածներ կը գրեն, որպէսզի անունն շահին:

10. Հայրս մեր նահանգի կառավարութեան մէջ բարձր պաշտօն մը ունի:

11. Պէտք է լուրջ աշխատիս, որպէսզի պարտականութիւններդ լաւ կատարես:

12. Գիրքերդ վերցո՛ւր սեղանին վրայէն, որպէսզի կարենամ ճաշի սեղանը պատրաստել:

13. Երանի գիտնայի ճիշտ պատասխանը:

14. Կ՚ուզեմ, որ իմ գիրքէս օրինակ մը ունենաս:

15. Գործաւորներուն ըսէ, որ երբ այդ գործը վերջացնեն, տուն թող չերթան:

16. Այս գիշեր հալու միս ուտենք:

17. Գործը իրեն ցուցընենք, տեսնենք ինչ կ՚ըսէ:

18. Բժիշկը դանդաղ կը խոսէր, որպէսզի հիւանդը հասկնար իր ըսածները:

19. Քիչ մըն ալ սպասենք, թերեւս գայ:

20. Մեր տան պատերը ինչ գոյն ներկենք:

21. Ուրիշներուն վրայ մի՛ խնդար, որպէսզի ուրիշներն ալ վրադ չխնդան:

1. All members of the organization must be present at the next meeting.

2. For the last ten years the value of this picture has been gradually increasing.

3. Our uncle used to play an important role in national affairs.

4. Fortunate are those who can eat meat once a week.

5. The entrance to the museum is on the other side of the building.

6. The following students should remain in class after the lesson.

7. I wish I could speak Armenian as well as you.

8. In the past the Armenians used to govern their country wisely and well.

9. Let's get off at the next stop.

10. Have you noticed how many new buildings are going up in Erevan?

11. When we arrived at the airport, nobody was waiting for us.

12. They are demanding that we pay our debts immediately.

13. She has been suffering for a long time from the same illness.

14. Mother did not want me to marry a poor student; she preferred that I marry a rich doctor.

15. I wish I had gone to Armenia when Ajarian was still alive.

16. Where (whence) are we to begin?

17. She is always asking us to shut the door more quietly.

18. He bought a car in order to be able to visit his girl friends more often.

19. Why don't we write to them and explain what happened?

20. Be careful lest you fall down the stairs.

21. We used to leave the house early on Sundays in order to buy flowers for Grandma.

22. It looks as though it's going to rain all day.

Uses of the Infinitive

The infinitive plays a large role in Armenian syntax, both as noun and verb. Infinitives are declined as nouns in the following way:

N/A	սիրել	խօսիլ	կարդալ
G/D	սիրելու	խօսելու	կարդալու
Abl.	սիրելէ	խօսելէ	կարդալէ
Instr.	սիրելով	խօսելով	կարդալով

Note that infinitives in *-իլ* change the *-ի-* to *-ե-* in declined forms.

A. Examples of the usage of declined forms:

Nom. Swimming is healthy. Լողալը առողջարար է:

(Note here the use of the definite article as in III 5b.)

Acc. I like dancing. Պարել կը սիրեմ:

(No def. art.; cf. III 5b.)

Gen. The time for playing is over. Խաղալու ժամանակը անցած է:

Dat. She is waiting for her   Իր ամուսինին ժամանելուն կը

  husband's arrival. սպասէ:

Abl. Are you afraid of dying? Մեռնելէ կը վախնա՞ք:

Instr. I spend my time reading. Ժամանակս կարդալով կ'անցընեմ:

B. The dative of the infinitive, normally with համար, is widely used for *purpose clauses* where the subject of the main and subordinate clauses remains the same:

E.g. We have come to see you. Ձեզ տեսնելու եկանք:

They will go to Armenia in Հայաստան պիտի երթան Մատենադարանը

order to visit the Madenataran. այցելելու համար:

A similar construction (without համար) is used for an action which will take

place or which must be done:

E.g. Tomorrow $\begin{bmatrix} \text{I am} \\ \text{I have} \end{bmatrix}$ to give Վաղը դասախօսութիւն մը տալու

a lecture. եմ:

C. The instrumental of the infinitive is used in several senses:

E.g. He came running. Վազելով եկաւ:

(Cf. above, A.)

For the third time... Երրորդ անգամ ըլլալով...

Note especially participial clauses:

E.g. Being unable to see, he fell Տեսնել չկրնալով, ջուրը ինկեր

into the water. է:

Cf. also the use of ըլլալով with participles in -ած, Lesson XVII la.

D. The infinitive is used as a complement for many verbs, e.g. "to want (to

do...), to be able to," etc.

I want to leave now. Կ'ուզեմ հիմա մեկնիլ:

The pupils began to write. Ուսանողները սկսան գրել:

Note, however, that some verbs govern cases other than the accusative. Thus:

Dative: մոռնալ (to forget), վախնալ (in the sense of being afraid to do some-

thing rather than of something).

E.g. He forgot to say that... Մոռցաւ ըսելու թէ...

I am afraid to come to your Կը վախնամ գիշերները ձեր

house at night. տունը գալու:

Ablative: ամչնալ (to be ashamed), խուսափիլ (to avoid), ձանձրանալ (to get tired of), վախնալ (to be afraid of)

Note, however, that ամչնալ and վախնալ may take either the dative or ablative.

E.g. Aren't you ashamed of swearing? Չես ամչնար հայհոյելու (հայհոյելէ)

I am tired of reading such books. Այսպիսի գիրքեր կարդալէ

ձանձրացած եմ:

I am afraid of dying (cf. §A Մեռնելէ կը վախնամ:

above).

E. Note that the negative չ- is prefixed directly to the infinitive:

E.g. We decided not to go. Որոշեցինք չերթալ:

Cf. also §C above: չկրնալով.

F. Պէս after the dative of the infinitive may render "as soon as." E.g.

as soon as you arrive հասնելուդ պէս

as soon as she arrives հասնելուն պէս

Note that the suffixes are obligatory.

Vocabulary: Lesson XXIV

ակումբ, -ի	club	հիանալ	to admire
ամչնալ	to be ashamed	հիւր, -ի	guest
անձնական	personal	ձանձրանալ	to grow weary, tired, bored (+ abl.)
առիթ, -ի	occasion, opportunity		
առողջարար	healthy (promoting health)	Մատենադարան, -ի	Madenatarán (manuscript library) in Erevan
գծել	to draw		
դանակ, -ի	knife	պարել	to dance
Եվրոպա, Եվրոպայի	Europe	սաստիկ	severe, strong
		վստահիլ	to trust, count on (+ dat.)
լողալ	to swim		
խուսափիլ	to avoid (+ abl.)	տարածել	to spread, extend (tr.)
ծառայել	to serve, wait upon (+ dat.)	փայլուն	bright, shining
		փոխանակ	instead of (preposition + gen.)
կազմել	to form		
կեղծ	false, feigned	փոխել	to change, alter
կարել	to cut	փրկել	to save, rescue
հավատք, -ի	faith, belief	քաշել	to pull
հետաքրքրու-թիւն, -եան	interest	քշել	to expel, drive (a car)

1. Մեծ Հօրդ անձնական նամակները ո՞ւր պահած ես։

2. Մայրիկին բաժակ մը թէյ տուՐ։

3. Քալելը առողջարար է բոլոր աննոց համար, որոնք սրտի հիւանդութիւն ունին։

4. Բոլոր ներկաները աղշկան պարելը տեսնելով՝ հիացան։

5. Մեր գալուն մի սպասեք, դուք ձեր ճաշը կերէք։

6. Վաղը առտու ծովեզերք պիտի երթանք՝ լողալու։

7. Կարդալէն ձանձրացայ։ Դուրս ելլենք՝ քիչ մը թարմ օդ առնելու։

8. Մեր դրացիին կինը մօրս առողջութեան մասին հարցուց՝ կեղծ հետաքրքրութեամբ մը։

9. Գծելով գքաղած պզտիկները խելօք կը նստին։

10. Սաստիկ անձրեւին տակ քշել չկրնալով, Արամ ամբողջ գիշերը իր ինքնաշարժին մէջ անցուց։

11. Եկեղեցի երթալու ժամանակ շմորունք մեզի հանդիպելու։

12. Հօրեղբայրս ճաշը ուտելէն ետք ակումբը կ'երթայ՝ հայերէն թերթեր կարդալու։

13. Վաչէին նուէր մը տալու ենք իր տարեդարձին առթիւ։

14. Փոխանակ տունը ընթրիք պատրաստելու՝ ճաշարան մը երթանք։

15. Վազելէն շատ շուտ կը յոգնիմ։

16. Միշտ խուսափած եմ կազմակերպուիւններու պատկանելէ։

17. Երեւանէն վերադառնալէս ի վեր հայերէն խօսելու առիթ չեմ ունեցած։

18. Այս խօսակցութենէն ձանձրացայ, նիւթը փոխենք։

19. Կը կարծէք որ հիւրերը ժամանակին պիտի ժամանեն։

20. Դանակը սպահով տեղ մը պահեցէք, որպէսզի պզտիկներուն ձեռքը չիյնայ։

21. Սեղանը քիչ մը այս կողմ քաշենք, որպէսզի մեր միւս ընկերներն ալ նստին։

1. This (now) is not the time to talk about such things.

2. I am going to the library to get some books on Armenian history.

3. It is a pleasure for us to serve you.

4. Aren't you afraid of climbing that dangerous mountain?

5. My friends are going to Europe next month to visit their family.

6. After her guests' departure, she continued her work.

7. He must settle his debts before he leaves tomorrow.

8. Aren't you ashamed to wear such a short dress?

9. It seems they have forgotten to tell you that I will not be coming home for dinner.

10. Instead of going by car, walk to the museum; it's healthier for you.

11. Avoid forming opinions on things you know nothing about.

12. Do you have anything to do this evening?

13. He has no right to curse at his older brother like that.

14. Hurry up, we have no time to lose.

15. I am looking for someone whom I can count on. This work is very important.

16. Is there no one here who can save us?

17. Ani is waiting for her friend so that they can go dancing together.

18. His faith is a shining example to us all.

19. Don't decide anything before hearing my proposal.

20. So many young men have deceived her that now she does not trust a soul.

21. Who spread that false news about my sister's future wedding?

The Passive

Passive forms are constructed by inserting *-ni-* between the stem and the ending. Note, however, the following further transformations.

1. Verbs with infinitives in *-ել* :

    a. The infinitive becomes *-ուիլ*

        սիրել – *սիրուիլ*; *խաբել* – *խաբուիլ*; *ըսել* – *ըսուիլ*

    b. The present and imperfect indicatives (and subjunctives) are then formed regularly from the passive infinitive:

        կը սիրուիմ   (I am loved)

        կը խաբուէին   (they were deceived)

    c. The aorist is formed regularly as with verbs in *-իլ* :

        սիրուեցայ; *խաբուեցայ*

(i.e. the *active* aorist stem is not used)

    d. The imperative is formed from the present and *(passive)* aorist stems in a regular manner:

        սիրուէ, սիրուեցէք; մի սիրուիր, մի սիրուիք

    e. The past participle is regular:

        սիրուած

Hence the perfect and pluperfect:

        սիրուած եմ, սիրուած էի

        խաբուած եմ, խաբուած էի

2. Verbs with infinitives in -ɧɭ :

These are straightforward (e.g. ընդունիլ to receive, accept)

a. ընդունուիլ

b. կ՚ընդունուիմ

c. ընդունուեցայ

d. ընդունուէ, ընդունուեցէք
   մի ընդունուիր, մի ընդունուիք

e. ընդունուած

Note that some active verbs in -ել have intransitive forms in -ɧɭ : E.g.

| այրել | to burn (something) | մարել | to extinguish |
| այրիլ | to burn, be burned | մարիլ | to be extinguished, go out; to faint |

Such verbs have no passives in -ուɧɭ :

Տունը այրեցաւ: The house burned.

Գիրքը այրեցի: I burned the book.

(Therefore, passives such as "the house was burned by X" are rendered by: "X burned the house.")

3. Verbs with infinitives in -wɭ :

These form the passive from the *aorist* stem:

a. կարդալ - կարդացուիլ
   բանալ - բացուիլ; մոռնալ - մոռցուիլ

Other forms are then derived from these infinitives as if they were regular infinitives in -ɧɭ .

b. կը կարդացուի; կը բացուի

c. կարդացուեցաւ; բացուեցաւ

d. *բացուէ̆, բացուեցէ̆ք; մի̆ բացուիր, մի̆ բացուիք*

e. *կարդացուած; բացուած*

Note the following "irregular" passive verbs (cf. §7 and 8 in Lessons XVI and XIX):

դնել – դրուիլ		(aor. stem)
տանիլ – տարուիլ		(aor. stem)
տալ – տրուիլ		(cf. *տուր* imperative)

For *ունել* the present passive is *ունուիլ* ; but a 3p.s. is found from the aorist stem: *ճաշը կերուեցաւ* the meal was eaten.

For the passive of factitive verbs see Lesson XXX.

---

4. A few verbs are passive in form but intransitive, reflexive or reciprocal in meaning. E.g.

վարժուիլ   to get used to, accustomed to (+ dat.)

սանտրուիլ   to comb one's hair (without *մազ* ; or *մազերը սանտրել*)

համբուրուիլ to kiss each other

---

5. The personal agent with a passive verb is expressed by the ablative or by the postposition *կողմէ* (+ gen.):

իր զաւակներուն կողմէ ⎱ *սիրուած է:*
իր զաւակներէն   ⎰ *կը սիրուի:*   She is loved by her children.

but: *Հրացանով սպաննուեցաւ:*   He was killed by a rifle.

In modern Armenian the 3 pl. is widely used to make general statements. The passive is used less frequently than it is in English.

E.g.   Such things are not done in the   *Այսպիսի բաներ չեն ըներ*
       presence of others.   *ուրիշներու ներկայութեան*
                                             (or *առջեւ*):

       In Erevan ice cream is sold   *Երեւանի մէջ ամէն տեղ պաղպաղակ*
       everywhere.   *կը ծախեն* (or *կը ծախուի*):

But: It is said that...   *Կ՚ըսուի թէ* (or *կ՚ըսեն թէ*)...

With passive verbs, when the subject is a noun singular in form but plural
in meaning, the verb is also singular.

E.g.   Ten thousand dollars *were* given   *Տասը հազար տոլար տրուեր է*
       to the poor.   *աղքատներուն*:

       Six people *were* killed.   *Վեց հոգի սպաննուեցաւ* (or
                                             սպաննուեր է):

Vocabulary: Lesson XXV

այրել	to burn (trans.)
այրիլ	to burn (intrans.)
արգիլել	to prohibit
բարեսէր	benevolent, kind
բժշկել	to cure
բժշկութիւն, -եան	medicine
բնութիւն, -եան	nature
գիր, -ի	letter, script
երեւոյթ, -ի	phenomenon
զանազան	various
ընկերութիւն, -եան	friendship, society
լուալ	to wash
կոչել	to name, call (+ *անունով* = name after)
կռիւ, -ի	fight, quarrel
հաւասար	equal
հետաքրքրուիլ	to take an interest in (+ instr.)
հիւանդանոց, -ի	hospital
հրացան, -ի	rifle
մարել	to put out, extinguish
մարիլ	to be extinguished; faint
ներկայութիւն, -եան	presence
նորէն	again, anew
շարժել	to move (trans.)
շարժիլ	to move (intrans.)
նյդ, -ի	force, strength, prowess
պահանջք, -ի	demand
պահուրիլ	to hide oneself
պառկիլ	to lie down
սանտրուիլ	to comb one's hair
սովորութիւն, -եան	habit, custom
վարժուիլ	to get used to (+ dat.)
վարուիլ	to act, behave
վիրաւորել	to hurt, wound
տակաւին	yet
ցոյց տալ	to show, indicate
քաղաքավարութիւն, -եան	politeness, civility
քար, -ի	stone
օրէնք, -ի	law

1. *Ազգականիդ նամակը չկրցայ կարդալ, որովհետեւ ռուսերէնով գրուած*
   էր:

2. *Անահիտ իր բոլոր բարեկամներէն սիրուած է, որովհետեւ բարեսէր ու*
   ազնիւ աղջիկ է:

3. *Կրակը ինչո՞վ մարեցին:*

4. *Իր ամբողջ ոյժը գործածելով` ճագիլ կրցաւ սեղանը տեղէն շարժել:*

5. *Ամէն կենդանիի միս չ'ուտուիր:*

6. *Ընդ հանրապես, հայրիկս քաղաքական խնդիրներով կը հետաքրքրուի:*

7. *Տղաս իր մեծ ճոր անունով Յակոբ կոչուած է:*

8. *Ընդ հանրապես օրէնքները զանազան յօդուածներու կը բաժնուին:*

9. *Վա՜շ, ոտքերը աթոռի մը դրած` կը քնանար:**

10. *Անահիտ տաքեն մարեր է, զաւաթ մը պաղ ջուր կը բերէք:*

11. *Կամաց կամաց կը վարժուինք այս երկրի սովորութիւններուն:*

12. *Քանի հայը կայ` հայերէնը պիտի չմոռցուի:*

13. *Իր առաջարկը տակաւին ընդունուած չէ:*

14. *Այսպիսի կեղծ պատմութեան մը ինչպէ՞ս կը հաւատաք:*

15. *Այս քաղաքը հայկական դպրոց կա՞յ: Եթէ կայ, ո՞ւր կը գտնուի:*

16. *Գողը երկրորդ անգամ ըլլալով բռնուեցաւ, բայց նորէն փախաւ:*

17. *Կոխիի մը ընթացքին քարով վիրաւորուած էր:*

18. *Աշխարհ\'ի ամենամեծ ընկերութիւնները Ամերիկայի մէջ կը գտնուին:*

19. *Մարդիկ ճաւասար կը ծնին:*

20. *Գիտութիւնը դեռ չէ կրցած բացատրել բնութեան բոլոր երեւոյթները:*

21. *Քեզմէ մեծերուն ճետ միշտ քաղաքավարութեամբ վարուէ:*

*Note the adverbial use of the participle.

1. He was named Hayg because of his strength.

2. By the time of our arrival, everything had already been prepared.

3. Only give fresh meat to the dog.

4. He has changed quite a bit since I first met him.

5. The room was painted a light color.

6. What was asked was more than what was needed.

7. Because he speaks so slowly, what he says is understood even by foreigners.

8. Smoking is prohibited in the hospital.

9. Thanks to modern medicine, we may be able to cure her.

10. This was not explained to me before.

11. My friend was wounded by the enemy during the last war.

12. The man was sought for three years before he was caught.

13. All the deceased man's money was given to the church for the building of a new school.

14. Such things are not said in the presence of children.

15. Show us the most intelligent of your pupils.

16. The book I found was written in ancient script.

17. Where are the children hiding? Tell them to come here at once.

18. Comb your hair and wash your hands before going to school.

19. Burn these personal letters lest they fall into anyone else's hands.

20. When we went to visit the sick man, he was lying down asleep.

21. The demonstrators made new demands every hour.

Conditional sentences

    "If" is rendered by եթէ. There are numerous varieties of conditional sentences, but the following categories indicate the most usual types:

1. *Statements of fact.* The indicative is found in both clauses for present and past statements; the subjunctive is used in the subordinate clause for future statements.

    a. *Present:*

եթէ կը մտածեմ, ուրեմն գոյութիւն ունիմ:	If I think, then I exist.
եթէ այդպէս է, դուն պէտք է անմիջապէս պատասխանես:	If that is the case, then you must reply immediately.

    b. *Past:*

եթէ այդ խնձորը կերար, պիտի հիւանդանաս:	If you ate that apple, you will be ill.
եթէ օգնած ես մեր թշնամիներուն, (ուրեմն) դուն դաւաճան մըն ես:	If you have aided our enemies, you are a traitor

    c. *Future*

եթէ այդ ուտես, կը հիւանդանաս OR պիտի հիւանդանաս:	If you eat that, you will be ill.
եթէ պատուհանը բանաս, պաղ օդ կու գայ ներս:	If you open the window, cold air will come in.

173

Եթէ վաղը գրադարան երթաս, ես   If you go to the library tomor-

    ալ հետդ պիտի գամ: row, I shall come with you.

Մեռնիմ եթէ սուտ խօսիմ: May I die if I tell a lie.

2. *Hypothetical statements.* The subjunctive is used in the subordinate clause, various tenses of the indicative or conditional mood in the main clause according to the sense.

The "conditional" mood is the imperfect or pluperfect with պիտի: պիտի ուզէի I would like; ուզած պիտի ըլլայի I would have liked.

E.g. Առանց իր օգնութեան պիտի   Without his/her help, I would not

    չկարենայի դասերս պատրաստել: be able to prepare my lessons.

    a. *Present* (two imperfects, or imperfect in the "if" clause and conditional in the main clause):

Եթէ չօգնէր, պիտի չկարենայի   If he didn't help, I would be

    դասերս պատրաստել: unable to prepare my lessons.

Եթէ այդ ուտէիր, կը հիւանդանայիր   If you were to eat that, you

    OR պիտի հիւանդանայիր: would be ill.

Note that in English "if" is sometimes omitted. E.g. "If you were to..." may be rendered: "Were you to...."

    b. *Past* (imperfect or pluperfect, and future perfect or conditional):

Եթէ շոգեկառքը փախցուցած   Had I missed the train, I would

    ըլլայի, ժողովէն ուշացած   have been late for the con-

    պիտի ըլլայի: ference.

Եթէ այդ արկածէն (արկածով)   If he had not died in that

    մեռած չըլլար, երէկ քսանմէկ   accident, he would have been

    տարեկան եղած պիտի ըլլար: 21 yesterday.

(21 տարեկան պիտի ըլլար [or   (...he would be 21 today)

    կ՚ըլլար] այսօր)

եթէ չանձրեւէր, պտոյտի մը   If it had not been raining, we

   գացած պիտի ըլլայինք: would have gone for a walk.

Note also the juxtaposition of a past condition with a present possibility:

եթէ իր եղբայրը ժամանակին հասած   If her brother had arrived in

ըլլար, մենք բոլորս միասին   time, we could all go to

կրնայինք թատրոն երթալ: the theater together.

Note that the English "unless" must be rendered in Armenian by "if not":

E.g.   Unless they arrive soon, we   եթէ շուտով չգան, առանց իրենց

      shall leave without them.   պիտի երթանք:

Negative of the Subjunctive

     The negative form of the subjunctive is widely used to render a prohibitive (in place of the imperative).

E.g.   Tell no one.   Մէկու մը չըսես (մի ըսեր):

This construction implies an exhortation or a warning entailing undesirable consequences.

Vocabulary: Lesson XXVI

այդպէս	thus, so	իմացնել	to let know, inform
Աստուած,	God	խելք, -ի	intelligence
Աստուծոյ		խորունկ	deep, profound
Աստուած չընէ	God forbid!	համարձակիլ	to dare, be bold (+ inf.)
Արաքս, -ի	Araxes (the river Araxes)	հարուած, -ի	blow (n.)
արկած, -ի	accident	հիւանդանալ	to fall ill
բախտ, -ի	luck, fate	մասամբ	in part, partly
գլխաւոր	chief, prime	միակ	only, single
գոյութիւն, -եան	existence	մտադրել	to intend
գոյութիւն ունենալ	to exist	յանցանք, -ի	fault, misdemeanor
դաւաձան, -ի	traitor	ներել	to forgive, excuse (+ dat.)
դիմանալ	to endure, stand up to (+ dat.)	ներողութիւն	apology; excuse me
եթէ	if	ներողութիւն խնդրել	to apologize
երիտասարդութիւն, -եան	youth (abstract noun)	ուշանալ	to be late (abl. be late *for*)
երջանկութիւն, -եան	happiness	պատարագ, -ի	liturgy, mass
զգուշութիւն, -եան	caution, attention	պատժել	to punish
		պտոյտ, -ի	walk
զօրաւոր	strong	պտոյտի երթալ	to go for a walk

տարեկան	annual; also used to render age	*փախցնել*	to miss (train, occasion, etc.); snatch
տկարանալ	to weaken (intrans.)		

1. Եթէ, Աստուած չընէ, արկած մը պատահի, մեզի հետաձայնէ՝

2. Եթէ դաւանանը քունուի՝ անմիջապէս պիտի պատժուի:

3. Եթէ խելք ունենար՝ այդպիսի չարութիւններ չէր ընէր:

4. Չհամարձակիս աՌնոր հետ կռուիլ, շատ զօրաւոր է:

5. Հայաստանէն քանի մը շիշ գինի բերին մեզի:

6. Պէտք է դիմանալ բախտի հարուածներուն:

7. Եթէ ներողութիւն չխնդրես՝ պիտի չներենք քեզի:

8. Մի ուշանար, որովհետեւ պիտի չկրնանք քեզի սպասել:

9. Եթէ այդ կոմՌերը երթաք, գողերէն զգուշացէք:

10. Իր կեանքը մեծ մասամբ զիՆդերու մէջ անցուցած է:

11. Եթէ զգուշութեամբ վարուիս՝ գործերդ աւելի լաւ Կ՚ըլլան:

12. Առանց Հայաստան երթալու, պիտի չկարենայի այսքան լաւ հայերէն խօսիլ:

13. Եթէ գիտնայիս, որ հոս ենք, եղբայրս եւ իր կինն ալ կու գային:

14. Քու բաձները միայն մասամբ ճիշդ են:

15. Մինչեւ պատարագին սկսիլը՝ շատ քիչ մարդ կար եկեղեցին:

16. Եթէ մտադրած ես նպատակիդ հասնի՝ աւելի լուրջ պէտք է աշխատիս:

17. Եթէ վարը չանձրեւէ, մեր տան առջեւի մասն ալ պիտի ներկենք:

18. Այդ ինքնաշարժի արկածէն ի վեր չի կրնար շտապ քալել:

19. Պզտիկ տղուն արգիլեցին խորունկ ջուրի մէջ լողալ:

20. ճիշդ է, որ երեսուն տարեկանէն եԹք մարդու խելքը կը սկսի տկարանալ:

1. If that is the case, one of us must be wrong.

2. If it rains tomorrow, there will be no class.

3. What would you do if you were to find a thousand dollars?

4. Our prime concern is that the others not arrive before us.

5. You should drive your car cautiously in order not to have an accident.

6. My brother informed me last night that their first child was born yesterday.

7. The Araxes is too deep for animals to cross (= so deep that animals cannot cross).

8. Take care that you don't fall ill again.

9. Let us know when you get back home.

10. If you intend to buy a car, it would be better to buy a new one.

11. The faults of his youth were only minor ones.

12. Next week I shall be thirty-seven.

13. Whatever you do, do not miss that opportunity.

14. If you haven't given him any money, he will not be able to buy what you wanted.

15. Were you to arrive at the time you said, you would find everyone out (= would not find anyone at home).

16. If you send that letter tomorrow morning, it will arrive the next day.

17. Do not do that unless you want to be punished.

18. They would know what we are talking about had they been present at our last meeting.

19. Since she began going for a walk every day, her health has greatly improved.

20. If you had informed us that you were intending to come by train, we would have gone to the station with the car.

Expressions of time

1. Nearly all nouns in modern Western Armenian that refer to periods of time or to seasons have a special declension in the singular. (Plurals are regular.) Thus:

N/A	օր	(day)	ժամ	(hour)	տարի	(year)
G/D	օրուան		ժամուան		տարուան	
Abl.	օրուընէ or օրէ		ժամուընէ or ժամէ		տարուընէ or տարիէ	
Instr.	օրով		ժամով		տարիով	

(Plurals: օրեր, ժամեր, տարիներ)

week	շաբաթ – շաբթուան
month	ամիս – ամսուան or ամսու
morning	առտու – առտուան; առաւօտ – (gen.) առաւօտեան, (dat. առաւօտ
noon	կէսօր (as օր)
evening	իրիկուն – իրիկուան
night	գիշեր – գիշերուան
daytime	ցերեկ – ցերեկուան or ցորեկ – ցորեկի, ցորեկուան
yesterday	երէկ – երէկուան
tomorrow	վաղը – վաղուան
time	ատեն – ատենուան

Irregular is երեկոյ (evening) – երեկոյեան.

But note the regular G/D in վայրկեան minute: վայրկեանի (or վայրկեանունւան

ժամանակ time: ժամանակի (or ժամանակունւան)

(մահ, "death," also belongs to this group: gen. մահուան

abl. մահէ (or մահուընէ)

The seasons are declined as follows:

spring	զարուն – գարնան	(adj.:	գարնանային)
summer	ամառ – ամռուան	(adj.:	ամառնային)
autumn	աշուն – աշնան	(adj.:	աշնանային)
winter	ձմեռ – ձմեռուան	(adj.:	ձմեռնային)

---

2. *Time of day*

What is the time?	Ժամը քանի՞ է:
It is two o'clock.	Ժամը երկու(քն) է:
(It is) eight (o'clock).	Ժամը ութը or ութն է; or simply ութը
It is half past three.	Ժամը երեքուկէս է:
It is a quarter past four.	Ժամը չորսը քառորդ կ՚անցնի:
It is a quarter to five.	Հինգին քառորդ կայ:
It is ten past six.	Վեցը տասը կ՚անցնի:
It is twenty-five to seven.	⎰ Վեցուկէսը հինգ կ՚անցնի: ⎱ Եօթին քսան հինգ կայ:
at two o'clock	Ժամը (acc.) երկուքին (dat.) [but երեքին etc.]
at eight o'clock	Ժամը ութին
at a quarter past nine (nine fifteen)	⎰ իննը քառորդ անցած ⎱ իննը տասնհինգ անցած
at a quarter to ten	տասնին քառորդ մնացած
at twenty past eleven	տասնմէկը քսան անցած
at thirteen minutes to twelve	տասներկուքին տասներեք վայրկեան մնացած

at noon	կէսօրին
at midnight	կէսգիշերին
at what time?	օ̂ր ժամուն (= ե̂րը)
in what month?	օ̂ր ամսուն
Cf. also	in the future	ապագային
	in the past	անցեալին
	on time	ժամանակին

These forms are in origin locatives, but the locative case is not distinguished from the dative in modern Armenian.

The exam lasted from a quarter past nine to eleven thirty (half past eleven).

Քննութիւնը ժամը իևը քառորդ անցածէն մինչեւ տասնմէկ ու կէս տեւեց:

Beginning tomorrow the class will meet three times a week.

Վաղուընէ սկսեալ շաբաթը երեք անգամ դաս պիտի ունենանք:

Up until yesterday they all attended regularly.

Մինչեւ երէկ բոլորն ալ կանոնաւոր կերպով կը յաճախէին:

All summer the university is closed.

Համալսարանը ամբողջ ամառը գոց է:

The New Year holiday occurs in winter.

Նոր տարուան արձակուրդը ձմեռը (or ձմեռուան մէջ) կ'ըլլայ:

The foliage falls in autumn.

Տերեւները աշնան կը թափին:

3. The adjectival forms in -ական can be used as adjectives (or nouns) and also sometimes in expressions of time.

E.g. օրական: daily, a day.

You should eat three meals a day.   Օրական (or օրը) երեք անգամ

պէտք է ուտէք:

ամսական: monthly; *as noun,* salary

տարեկան: yearly, annual (also used for age; cf. Lesson XXVI)

The annual meeting of our society takes place in autumn.	*Մեր կազմակերպութեան տարեկան ժողովը տեղի կ'ունենայ աշնան:*

ժամական: hourly, per hour

50 miles an hour	*ժամական յիսուն մղոն*

184

Vocabulary: Lesson XXVII

ամառ, -ուան	summer	*կեսգիշեր,*	midnight
ամսական, -ի	monthly salary	*-ուան*	
Անգլիա,	England	*կեսօր, -ուան*	mid-day, noon
Անգլիոյ	(cf. Appendix on	*կեսօրէն ետք*	afternoon
	Geographical Names)	(or *վերջ*)	
աշուն, աշնան	autumn; fall	*Հանդէս*	Handes Amsorya: a
առջի օր	the day before yester-	*Ամսօրեայ*	scholarly review of
	day		Armenian studies
արագութիւն,	speed	*ձմեռ, -ուան*	winter
-եան		*ծրի*	free, without charge
արձակուրդ, -ի	holiday(s)	*միջոց, -ի*	means
բնակութիւն	to settle	*մղոն, -ի*	mile
Հաստատել		*յաջողիլ*	to succeed; (with
գարուն,	spring		abl.) to pass
գարնան			(exam, etc.)
դիմել	to apply to (+ dat.)	*սկսեալ*	beginning (postposi-
երեկոյ,	evening		tion + abl.)
երեկոյեան		*վայրկեան, -ի*	minute
թափել	to spill (trans.)	*տերեւ, -ի*	leaf
թափիլ	to overflow; fall (of	*ցերեկ, -ուան*	daytime
	leaves)	(also *ցորեկ,*	
ժամական	hourly	*-ուան* or *-ի*)	
կանոնաւոր	regular, proper	*քննութիւն,*	examination
կերպով	(in) fashion, way, man-	*-եան*	
	ner (instr. case of	*օրական*	daily
	կերպ)		

1. Աշնան տերեւները տարբեր գոյներ կ'ունենան:

2. Երեւանը շատ գեղեցիկ է գարնան:

3. Կէսգիշերէն առաջ տունը պէտք է ըլլաս:

4. Վաղուընէ սկսեալ դասերը աւելի կանուխ պիտի սկսին:

5. Ժամը երկուքին ամէն մարդ ճաշէն վերադարձաւ:

6. Մինչեւ ժամը հինգ, բոլորդ ալ վերադարձած պէտք է ըլլաք:

7. Օրը քանի՞ ժամ կը բնանաք:

8. Ձեր գործաւորները ո՞ր ամսուն արձակուրդ կ'առնեն:

9. Առտուները ժամը քանի՞ին կ'արթննայ մայրդ:

10. "Հանդէս Ամսօրեայ"-ի այս ամսուան թիւը կարդացած ես:

11. Այս շաբթուան քաղաքական լուրերը լաւ չեն:

12. Գիշեր-ցերեկ աշխատեցաւ, որպէսզի գործը այս ամիս լմնցնէ:

13. Այն տատենուան սովորութիւնները հիմա մոռցուած են:

14. Անոր մանուան պատճառները մինչեւ հիմա չենք գիտեր:

15. Հայերը շատ կանուխէն բնակութիւն հաստատած են շատ մը օտար
    երկիրներու մէջ:

16. Եթէ չես կրնար այդ գործը կատարել, մի՛ խոստանար:

17. Ո՞ր ժամուն, կը կարծէք, որ ձեր բարեկամները պիտի գան:

18. Տարին աոնուագն անգամ մը պէտք է քժիշկի երթալ:

19. Կառավարութիւնը քաղաքական ի՞նչ միջոցներու պիտի դիմէ, այդ հարցին
    լուծում մը գտնելու համար:

20. Սովորաբար, եղբայրս ժամական վախսուն մղոն արագութեամբ կը քշէ
    իր ինքնաշարժը:

21. Օրականո՞վ կ'աշխատիք, թէ ամսականով:

22. Այս իրիկուն գբաղած եմ, վաղը ցերեկը կրնա՛ք գալ:

1. Generally, the summers are long and hot in Boston.

2. Where are you intending to go for your winter holidays?

3. In England shops are usually closed from one to two in the afternoon.

4. He spends his evenings working and his mornings sleeping.

5. Many people wrongly suppose that noon is the hottest time of the day.

6. The population of Armenia is now 3,147,859.

7. Each day has twenty-four hours, and each hour sixty minutes.

8. He gives a quarter of his monthly salary to the poor of his village.

9. Students must pass all their examinations before moving into a higher class

10. It is three o'clock; it is seventeen minutes past five; it is half past
    eleven; it is twenty-one minutes to seven; it is a quarter to eight.

11. The meeting will begin promptly at 8:15 in the evening.

12. At what time do you usually have breakfast?

13. Today the shop will be closed from midday until 3:30.

14. Look out or you will burn yourself.

15. Unless you attend classes regularly, it will be difficult for you to finish
    the Armenian course.

16. For many years, the population of the world has been rapidly increasing.

17. She has not eaten anything since yesterday.

18. How many free copies of his book does an author usually receive?

19. Three apples fell from heaven.

20. For the last seventeen years that writer has been busy writing a novel about
    life in modern Armenia.

21. I last saw your friend the day before yesterday.

LESSON XXVIII

1. *Present Participles*

a) There is a present participle in *-nη* (passive in *-ηιnη*) which is used as an adjective or substantive and can be declined. The suffix *-nη* is added to the present stem of verbs in *-ɓl* and *-ɦl*, and to the aorist stem of verbs in *-wl*. Thus:

սիրել > սիրող; սիրուող	loving, lover; beloved
խոսիլ > խոսող	speaking, speaker
կարդալ > կարդացող; կարդացուող	reading, reader; being read
խաղալ (> խաղացող) > խաղցող	playing, player
տալ > տուող; տրուող	giving, giver; given

Examples of usage:

երկու կին ունեցող մարդ մը	a man with two wives
լսողները	the audience
գրողներու միութիւնը	the writers' union
Պոսթոն զանուող հայերը	the Armenians (living) in Boston

(Note that the Armenian participle in *-nη* cannot be used to render the English present participle in such clauses as "crossing the street I saw...." This may be rendered: ձամբան անցնելու ատեն, տեսայ....)

b) There is also a participle in *-ɦ¿* added to the present stem of "regular" verbs in *-ɓl* and *-ɦl* which indicates an actor or agent. It is only found with some verbs. E.g.:

երգել > երգիչ	singer
բնակիլ > բնակիչ	inhabitant

187

But   ներկայացնե լ >   representative (see further below Lesson

      ներկայացուցի՞   XXX for causative verbs in -ցնե լ)

2. *Future participles*

There are two future participles, one verbal and one adjectival. They
are formed by adding -ու and -իք respectively to the infinitive, save that
verbs in -ի լ have future participles in -ե լու, -ե լիք. Thus: գրե լու,
խոսե լու, կարդա լու; գրե լիք, խոսե լիք, կարդա լիք:

a) *Participle in -ու*. This is the same in form as the dative of the infinitive. See Lesson XXIV above for the use of this participle in purpose clause

The participle in -ու can also express a supposition: E.g.

Մինչ եւ հիմա մեկնած ըլլա լու է: He must have left by now.

b) *Participle in -իք*. This participle is used as an adjective, indicating something to be done:

Պատմե լիք ունիմ քեզի: I have something to tell you.

կարդա լիք գիրքերս   the books I have to read

(cf. կարդացած գիրքերդ   the books you have read)

ուտե լիք, խմե լիք   food, drink

3. *Verbal adjectives in -ի*

These correspond to the English "-able" and are formed by adding -ի to
the infinitive. But note the change to -ե լի in -ի լ verbs. E.g.

սիրե լ > սիրե լի   lovable

ընդունիլ > ընդունե լի   acceptable

պաշտե լ > պաշտե լի   adorable, darling

(Note that բանա լի is a noun, "key," from բանալ to open.)

Some of these verbal adjectives may be used as substantives in certain
situations. E.g.

սիրելիներս	my dear ones!
պաշտելիս	my darling
Կասկածելին փախաւ:	The suspect escaped.

Vocabulary: Lesson XXVIII

այլ	other
անընդունելի	unacceptable
անհոգ	negligent
անհոգութիւն, -եան	negligence
բանալի, -ի	key
բնական	natural
բնակիչ, -ի	inhabitant
գտնուիլ	to be situated
գրութիւն, -եան	writing, literary piece
ընդունելի	acceptable
իբր թէ	supposedly
խմելիք, -ի	drink, beverage
ծառայութիւն, -եան	service
ծիծաղելի	ridiculous
կասկածելի	suspect
Համլեթ	Hamlet
հայելի, -ի	mirror
հանրային	public (adj.)
հաւաքել	to collect, assemble (trans.)
հաւաքուիլ	to assemble (intrans.), come together
հետեւաբար	consequently, so, accordingly
մեծագոյն	greater, very great, greatest
միութիւն, -եան	union
միտք, մտքի	mind, thought
մշակոյթ, -ի	culture
մշակութային	cultural
յանկարծ	suddenly
ներկայացնել	to introduce, represent, perform (a play)
ներկայացուցիչ, -ի	representative
շարժում, -ի, շարժման	motion, movement, gesture
շրջակայք, -ի	neighborhood
ուտելիք, -ի	food
ուրանալ	to deny, renounce
պաշտելի	adorable
պաշտօնեայ, -ի	official
պարագայ, -ի	circumstance
պետութիւն, -եան	state

1. Անձնական պատմաններով չկրցայ ժողովին ներկայ զանուիլ:

2. Բացի անկէ, այլ խնդիրներով ալ զբաղեցանք:

3. Այդ գրողի գրութիւնները ալ չեմ կարդար, որովհետեւ չեմ հասկնար
   զանոնք:

4. Հանրային գործերով զբաղողները եւ ժողովուրդէն ընտրուած բոլոր
   ներկայացուցիչները պէտք է կարդան այդ կարեւոր յօդուածը:

5. ներկայ եղողներուն մեծագոյն մասը ընդունեց անոր առաջարկը:

6. Իր շարժումները բոլորովին ալ բնական չեն:

7. Տիգրան ուրացաւ անցեալ ամսուան քաղաքական ժողովներուն մասնակցած
   ըլլալը:

8. Կառավարութեան պաշտօնեաները յայտնեցին, որ ազգային պարտքը
   քանի մը միլիոնով աւելցած է:

9. Պարագաները ստիպեցին զինք իր հին տունը ծախելու:

10. Գործ չունեցողները պետութեան օգնութիւնը պէտք է խնդրեն:

11. Եթէ այդ կողմերը պատոյաի երթալու ըլլաք,* ձեր ուտելիքներն ու
    խմելիքները ձեզի հետ տարէք՝ որովհետեւ խանութներ չկան հոն:

12. Ըսելիքներ շատ ունիմ: Որ մը հանդիպինք, որպէսզի բոլորն ալ
    պատմեմ քեզի:

13. Գիտնալու էք, որ քննութիւնը շատ դժուար պիտի ըլլայ:

14. Ձեր ըսածները պարզ են, կրկնելու պէտք չունիք:

15. Հայրս գործի երթալէ առաջ մեզ կը հաւքուրէ:

16. Քանի մը վայրկեանէն նամակատուն պիտի երթամ: Եթէ դրկելիք
    նամակներ ունիք՝ տուէք, տանիմ:

17. Զբաղելու միջոց մը գտնելու է, այլապէս քան մը շրնելով պիտի
    ձանձրանաք:

18. Միութեան անդամները ո՞ւր պիտի հաւաքուին գալ շաբաթ:

* = երթաք.

19. Մեծ հայրդ հիւանդ էր թէ բնական պատՃառներէ մեռաւ:

20. Յանկարծ, առանց որեւէ պատՃառի, Պրն. Յակոբեան քաղաքէն մեկնեցաւ

1. Most of the town's paper factories are situated on the right-hand bank of the river.

2. A man with a watch does not need to ask strangers the time.

3. Following her husband's death, she lost her former happiness.

4. He came supposedly to help us, but in reality he did more harm than good.

5. Because of the services he has rendered everyone, he is liked by all.

6. That man is suspect; keep away from him.

7. Our daughter wants to become a famous writer.

8. She has read too many novels, consequently her ideas about life are ridiculc

9. Wherever Armenians are to be found, they always form various cultural unions

10. Our Armenian teacher has written many books on the history of Armenian thought.

11. Last night the members of the Armenian theater performed "Hamlet" for the third time this month.

12. The inhabitants of our neighborhood come from various countries of the world.

13. He broke the key trying to open the door.

14. How many letters do you have to write this week?

15. I have a lot of things to do; you will have to wait a few more minutes.

16. The enemies' proposals were quite unacceptable, so the war continued.

17. He is a very rapid speaker, so the lecture should not last long.

18. My elder sister spends hours in front of the mirror combing her hair.

19. Dikran is a very quick reader; he would have finished that novel long ago.

20. Due to his negligence, he soon lost his position.

1. *Result clauses*

Clauses of result are introduced by the particle *որ*. "So that" is rendered by *այնանկ որ* (or *այնպէս որ*). The verb of the subordinate clause is in the indicative mood.

Distinguish, therefore, between purpose and result:

Purpose: She opened the window so that fresh air could come in.

Պատուհանը բացաւ, որպէսզի թարմ օդ գար ներս:

Result: She opened the window so that cold air came in.

Պատուհանը բացաւ, անանկ որ պաղ օդ մտաւ ներս:

Further examples:

The book was so long that I could not finish it.	Գիրքը այնքան երկար էր, որ չկրցայ (զայն) վերջացնել:
My grandfather is so old that he cannot walk unaided.	Մեծ հայրս այնքան ծեր է, որ չի կրնար քալել առանց օգնութեան:
The train was so late that we did not arrive on time.	Շոգեկառքը այնքան ուշացաւ, որ ժամանակին չ հասանք:

2. *Concessive clauses*

A. "Although" is rendered by *թէեւ* (*թէպէտ* and *թէպէտեւ* are also found): E.g.

He continued to sing, although no one was listening to him.	Ան կը շարունակէր երգել, թէեւ ոչ ոք մտիկ կ'ընէր իրեն:
Although he bought the tickets, his friends did not even say thank you.	Թէեւ ինք գնեց տոմսակները, իր ընկերները շնորհակալութիւն իսկ չ յայտնեցին իրեն:

193

If the concessive clause comes first, բայց often precedes the main verb:

Although I liked the picture, I   Թէեւ հաւնեցայ նկարը, (բայց) չկրցայ

    couldn't buy it as I had no money.   զնել զայն որովՀետեւ դրամ չունէ.

    B.   "Despite" is rendered by Հակառակ. A following noun is put into the genitive. "Despite the fact that" is rendered by Հակառակ plus an infinitive (in the gen. case) or Հակառակ անոր որ. E.g.

Despite the rain we went for a   Հակառակ անձրեւին, պտոյտի

    walk.   գացինք:

(But in Armenian this could also be translated: Հակառակ անոր որ

կ'անձրեւէր, պտոյտի գացինք:

Despite being ill, Boghosian   Հակառակ Հիւանդ ըլլալուն, Պողոսեան

    attended the meeting.   ներկայ գտնուեցաւ ժողովին:

Despite the fact that he was   Հակառակ անոր որ Հիւանդ էր,

    ill, Boghosian...   Պողոսեան...

Despite his illness, B...   Հակառակ իր Հիւանդութեան, Պ...

3.   *"Please"*

    In a more formal sense կը Հաճիք (կը Հաճիս for intimate friends) is used, followed by the infinitive.

E.g.   Would you please give me a   Կը Հաճիք (կը Հաճիս) գաւաթ մը

    glass of water.   ջուր տալ:

    In a less formal sense Հաճիս and Հաճիք are put at the end or beginning of the sentence, which then has the verb in the indicative:

                 Գաւաթ մը ջուր կու տաք, Հաճիք:

                 Հաճիս, գաւաթ մը ջուր կու տաս:

Very formal is *հաճեցէք* with the infinitive, used primarily in writing.

E.g.   Please accept our best wishes   *Հաճեցէք ընդունիլ մեր լաւագոյն*

for the New Year.   *մաղթանքները Նոր Տարուան առթիւ:*

Խնդրեմ with the imperative is used mainly for invitations.

E.g.   Come in, please.   *Ներս եկէք, խնդրեմ:*

In a similar sense note *հրամմէ , հրամմեցէք,* a general invitation mean-

ing - according to the situation - "come in, help yourself, sit down, etc."

Vocabulary: Lesson XXIX

աղբիւր, -ի	source, fountain	հրամմէ,	[see above, §3]
աղտոտ	dirty	հրամմեցէք	
այնպէս	so	ձիւն, -ի	snow
անանկ	so	ձիւն գալ	to snow
անանկ որ	so that	մաղթանք, -ի	wish (as greeting)
անհամբերութիւն,	impatience	մութ	dark (adj.)
-եան		մտիկ ընել	to listen to, pay
անձամբ	in person		attention to (+
արթննալ	to wake up		dat.)
բարձրութիւն,	height	մօտաւորապէս	about, approximately
-եան		ներս	inside, interior
ըստ	according to (prepo-		(noun)
	sition + dat.)	նոյնպէս	likewise
թէեւ, թէպետեւ	although	շուք, -ի	shade, shadow
ինչպէս...	as...so (often =	ստոյգ	reliable, real
նոյնպէս	both...and)	ստուգել	to verify
(or այնպէս)		վերադարձ, -ի	return (noun)
իսկ	but, whereas	վստահութիւն,	trust, confidence
կանոն, -ի	rule, regulation	-եան	
հակառակ	(the) opposite (noun)	տոմսակ, -ի	ticket
հաճիլ	to be pleased	ցոյց, -ի	demonstration
հեռաւորութիւն,	distance	քայլ, -ի	step, footstep
-եան		քիլոմեթր, -ի	kilometer

1. Անծրելէն եռք այնքան ձիւն եկաւ, որ չկրցանք գիշերը տուն
   վերադառնալ:

2. Այնքան բարկացած կ՚երեւէր, որ չ՚համարձակեցայ իրեն մօտենալու:

3. Սենեակը այնքան մութ էր, որ պատին զարնուեցայ:

4. Տան ներսը մաքուր էր, իսկ դուրսը՝ աղտոտ:

5. Ինչպէս աննս, նոյնպէս եւ մենք՝ կ՚եսօրները ճաշ չ՚ենք ուտեր:

6. Դժբախտաբար շատ ուշ է, ալ չ՚ենք կրնար իր տուած տեղեկութիւնները
   ստուգել:

7. Մեծ անհամբերութեամբ ծնողին վերադարձին կը սպասէ:

8. Հակառակ իր բաձնԵերուն, ես այդպիսի մարդոց նկատմամբ վստահութիւն
   չ՚ունիմ:

9. Օրուան աշխատանքը վերջացնելէ եռք, ան ամէն իրիկուն պատյտի մը
   կ՚երթայ:

10. Ձեր մարղը դանդաղ քայլերով շուկայ կ՚երթար:

11. Ակնլութիւն ունեցէք եւ ճշմարտութիւնը ըսէք:

12. Ասիկա ճայկական ճաշ մըն է, յուսամ* կը ճանիք: Բարի ախորժակ:

13. Գողը փախաւ եւ մութին մէջ անճետացաւ:

14. Հակառակ մեր սովորութեան, երէկ կանուխ քնացանք, որպէսզի այսօր
    շուտ արթննանք եւ գործը ժամանակին վերջացնենք:

15. Ամերիկացիները դժուարութեամբ կ՚արտասանեն շատ մը ճայկական
    անուններ:

16. Իրեն ճամար մեծ ճաճոյք է արձակուրդը առանձին անցընելը:

17. Հակառակ շատ ձեր ըլլալուն, ամէն տարի անձամբ իր տունը կը ներկէ:

18. Կը ճաճիք այս թուղթերը սեղանին վրայ դնել:

19. Այդ աթոռը ճոս կը բերես, ճաճիս:

20. Հաճեցէք նամակիս անմիջապէս պատասխանել:

*յուսամ and յուսանք are often found without կը ; cf. Lesson VIII 3.

1. He was so weak that he could not even lift the chair.

2. What is the height of Mt. Ararat? I am not sure, but I think that it is between 5,150 and 5,160 meters.

3. The rules of the organization were accepted by its members at the last meeting.

4. The distance between Erevan and Moscow is about 3,000 kilometers.

5. The teachers informed their students that not one had passed the history examination.

6. The sad girl sat down in the shade of the old apple tree.

7. Fish is so expensive now, that we have not bought any for several weeks.

8. According to reliable sources, at least three people were killed in yesterday's demonstration.

9. Since I was unable to buy tickets for the theater, we had to change our plans at the last moment.

10. In summer the days are longer than the nights, but in winter the opposite is the case.

11. I'm free, so let's have a beer somewhere.

12. Although the windows were closed, he could still hear the noise from (= of) the street.

13. I cannot talk to you now, because I am in a hurry.

14. Despite the fact that as a child he had had no opportunity to attend school regularly, he succeeded in life.

15. Kindly explain to me how you lost your shoes on the way (= while coming) home

16. Because he was not paying attention, the wine glasses he was carrying all fell to the floor.

17. Although I am satisfied with your work, you will have to work harder if you want to be the best in the class.

18. Although she is very clever, she was unable to grasp the meaning of the teacher's remarks.

19. The quickest way to reach the university is by bicycle.

LESSON XXX

Causative verbs

A causative verb is formed by adding the suffix *-gʰᵘᵉᵗᵢ* to a root, e.g.
adjectives or verbal stems:

կարճ short: կարճգնել to shorten; հագ- (√to dress): հագգնել to clothe.
Sometimes with verbal roots an -ե- is inserted before the causative suffix for
verbs in -ել and -իլ , and an -ա- for verbs in -ալ:

լնել	to be silent:	լնեգնել	to silence
նստիլ	to sit:	նստեգնել	to seat
խնդալ	to laugh	խնդագնել	to make someone laugh

Verbs that have the suffixes -ն-, -ան-, -են- or -չ- between the root
and the infinitive ending lose the consonant in the causative:

մտնել	to enter:	մտգնել	to bring in
հագնիլ	to dress (oneself):	հագգնել	to dress someone
փախչիլ	to flee:	փախգնել	to miss; snatch away
(or փախիլ)			
տկարանալ	to be weak:	տկարագնել	to weaken
մօտենալ	to approach	մօտեգնել	to bring near
մեռնիլ	to die:	մեռգնել	to put to death

Irregularities:

փրթիլ	to come off:	փրգնել	to detach, pick off
հանգչիլ	to rest:	հանգչեգնել	to put to rest
ուտել	to eat:	կերգնել	to make someone eat, feed

200

անցնիլ   to pass: *անցընել*   to take past (and many spe-

cial meanings)

կենալ   to stop: *կեցնել*   to bring to a stop; park

(a car)

դառնալ   to turn (intrans.): *դարձնել*   to turn (trans.)

The aorist of verbs in *-գնել* is *-գուցի* (cf. Lesson XIX, cat. 6).

E.g. *տկարացնել* - *տկարացուցի*

կեցնել - *կեցուցի*

But note: *անցընել* - *անցուցի*

անցնիլ - *անցայ*

դարձնել - *դարձուցի*

The imperatives follow the regular pattern of Lesson XXII, cat. 6.

E.g. *կեցնել* - *կեցունր, կեցուցէք*

(*մի կեցներ, մի կեցնէք*)

անցընել - *անցունր, անցուցէք*

դարձնել - *դարձունր, դարձուցէք*

The classical causative in *-ուցանել* is rarely found in spoken Armenian:

մատուցանել   to offer

ծանուցանել   to notify

The aorist is in *-ուցի*. E.g. *ծանուցի* etc.

Examples of usage

The tailor shortened my jacket.   *Դերձակը բաճկոնս կարճցուց:*

You make us work long hours.   *Մեզ երկար ժամեր կ'աշխատցնես:*

The speaker silenced the opposition.	*Խոսողը լռեցուց իր հակառակորդները:*

Note *անցնիլ* and *անցընել*:

We passed them on the road.	*Ճամբան անոնց անցանք:*
We took the children across the river.	*Պզտիկները գետին մէս կողմը անցուցինք:*

Some causative verbs can take two objects; then the actor is put into the dative case:

They made him drink wine.	*Գինի խմցուցին անոր:*

More common is the use of the verb *տալ* in a factitive sense: "to have someone do something." The actor is put into the dative case, and the infinitive of the secondary verb remains in the *active* mood.

E.g. He had a house built.	*Տուն մը շինել տուաւ:*
My parents had those workmen build their house.	*Ծնողքս իրենց տունը այդ գործաւորներուն շինել տուին:*
He had the barber cut his hair short.	*Իր մազերը կարճնել տուաւ սափրիչին:*

The passive of causatives

Generally, the passive is formed from the present stem without the *-ն-* of the causative suffix.

E.g. *կարճ* short: *կարճցնել* to shorten: *կարճցուիլ* to be shortened

վերադարձնել to return: *վերադարձուիլ* to be returned

Causatives in *-ուցանեմ* lose *-ան-* in the passive:

մատուցանել to offer: *մատուցուիլ* to be offered

Some causative verbs build the passive from the root:

կորսնցնել to lose: *կորսուիլ* to be lost (not * *կորսնցուիլ*)

However, passive causative verbs are not very common; the impersonal 3rd

person plural usually renders such expressions. E.g.

The speaker was introduced.   *Խօսողը ներկայացուցին:*

(rather than *ներկայացուեցաւ*)

Note: Although *հարցնել* (to ask) is not a causative, the passive (3p. only is

found) follows this pattern: *հարցուեցաւ.*

Vocabulary: Lesson XXX

աշխատցնել	to make (someone) work, put into action, start	հագցնել	to clothe, dress
		հակառակորդ, -ի	opponent
բաճկոն, -ի	jacket	հայրենակից, -ի	compatriot, fellow-countryman
բացական	absent		
գետ, -ի	river	հայրենակցական	compatriotic
գոհացնել, -ցուցի	to satisfy, please	հրամցնել	to offer
		մատուցանել	to offer
դարձնել, դարձուցի	to turn (trans.)	մեծցնել	to enlarge
		մացնել	to bring in
դերձակ, -ի	tailor	մոտեցնել	to bring near
զարմացնել, -ացուցի	to astonish, surprise	նախագահ, -ի	president, chairman
		նստեցնել	to seat
ընտրութիւն, -եան	election	պառկեցնել	to lay down, put to bed
լռել	to be silent	պարահանդէս, -ի	dance (noun); ball
լռեցնել	to silence	սառիլ	to freeze (intrans.)
խմցնել	to make (someone) drink	սափրիչ, -ի	barber
		սորվեցնել	to teach
ծանուցանել	to notify	տաբատ, -ի	(pair of) trousers
ծանօթացնել	to introduce	տեղեկացնել	to inform, notify
կարճցնել	to shorten	տկարացնել	to weaken (trans.)
կերցնել	to feed	փրթիլ	to come off
կեցնել	to stop (trans.); park	փրցնել	to detach, pick off
կորսուիլ	to get lost, disappear		

1. Օրը պադ ըլլալուն ինքնաշարժը չկրցանք աշխատցնել:

2. Ծոյլ ուսանողները չեն կրնար գոհացնել իրենց ուսուցիչները:

3. Կարեւոր ըսելիք ունեցողները լռեցնելը լաւ չէ:

4. Եթէ այս կողմէն երթանք, ճամբան կարճուցած կ՚ըլլանք:

5. Կրրսուլէ՞ ասկէ,* չեմ ուզեր քեզ տեսնել այլեւս:

6. Պզտիկը կը փախէր, որպեսզի մայրը չկրնար զինք հագցնել:

7. Սարգիսեանները ի՞նչ հրամցուցին իրենց հիւրերուն երէկ գիշեր:

8. Դուրսը սպասողները եւելի դռնէն ներս մոցուցէք:

9. Դուք ո՞ր կուսակցութիւնը կը ներկայացնէք:

10. Մինչեւ վերջին վայրկեանը, առաջնորդը չէր գիտեր, թէ զինք ո՞ւր պիտի նստեցնեն:

11. Տարին քանի՞ անգամ սափրիչի կ՚երթաս:

12. Հին ատեն աղջիկ փախցնելը սովորական էր:

13. Հակառակ յօգնած ըլլալուս, քանի մը երգ երգել տուին ինծի:

14. Անգլերէն չգիտնալուն պատճառաւ, նամակները ուրիշներուն գրել կու-
    տայ:

15. Ինծի մի՞ լիշեցներ անոր պատճառած դժուարութիւնները:

16. Կը յուսամ, որ նախագա՞հը մեր ամսականները կ՚աւելցնէ զալ տարի:

17. Հայ ժողովուրդի պատմութեան մասին անոր գրած յօդուածները միշտ
    կը բարկացնեն զիս:

18. Ինչէ՞ն կ՚ենթադրէք, որ դուք ծիշտ էք, իսկ ես՝ սխալ:

19. Աշնանային երկար երեկոները վեպեր գրելով կ՚անցընէր:

20. Բացականերուն ո՞վ պիտի տեղեկացնէ մեր որոշումները:

*ասկէ, a common variant of այս տեղէն.

1. He entered the tailor's shop in order to buy a new pair of trousers and a jacket.

2. In Armenia the rivers usually freeze in winter.

3. Vache, turn the pages of that book one at a time, please.

4. The results of the elections completely astonished the entire population of the city.

5. Because of his political ideas, he has many opponents.

6. Do not make people drink if they do not wish to drink.

7. An old friend introduced me to my future husband at a New Year's dance.

8. What kind of food do you feed your cat?

9. In every country there is at least one Armenian compatriotic society named after some Armenian town.

10. Every Sunday a priest offers the liturgy in our church.

11. Bring your chairs nearer if you wish to see better.

12. Who will introduce our speaker this evening, as our chairman is absent?

13. What time do you normally put the children to bed? The bigger goes to bed at 8:45, the little one at 7:30.

14. How many languages are taught at your school?

15. His last illness has so weakened him that now he can hardly walk.

16. In the heat of the summer we like to lie in the garden picking fruit from the trees.

17. It is forbidden to park cars on this street at night.

18. Do not forget to inform us of your plans for the coming holidays.

19. There is no doubt that in past times people were made to work longer hours than now.

20. We had the picture of the children enlarged for their grandmother.

LESSON XXXI

Days and Months

Sunday	Կիրակի	Thursday	Հինգշաբթի
Monday	Երկուշաբթի	Friday	ուրբաթ
Tuesday	Երեքշաբթի	Saturday	շաբաթ
Wednesday	Չորեքշաբթի		

Usage

Acc. for day on which:

Let's meet on Monday.

On Sundays I go to church.

He spends his Saturdays

    playing tennis.

    Gen.

Have you seen Tuesday's paper?

    Abl.

from Wednesday to Wednesday

Since last Friday...

Երկուշաբթի հանդիպինք։

Կիրակի օրերը եկեղեցի կ'երթամ։

Շաբաթ օրերը թենիս խաղալով

    կ'անցընէ։

Երեքշաբթի օրուան թերթը տեսած ես։

Չորեքշաբթիէն մինչեւ չորեքշաբթի

Անցեալ ուրբաթէն (or ուրբաթ օրուընէ)

ի վեր...

January	Յունուար	July	Յուլիս
February	Փետրուար	August	Օգոստոս
March	Մարտ	September	Սեպտեմբեր
April	Ապրիլ	October	Հոկտեմբեր
May	Մայիս	November	Նոյեմբեր
June	Յունիս	December	Դեկտեմբեր

Usage:

In January it snows a lot.   Յունուարին (or Յունուար ամսուն) շատ

ձիւն կու գայ:

from March to May   Մարտէն (մինչեւ) Մայիս:

DATES

What is today's date?   Ամսուն քանի՞ս է այսօր:

Today is the twenty-fifth.   Այսօր 25 (քսան հինգն) է:

Today is the thirteenth of April.   Այսօր Ապրիլի 13 (տասներեքն) է:

on the seventh of March   Մարտի 7-ին (եօթին)

from the seventeenth of June   Յունիսի տասնեօթէն (17-էն) մինչեւ

to the last day of August   Օգոստոսի վերջին օրը

AGE

How old are you?   Քանի՞ տարեկան ես:

I am fifteen (years old).   Տասնհինգ տարեկան եմ:

Since (she was) eighteen she   18 (տասնրուլթը) տարեկանէն ի վեր

has been in poor health.   վատառողջ եղած է:

At the age of five he began   5 (հինգ) տարեկանին սկսաւ դպրոց

(going to) school.   երթալ:

a girl of about nineteen   Մօտաւորապէս 19 (տասնրինը) տարեկան

աղջիկ մը

Vocabulary: Lesson XXXI

արտայայտե լ	to express	ճառ, -ի	speech
աւելցնե լ	to increase (trans.)	մանաւորապէս	especially, above all
բարեկամական	amicable, friendly	մարդկային	human (adj.)
բարձրացնե լ	to lift, raise	մարմին, -ի	body
գեղեցկանա լ	to become beautiful	միւակ (+ per-	alone, by oneself
զատ	separate, apart; +	sonal suffixes)	
	abl., aside from,	յստակ	clear, plain
	besides	նահանջ տարի	leap year
զգացմունք, -ի	sentiment, feeling	շրջանակ, -ի	circle, set of
թագաւոր, -ի	king		people
թենիս	tennis	որքան (or	so much, as much;
իշխան, -ի	prince	ինչքան)	also interrog.
իսկապէս	really	ուղղակի	straight, directly
ծանոթ, -ի	acquaintance; known	սուր	sharp
կարգ, -ի	row; class, rank;	վատառողջ	in poor health
	queue	տարբերութիւն,	difference
կարելի	possible	-եան	
կարելի	as much as possible	տարօրինակ	strange, odd
եղածին չափ		տեսք, -ի	appearance
հասակ, -ի	height (of a person)	փորձ, -ի	try, attempt (noun)
հով, -ի and	wind, breeze	փչել	to blow
-ու			

Learn also the names of the months, as above.

1. Այս տարի, Դեկտեմբերը սովորականէն աւելի պաղ է:

2. Այդ սեղանը չես կրնար մինակդ բարձրացնել, թող եղբայրներդ ալ օգնեն քեզի:

3. Բոլոր ուսուցիչները առաջին կարգը նստան, իսկ աշակերտները՝ ետեւի կարգերը:

4. Քու տարիքիդ՝ տղոց հասակը մոտաւորապէս մէկ մեթր քանիհինգ կ՚ըլլայ:

5. Մորեքբայրս բոլոր օգնութեան կարոտ եղողներուն կ՚օգնէ, մանաւորապէս իր հայրենակիցներուն:

6. Յստակ կերպով բացատրէ՛ մտքերդ, որպէսզի զանոնք կրկնել պէտք չըլլայ:

7. Ինչքան գեղեցկացեր է այդ աղջիկը: Վստահ եմ որ շուտով կ՚ամուսնանա:

8. Երբեմն թուղթը սուր դանակի պէս մարդու մատ կը կտրէ:

9. Ոչ մէկ տարբերութիւն զտայ ձեր եւ անոնց ըսածներուն միջեւ:

10. Պատերազմէն վերադարձող զինուորները շատ յոգնած եւ խեղճ տեսք մը ունէին:

11. Իր տարիքի մարդոցմէն շատ աւելի մեծ ոյժի տէր է:

12. Այստեղի երիտասարդները սովորաբար քանի՞ տարեկանին կ՚ամուսնանան:

13. Անցեալ Մայիսէն ի վեր չենք հանդիպած: Ո՞ւր էիր, կը ճամբորդէ՞իր:

14. Կ՚ուզենք գիտնալ, թէ դասերը ամսուն քանի՞ն պիտի վերսկսին, որպէսզի կարելի եղածին չափ լալ պատրաստուինք:

15. Չորաքոյրս միայն Կիրակիէ Կիրակի կերթայ եկեղեցի:

16. Բացի Երկուշաբթի եւ Հինգշաբթի օրերէն, ամբողջ շաբաթը ազատ եմ:

17. Պատէն կախուած նկարը քիչ մ՚ըն ալ բարձրացուցէք, որպէսզի պզտիկները հեռը չխաղան:

18. Հակառակ վատառողջ ըլլալուն, շատ ուրախ աղջիկ մըն է:

19. Մարդկային մարմինը շատ մը կենդանիներու մարմիններէն տկար է:

20. Հիմա կը հասկնամ, թէ ինչո՞ւ այդքան դժուարութիւններ ունեցայ անցեալ տարի:

1. By how much do you intend to increase our salaries next year?

2. Apart from my brother and myself, there were 27 people present at the meeting.

3. We always play tennis together on Tuesday evenings.

4. For several centuries there have been no kings or princes in Armenia.

5. Last night it snowed for the first time this winter.

6. His circle of acquaintances is surprisingly narrow.

7. They went straight to the station without even having dinner.

8. What a marvelous speech Mr. Sarkisian gave the other evening!

9. What strange opinions your uncle has on today's most important political problems!

10. Let us make a final attempt to find an amicable solution.

11. From which direction does the wind usually blow in summer?

12. I last saw my grandfather when I was a boy of seven.

13. On the twenty-seventh of next month I have to go to New York on business (instr.).

14. Every year we take our summer holidays in the last two weeks of August.

15. Thirty days have September, April, June, and November; all the rest except for February have thirty-one.

16. I intend to stay there until the third of the following month.

17. He is the sort of man who never expresses his inner feelings.

18. Did you really spend last night studying in the library all alone?

19. In the middle (*կէս*) of next month, let's get together somewhere.

20. February has 28 days, and 29 in each leap year.

Nerses Virabian is a contemporary writer living in Beirut. This story is
taken from Նոյն Թաղի Մարդիկ, a collection of short stories published in
Beirut in 1968. The title "The Old Maltese" refers to a short story by Hrand
Asadour (1862-1928), in which the famous novelist Dzerents (Dr. Hovsep Shish-
manian, 1822-1888) is mistaken for a Maltese sailor on a ferryboat in Constantinople.

Ծերուկ Մալթզը

Ամէն ՀանդԷս, Հարսնիքէ կամ Թաղումէ ետք, երբ դպրոցական Հին
աշակերաններս իրարու քով գայինք, առաջին խօսքը պարոն Տիրապետեանին
մասին կ'ըլլար.

— Կը յիշես Տիրապետեանը...

Ու կը պատմէինք իրմէ մնացած զանազան յիշատակներու մասին, որոնք
կարծես երեք պատաՀած ըլլային:

Ծեր, բարի մարդ մըն էր, խոշոր, լիալուսնի նմանող գլուխով: Սեւ
ակնոցներ[1] ունէր ու ձեռքին՝ անխուսափելի պայուսակ մը, որուն մէջ իր
ունելիքը կ'ըլլար:

Առաւ, միշտ միեննոյն ժամուն կու գար դպրոց, դանդաղ քայլերով:
Մեղմ, Հանգիստ բնաւորութիւն մը ունէր: Կու գար դասարան, կը-
կայնէր[2] շիտակ ու Հոր մը Հոգածութեամբ կը սկսեր դասին:

Տադիներով, տասնրվեց տարեկանէն սկսեալ ուսուցչութիւն ըրած էր
զանազան քաղաքներու մէջ: Վերջին տասնամեակը անցուց մեր դպրոցին մէջ:
Եղբոսս դասախարակը եղած էր: Յետոյ քրոջս ուսուցիչը եղաւ:
Երրորդ դասարանէն սկսեալ ես ալ աշակերտեցայ իրեն:

---

1. Although ակնոց is sometimes used in both sing. and pl., sing. is preferable
2. Կը կայնէր: or կը կենար.

Տարիներ շարունակ, հայերէնի մէկ ուսուցիչ ունեցած ենք՝ ի՛նքը,
ու մէկ դասագիրք՝ իրեն հետ մեր դպրոցէն ներս մտած Հրանտ եւ Զապէլ[3]
Ասատուրներու "Նոր Թանգարան"ը։ Առաջին անգամ եղբօրս դասագիրքը
եղաւ, յետոյ քրոջս սկսաւ գործածել գայն, ապա քրոջս կողմէ ինծի
փոխանցուեցաւ։ Մաշած, թերթերը եւած, քանի մը անգամ նորոգուած ու
վերակազմուած գիրք մըն էր, գոր կը պահէմ տակաւին, ի յիշատակ[4] պարոն
Տիրապետեանին։

ծերո՛ւկ Մալթըզը։

Այդ անունը դրած էին իրեն աշակերտները։ Իրապէս, որքան կը-
նմանէր Հրանտ Ասատուրի "ծերուկ Մալթըզ"ին։ Ութսունական թուականներու
գրագէտը կարծես ուղղակի մեր ուսուցիչը նկարագրած էր։

Իր անունը շատ կը հոլովուէր մեր տան մէջ։ Եղբայրս ու քույրս
միշտ պատմելիք բան մը կ'ունենային իրմէ։ Ետքը ես ալ միացայ անոնց։

Գլուխը հակած գիրքին՝ ուշի ուշով կը հետեւէր մեր ընթերցանութեան,
մատը տողերուն հետ սահեցնելով։ Երբ լաւ կարդայինք, գլուխը կ'ելլեր-
կ'իջնէր, լաւ է ըսելու պէս, իսկ եթէ սխալ կարդայինք կամ կմկմայինք՝
— Թաւական է, նստէ՛, — կ'ըսէր։

Լաւ կը ճանչնար Պետրոս Դուրեանը։[5] Ամէն անգամ որ եղերաբախտ
բանաստեղծին մէկ բանաստեղծութեան հանդիպէինք, դասը կը կեցնէր, կը-
կենար շիտակ, խոշոր թաշկինակով ակնոցը կը սրբէր ու խոր յուզումով կը-
պատմէր անոր կեանքը։

— "Տրտունջքը" գրած է մեռնելէն երեք օր առաջ։ Ամէն հայ տղայ

---

3. Զապէլ Ասատուր, also known as Սիպիլ; wife of Hrand Asadour and a writer,
   1863-1934.

4. ի յիշատակ: a classical Armenian phrase, "in memory of."

5. Պետրոս Դուրեան: a talented Armenian poet and playwright, 1851-1872.

զոց պէտք է սորվի այդ գոհարը, - կ'ըսէր ու այդ պարտականութիւնը կու֊
տար մեզի:

Ամբողջ չորս տարիներու ընթացքին մենք կրցանք միայն Դուրեանին
եւ բիչ մըն ալ Մեծարենցի[6] մասին զգապար կազմել: Իրմէ իմացանք նաեւ
որ Գրիգոր Զոհրապ[7] անունով գրագէտ մը ունեցած ենք, որուն գլուխը
ծգմեր են թուրք դահիճները:

Աշխարհագրութեան դաս ալ կու տար մեզի պարոն Տիրապետեանը:
Աշխարհագրութեան դասին կը պահանջեր որ զոց սորվինք բոլոր քաղաքներուն
անունները, նոյնիսկ յետին քաղաքներունը եւ երբ զինք գոհ ձգէինք,
կ'ըսէր.

- Տեսէք, տղա՛քս, հիմա բոլոր քաղաքներուն, գետերուն, ծովերուն
անունները գիտէք, բայց երբ դպրոցէն ելլէք, շատերը պիտի մոռնաք, իսկ
երբ ծերանաք՝ հագիւ պիտի յիշէք Մեռեալ ծովը:[8]

Անկեղծ մարդ մըն էր:

Չէր ուզեր որ աշակերտ մը թերանայ իր պարտականութեան մէջ, ուշանա
դպրոցէն, բայց ուշացողին ալ ծեծ չէր քաշեր, այլ հոր մը պէս կը֊
խրատէր, իր կանուխ ելլելը կը պատմէր անոր եւ երկաորէն կը խօսէր
գերմանական կրթութեան մասին: Որեւէ անկարգապահութիւն որ նշմարէր,
անպատճառ գերմանացիներէն տիպար օրինակ մը կը յիշէր: Գերմանացիներուն
ծշղապահ ըլլալը, անվերապահօրէն իրենց մեծին հնազանդիլը մեծապէս
ագղած էին վրան: Կը յիշէր օրինակ մը եւ կ'աւելցներ.

***

6. *Միսաք Մեծարենց:* a gifted Armenian poet, 1886-1908.

7. *Գրիգոր Զոհրապ:* famous writer of short stories, 1861-1915, killed in the
   massacres of 1915.

8. *Մեռեալ:* a classical form, "dead."

– Գերմանացիներուն պէս եղէք:

Պաշտամունքի տաեն, երբ իրեն աղիթ տրուէր քանի մը խօսք ըսելու, կամքի, աշխատանքի եւ կորովի մասին կը խօսէր եւ կ'ուզէր որ կամքի, աշխատանքի եւ կորովի տէր մարդ ըլլանք:

Դասի պահուն չէր ուզեր որ շշուկ մը իսկ լսուի: Մանաւանդ չէր ախորժեր յօրանջողներէն: Սաստիկ կը բարկանար յօրանջողներուն վրայ ու իր ջղայնութեան սաստկութենէն ծաղատ գլուխը կը կարմրէր, լուսնի խալարում տեղի կ'ունենար: Բարկութենէն եաք՝ դասը չէր կրնար շարունակել: Խիղճը կը տանջէր գինք: Կը սկսէր խրատի, կը շոյէր գինք գայրագնող տղան, իսկ դաղարին ալ գլուխը ծնօտերուն մէջ կ'առնէր, հաշտութիւն կը-գոյացնէր: Երբեք չէր ուզեր որ մէկը նեղուի իրմէ:

Եթէ պատահէր որ ամբողջ դասարանով տրուած դասը չգիտնայինք, կ'ըսէր.

Սեռական, տրական, հայցական,
Դասերնիդ սորվիք չսորվիք,
Տիրապետեան կ'առնէ ամսական:

Առանկ կ'ըսէր, սակայն իր խանունուածքը թուլորովին տարբեր էր, կը-գուրգուրար ամէն մէկ աշակերտի վրայ: Կ'ուզէր որ աննոք գուր տեղը դպրոց եկած չըլլային:

– Տեսէք, տղա'քս, ձեր հայրերը արիւն-քրտինքի մէջ կը մոեն, պարտքի դրամ կ'առնեն ձեզ դպրոց որկելու համար: Չեզմէ շատերուն հայրերը որբանոցէն կը ճանչնամ, մեղքցէք աննոց, աշխատեցէք, մարդ եղէք...

Կը խօսէր երկար, պահն ալ կ'երկննար, մինչ ուսուցչուհիները դուրսը կը սպասին... Մեեք շատ գոհ կը մնայինք ատկէ, որովհետեւ ընդհանրապէս հայերէնին յաջորդող դասը չէինք սիրեր:

Պարոն Տիրապետեան լալ կը ՟ետեւէր նաեւ ժամանակին։ Ամէն անգամ որ օրերը երկննային կամ կարճնային, մեզի լուր կու տար։

— Գիտէք, տղա՛ք, այսօր ամէնէն կարճ օրն է, վաղուընէ սկսեալ օրերը կամաց-կամաց կ՚երկննան...

— Այսօր ամենաերկար օրն է, վաղուընէ սկսեալ օրերը կամաց-կամաց կը կարճնան...

— Այսօր ցերեկը եւ գիշերը ՟աւասար են...

Խօսած ատեն կալիՕը ձեռքը կ՚ըլլար եւ թիւերը մէկ-մէկ կը գրեր գրատախտակին վրայ, կ՚ուզէր որ մենք ալ մեր տետրակներուն մէջ արձանագրենք՝

"Դեկտեմբեր 21-ը ամէնէն կարճ օրն է,

Մարտ 21-ին գիշերը եւ ցերեկը ՟աւասար կ՚ըլլան,

Յունիս 21-էն եԵop oրերը կը սկսին կարճնալ"։

Երբ ՟արցուՍ մը ընէինք, մանրամասնoրէն կը բացատրէր։ Շատ կը-սիրէինք զինք։ "Տղաքս" ըսելով կը խoսէր մեզի ՟եա։

Իր ընտանիքին մասին զաղափար չունէինք. գիտէինք միայն որ Զանզիպար կղզիին մէջ աղջիկ մը ունի։ Աշխար՟ագրութեան դասին, երբ նիւթը Ափրիկէն ըլլար՝ քարտէսին վրայ անպատճառ ցոյց կու տար Զանզիպարին տեղը։

— Եթէ օր մը ՟ոն երթանք, կ՚ըսենք որ Տիրապետեանի աշակերտ եղած ենք, — կ՚ըսէինք մենք ու ինք գո՟ կը ժպտէր։

Ամավերջի ՟անդէսին, երբ իրրեւ շրջանաւարտ վկայական պիտի առնէինք քովը կանչեց մեզ ու ըսաւ։

— Եթէ շուարելու ըլլաք եւ չկրնաք յիշել ձեր արտասանութեան բառերը, առանց յայտնի ընելու անցէք միւս տողը։ Բնաւ մի կենաք եւ սպասէցէք, թէ ձեր դիմաց մարդ չկայ։

Փորձի ժամանակ տարբեր քան կ'ըսէր մեզի։ Փորձի ժամանակ յածախ
կը կրկներ։

— Անանկ սեպեցէք, որ ձեր դիմաց Հազարաւոր Հոգիներ կան։

Մեր վկայական առնելէն երեք ամիս եթք, դպրոցական յաջորդ տարեշրջանի
սկիզբը, նոր Հոգաբարձուներ եկան եւ նոր Հոգաբարձուները նոր ու
երիտասարդ ուսուցիչներ Հրաւիրեցին պաշտօնի։

Պարոն Տիրապետեան չափէն աւելի ձեր էր եւ Հանգստեան կոչեցին
զինք։ Այդպէ՛ս։ Իր ձեռքէն վերջին անգամ վկայական առնողները մենք
եղանք։ Անկէ եթք բնաւ չտեսանք զինք, բայց միշտ կը յիշէինք իր անունը,
մեր սիրելի Տիրապետեանը, իր անբժան Հացի պայուսակին Հետ, սեւ
ակնոցներուն, դանդաղ քայլուածքին, շիտակ կեցուածքին, Հայրական իր
գուրգուրանքին, մեղմ-մեղմ արտասանած բառերուն, յուզումներուն ու
խանդավառութիւններուն Հետ։

Ամէն անգամ որ դպրոցական ընկերներս իրարու Հանդիպէինք, մեզմէ
մէկը անպատձառ կը բանար խօսքը։

— Գիտէ՞ք, — անցեալ օր պարոն Տիրապետեանը տեսայ...

Ատիկա կը բաւէր որ աւելի մտերմայինք լուրը տուողին, Հարցումներու
տարափ մը տեղացնէինք վրան...

Իր Հանգստեան կոչուելէն տարիներ յետոյ, երբ թերթի մը Հին
թիւերը կը թղթատէի, Հանդիպեցայ իր մէկ գրութեան՝ "ի՞նչ պիտի ըսէի,
եթէ նորէն պատանի ըլլայի"...

— Ուսուցչութի՛ւն, — անցալ մտքէս։

Խեղձ պարոն Տիրապետեան, որքա՜ն կը սիրէր ուսուցչութիւնը...

Ն. Վիրաբեան

LESSON XXXIII

Vahram Mavian is a contemporary writer living in Lisbon. The following are extracts from Անկապ Օրագիր, a collection of reflections and reminiscences in the form of a diary published in Jerusalem in 1968.

ՆՈՅԵՄԲԵՐ 30

Եղօն[1] կենդանի պատմութիւնն է Բուժարանին:[2] Վանեցի,[3] որբ, նախկին հիւանդ մը ինք ալ, քան տարի առաջ դարմանուելէ ետք մնացած է այստեղ հիւանդներուն ծառայելու համար: Համակրելի, ղիւրահաղորդ ու լուռ մարդ մը, աննոցմէ՝ որոնք կը շարունակեն տղայ մնալ հոգիով, հակառակ իրենց յառաջացող տարիքին ու սպիտակող մազերուն:

Ամէն անգամ որ կանչուի հիւանդներէն մեկուն կամ միւսին կողմէ խնդրանքի մը համար, պատասխանը նոյնն է միշտ:

— Սիրով ձանս,[4] հիմա, անմիջապէս:

Այդքան սակայն, որովհետեւ սենեակէն դուրս ելլելէ եւք արդէն մոռցած է ե՛ւ հիւանդը ե՛ւ անոր ներկայացուցած խնդրանքը:

Անցնող քան տարիներու ընթացքին Բուժարան մտած թուլոր հիւանդները, բուժուած կամ մահացած, կը յիշէ տակաւին մեկիկ մեկիկ, իւրաքանչիւրը իրեն յատուկ նկարագրի գիծով, քմայքներով, սենեակին թիւով ու պատահած՝ յաճախ աննշան դեպքերով: Եղօն հիւանդները կը ձանչնայ այլեւս շատ աւելի լաւ քան բժիշկները: Պաղարիւնով կը մօտենայ ուրիշներու կողմէ լուրջ նկատուած պարագաներո'ւն անգամ:

---

1. Եղo, gen. Եղoյի: diminutive of Եղիա.
2. Բուժարան: the Azuniye sanatorium in Lebanon.
3. Վանեցի: a native of Van.
4. ձանս: "my dear," a friendly, informal expression.

218

- Կը վարժուին, տակնուվրայ ըլլալու պէտք չկայ, ժամանակի ինդիր է եղածը, քանի մը շաբաթէն կը հաշտուին կացութեան հետ։ Բոլոր նոր եկողները այդպէս կ'ըլլան սկիզբը։ Իրեն պէս քանինե՞ր տեսած ենք մենք։

Եղոն կ'արձակէ տակաւին բժշկական իր վճիռները նոր հասած հիւանդներուն մասին։

- Ես սա Ջահլէէն[5] նոր եկողին վիճակը շատ չեմ հաւնիր կոր։[6] Երկու կողմէն է եղեր։ Ասանկները գործողութիւն անգամ չեն ըլլար։ Մէկ-երկու ամիսէն յայտնի կ'ըլլայ վիճակը։ Նայինք մարդը ինչ պիտի ըսէ Երեքշաբթի օր։

Մարդը՝ բժշկապետան է անշուշտ, որուն համակրանքը կը վայելէ Եղոն բացատրաբար՝ իր հեզ բնաւորութեան եւ տարիներու հալատարիմ ծառայութեան շնորհիւ։

Էմիլիոն մահոզ է քանի մը օրէ ի վեր։ Անշի օր չքնացաւ մինչեւ առաւոտ։ Երեկ գիշեր ուշ ատեն արթուն էր։ Ի վերջոյ[7] մատով դպաւ բարձին քովէն կախուած պզտիկ կոճակին ու քանի մը վայրկեան ետք Եղոն, որ գիշերապահ է այս շաբաթ, երեւաց դրան մէջ։

- Եղո, ինծի մորֆին մը բեր, Աստուծոյ սիրոյն,[8] երկու գիշեր է չեմ կրնար քնանալ։

- Սիրով, Պրն. Էմիլիո, միայն թէ արտօնուած չենք։ առանց բժիշկին հրամանին չեմ կրնար, իսկ բժիշկն ալ դիւրաւ հրաման չի տար։

Էմիլիո, որ փորձառութեամբ ծանօթ էր շիճուկին տալիք երանաւէտ

---

5. Ջահլէ: town in central Lebanon.

6. կոր: an expression in colloquial Armenian that indicates continuity.

7. ի վերջոյ: "finally."

8. Աստուծոյ սիրոյն: "for the love of God; for God's sake."

Հանգիստին, լիբանանեան երկու թղթոսկի սահեցուց Եղոյին սպիտակ գօգնոցին գրպանը:

Հասկցան կարծես գիրար ու Եղոն դուրս ելաւ՝ իբրե՛ւ թէ առանց նկատելու Էմիլիոյին ...վեհանձնութիւնը: Հինգ վայրկեան վերջ վերադարձաւ ապիին մէջ ներարկումի ասեղը պահած, գաղտնի արարքի մը մէջ զանունող մարդու զգուշաւորութեամբ, խորհրդաւորութիւնով:

Տասը վայրկեան ետք Էմիլիոն արդէն ինկած էր խոր քունի մէջ եւ այդպէս ալ մնաց մինչեւ առաւoտ, նախաճաշի ժամը:

Գիտէի թէ մորֆինի սրուակները քծիշկը կը պահէր անձամբ, եւ շատ բացատիկ պարագաներու տակ էր միայն որ կ՚արտonէր աննոց գործածունթիւնը: Չկրցայ ուրեմն ես ինձի բացատրել թէ ուրկէ՞ կրցած էր Եղոն ձեռք ձգել[9] զայն նախորդ գիշեր:

Առաւoտուն, նախաճաշէն ետք երբ Վարդանին հետ նստած էինք իր գրասենեակը, Եղոն մտաւ ներս՝ տուն մեկնելէ առաջ նախորդ գիշերnւան սովորական իր "տեղեկագիրը" ներկայացնելու.

- Մասնաւոր բան մը չկար երեկ գիշեր, Sօքթոր, հանգիստ ընացան բոլորը: Միայն Էմիլիոն էր որ արթուն էր երկար ատեն: Գլուխս կերաւ[10] մինչեւ առտուան ժամը երկուքը եւ մորֆին ուզեց: Տեսայ որ կարելի չէր ազատիլ ձեռքէն, եւ ալ իրբել մորֆին՝ թորեալ ջուր զարկի:[11] Մարդը մինչեւ առտու ընացաւ, մէկ կտոր:[12]

- Նոր բան մըն ալ սորվեցանք, ըսաւ Վարդան, գլուխը oրoրելով:

---

9. ձեռք ձգել: "to get hold of, obtain."

10. գլուխ ուտել: "to kill," here "to nag."

11. զարնել: here "to inject."

12. մէկ կտոր: cf. English "of a piece."

ՊԵՅՐՈՒԹ, ԱՊՐԻԼ 18

— Բարեւ ձեզ:

— Բարեւ:

— Ձեր առաջին այցելութիւնն է Պէյրութ:

— Ո՛չ, բազմաթիւ անգամներ եղած եմ այստեղ ուրիշ առիթներով:

— Ո՞ր կողմերէն էք արդեօք:

— Լիզպոնէն:

— Ի՞նչ կ՛ըսէք ...Լիզպոնի մէջ հայ կա՞յ:

* * *

— Լսեցի՞ք, Ալպեաններուն վրայ տեղի ունեցած օդանաւի արկածին մասին. 98 մեռեալ:

— Իսկապէ՞ս ...սարսափելի է, եղբայր: Մեռնողներուն մէջ հայ կա՞յ արդեօք:

* * *

— Անցեալ տարի քանի մը օրուան համար ճիպրալթար հանդիպեցայ: Ափ մը[13] տեղ է՝ տեսնեմ. խաղա՛ղ, շատ գեղեցիկ բնական տեսարանով:

— Այդպէ՛ս է եղեր: Ինչ պիտի ըսէի ...առիթ ունեցա՞ր ճետաքրքրուելու թէ հայ կա՞յ ճիպրալթարի մէջ:

* * *

— Ամերիկա՞ կ՛երթաք:

— Ո՛չ, Ամերիկայէն կու գա՞նք: Այս առաւօտ ճասանք եւ վաղը կը-մեկնինք Մարիա՝ վիրաբուժական միջազգային ճամագումարին ներկայ ըլլալու:

— Կ՛ենթադրեմ թէ աշխարհի բոլոր կողմերէն եկողներ կ՛ըլլան այդ առիթւ:

---

13. ափ մը : "small."

– Քանի մը Հարիւր Հոգի պիտի ըլլան կարծեմ:

– Մասնակցողներուն մէջ ուրիշ Հայ կա՞յ:

* * *

– Շաբաթ գիշեր պիտի երթա՞ս Պուշոյի ներկայացումին:

– Պուշոյը պիտի գայ:

– Հո'ս է արդէն: Երեկ գիշեր ներկայ եղայ իրենց առաջին ելոյթին խենթենալիք բան է պարզապէս:

– Յայտագրին ուշադրութեամբ նայեցա՞ր. պարողներուն մէջ Հայ կա՞յ:

* * *

Անծանօթ ու օտար ափերու վրայ, նոյն յանձախնքէն միշտ Հալածուած այսպէս՝ դուն, ես, ամբողջէն ակամայ փրթած մասնիկներ, մեր արեան ձայնին կարօտով, մեր Հողէն ու Հարազատներէն Հեռու, շա՛տ Հեռու, բիւրաւոր քառուղիներէն՝ Հազար կանչով պիտի զիրար, պիտի զՄե՛զ որոնենք

– Ըսէ'ք, Հայ կա՛յ...:

Վ. Մավեան

LESSON XXXIV

Antranig Dzarugian is a contemporary writer and journalist living in

Beirut. The following story is taken from Մանկութիւն Չունեցող Մարդիկ,

published in Beirut in 1955. The book is a collection of short stories de-

picting life in an orphanage, where he spent some of his years as a child.

Կաղանդ

Կաղանդի պէս օր մըն էր: Նոր Տարի չէր, Զատիկ ալ չէր, բայց

կայծակի արագութեամբ տարածուեցաւ լուրը շէնքէ շէնք, սենեակէ սենեակ:

Կաղանդ պիտի ունենայինք: Կաղանդ ունենալ՝ կը նշանակէր տոպրակի

վերածուած գուլպայ մը, մէջը շաքար, ընկոյզ, չամիչ ու թերեւս նաեւ

թաշկինակ մը:

Նախ, լուրը առինք թերահաւատութեամբ, չհաւատալ կեղծելով եւ ամէն

րոպէ հաւատացողներուն պնդումը ըմբոշխնելով: Ընթրիքն աւետիսը

պաշտոնականացաւ: Մայրիկը[1] յայտարարեց, թէ երկու օր ետք, շաբաթ

կէսօրին, կաղանդ պիտի ունենանք: իրազեկներ մանրամասնութիւններ

հաղորդեցին: Կաղանդը, այս անգամ, ոչ Մայրիկին նուէրն էր, եւ ոչ ալ

Հայրիկին: Դուրսէն, ուրիշ քաղաքէ մը մէկը եկած էր ու իրեն հետ բերած

կաղանդը:

Հաւասատի աղբիւր մը - հակիչ Յարութիւն - խորհրդաւոր ժպիտով

նոյնիսկ յայտնած էր քաղերարին անունը, բայց լսողները չէին կրնար

յիշել. ու եթէ յիշէին իսկ, այդ անունը որեւէ նշանակութիւն չունէր

մեզի համար: Բայց որոշ կերպով իմացուած էր հակիչ Յարութիւնէն, թէ

այցելուն նշանաւոր մէկն էր, շատ մը գիրքեր գրած էր եւ միշտ կը խնդար

ու կը խնդացնէր: Այս կէտը կրկնապէս հաւակրելի կը դարձներ անձանօթ

---

1. Մայրիկ : "mother"; here the supervisor of the female employees of the
    orphanage.

բարերարին դէմքը, ու անհամբեր կը սպասէինք շաբաթ օրուան:

Առեւտուրը սկսած էր արդէն: Համաձայնութիւններ կը կնքուէին անկիւններու մէջ: Կաղանդի անխուսափելի սովորութիւնն էր, որ կը-կրկնուէր տեննդոտ ու զուարթ եռուզերի մը մէջ: Մէկը ընկոյզը կը փոխէր շամիշով, ուրիշ մը զուլպան կը ծախէր շաքարով: Ամէնէն աւելի մատուցուած ապրանքները՝ զուլպաներն էին: Միշտ անկումի մէջ էր աննց գինը: Երբ կօշիկ չկար, անիմաստ պերճանք էր զուլպան: Կային,[2] որ ստացուելիք ամբողջ նուէրը ծախած էին կանխիկ հացով մը: Մինչեւ շաբաթ կէսօր՝ ծախուելիք բան չէր մնացած:

Այս անգամ հաւաքուեցանք որբանոցին չպատկանող եւ մեզի անծանօթ շէնքի մը մէջ, որ դաշտի նման ընդարձակ բան մը ունէր, մէկ կողմը բարձր, բեմի պէս տեղով մը, ու մասամբ ծածկուած թիթեղդ տանիքով: Հակառակ սովորութեան, խմբուած էին բոլոր շէնքերու որբերը առանց բացառութեան, Մանկապարտէզէն մինչեւ արհեստաւորները[3] եւ մեծ աղջիկներ մինչեւ դպրոցականները: Հազարաւորներու բազմութիւն մը խունուած էր ամէն կողմ, մինչեւ պատուհանները եւ կողմնակի սենեակները: ծակատը, բեմին առջեւ, տեղաւորուած էին Մանկապարտէզի փոքրերը: Մեր եւտել՝ մեծ աղջիկներն էին, նոյնպէս շարքով նստած տախտակէ նստարաններու վրայ Մնացեալները ոտքի էին, սեղմուած իրարու:

Բեմին վրայ աթոռներով շարուած էին մայրիկները եւ քանի մը ակնոցաւոր ամերիկացի օրիորդներ: Կեղրոնը՝ Հայրիկին[4] սեղանն էր, երկու կողմերը երկու պարապ աթոռներով: Բեմին մէկ մասը գրաւած էր լեցուն զուլպաներու հսկայ բլուրը:

---

2. Կայ ին, որ: or կայ ին աննը որունը.
3. արհեստաւոր: older child who was learning a craft.
4. Հայրիկ: "father"; here the director of the whole orphanage.

Հայրիկը բեմ մաալ կողմնակի դունէ[5] մը, ընկերակցութեամբ իրեն պէս սեւ հագուած մարդու մը։ ժխորը աստիճանաբար դադրեցաւ, հովին դէմ տատանումով մարող մոմի մը պէս։ Հայրիկը եւ հիւրը գրաւեցին պարապ աթոռները։ Հայրիկը զանգակը ծեռք առաւ, բայց յետոյ տեղը դրաւ, առանց զարնելու։ Լռութիւնը կատարեալ էր։

Կը սպասէինք, որ հիւրը ոտքի ելլէ ու խօսի անմիջապէս։ Բայց Հայրիկն էր որ խօսեցաւ։ Մեզի համար թուրորվին անհասկնալի բաներ ըսաւ հիւրին մասին, եւ ծեռքի թուղթին նայելով, յաջորդաբար բեմ կանչեց արտասանողներու եւ երգողներու անվերջանալի շարք մը։ Ընդհանրապէս տղաքը կ'արտասանէին եւ աղջիկները կ'երգէին։ Բոլորն ալ մեծերէն էին։ Մանկապարտէզէն մէկ արտասանող միայն կար, ծերմակ Արսէնը, որ Մայրիկին ու հակիշներուն սիրելին էր, ծերմակ մորթին ու գեղեցիկ դեմքին պատճառով։

Երբ վերջացուց արտասանութիւնը, հիւրը քովը կանչեց Արսէնը, շոյեց այտերը, զգուեց, եւ գրկելով` բեմէն վար կախեց, մեր մէջ. յետոյ դարձեալ նստաւ տեղը։ Մենք նախանձով կը դիտէինք Արսէնը։ Իսկ այս վերջինս, արդէն իսկ շփացած ընդհանուր գուրգուրանքէն, պզտիկ հնդկահալի մը կեցուածքը առաւ, աչ ու ձախ դարձնելով գլուխը, ժպտելով եւ ուշադրութիւնները կեդրոնացնելով իր վրայ։

Հայրիկին զանգակը վերահաստատեց խանգարուած լռութիւնը։ Կարգը եկած էր հիւրին։ Հայրիկը կը ստիպէր, միւսը կը մերժէր։ Մեծ դժուարութեամբ յաջողեցան ոտքի հանել հիւրը, որ նեղուած ու անհանգիստ երեւոյթ մը առած էր։ Ճետելէն, մեծ տղաքը սկսան ծափահարել ու մենք հետեւեցանք իրենց։ Հայրիկը, ծափերուն վրայ, բազմապատկեց պնդումները։

---

5. դունէ: abl. of դուն.

ի վերջոյ հիւրը անցաւ սեղանին առջեւ։ Ծափերը անգամ մըն աւ
փոթորկեցան եւ լռեցին։ Քիչ մը հետագաւ սեղանէն, երկու քայլ առաջացաւ
բեմին վրայ, Թաշկինակով սրբեց ճակատը, ծօծրակը։ Թաշկինակը գրպանը
դրաւ, թեւերը կախեց առջեւ, մատները իրար հիւսելով եւ ափերը գետին
դարձուցած։ Այդ վիճակով կեցաւ պահ մը, հազաց ու լուռ մնաց։

Գլուխը ճաղատ էր եւ փայլուն, Հայրիկին պէս։ Շատ խոշոր եւ սուր
քիթ մը ունէր։

Կը սպասէինք որ խոսի, ինդայ եւ ինդացնէ։ Պատրաստ էինք ինդալու
անմիջապէս որ բան մը ըսէր։ Մեր երեւակայութիւնը հազար տեսակ
յատկութիւններ տուած էր միշտ ինդացող մարդուն, մինչդեռ մեր դիմացը
կեցողը լուրջ եւ մտածկոտ յատկութիւն մը ունէր, ճիշդ Հայրիկին նման
սեւ հագուստով։ Յուսախաբութիւնը կատարեալ պիտի ըլլար, եթէ հըլլար
քիթը։ Փոքրերուս ուշադրութիւնը կեդրոնացած էր միայն անոր քիթին
վրայ, իբրեւ խոսացուած գուարծնութեան կարելի միակ աղբիւրը։

Երկար, տաժանելի ճիգէ մը վերջ, մարդը բացաւ բերանը։

– Տղաքնե՛ր, որբե՛ր...

Լռեց դարձեալ։ Չերքերը քակեց, կրկին ճանեց Թաշկինակը, վեր
նայեցաւ, փորձեց եռ դառնալ ու տեղը նստիլ, բայց Հայրիկը Թոյլ չտուաւ։
Ամէնէն փոքրերը սկսան ինդալ, կարծելով թէ ինդալիք բան մը տեղի
ունեցաւ ու ճարկ էր ինդալ։ Բայց երբ տեսան մայրիկներուն խոժոռ
դէմքերը, իսկոյն քարացան։

Հիւրը երկրորդ անգամ փորձեց խոսիլ, ու քիչ մը աւելի բարձր
ծայնով.

– Որբե՛ր, ես ձեզ շատ կը սիրեմ...

Այլեւս բառ մը չարտասանեց։ Վերաղարծաւ ու նստաւ տեղը, Թաշկինա
աչքերուն։ Հայրիկը չպնդեց այս անգամ։ Բեմ կանչեց մեծ աղջիկներէն

օրիորդ Զապէլը, որ երգէ կրկին։ Ամէնէն քաղցր ու անոյշ ձայն ունեցողն էր օրիորդ Զապէլը ու շատ գեղեցիկ էր։ Կ՚րսուէր թէ նշանուած է եւ Ամերիկա պիտի երթայ շուտով։ Բոլորը կը սիրէին զինք անոյշ ձայնին, անոյշ դէմքին եւ անոյշ բնաւորութեան համար։ Մեծ տղաքը օրը կը–թռնդացնէին ծափերով եւ սուլոցներով, երբ օրիորդ Զապէլ բեմ ելլէր։ Իսկ մենք բաղնիքին մէջ իրարու հետ կը կռուէինք, որպէսզի օրիորդ Զապէլը ըլլայ մեզ լոգցնողը։

Այդ օր, օրիորդ Զապէլ երգած էր "Կունկ"ը։[6] Երկրորդ անգամ բեմ գալուն, ո՛չ ոք ծափահարեց։ Օրիորդ Զապէլ այս անգամ սկսաւ երգել "Պարզի՛ր Աղբիւր"ը,[7] իր կախարդական ձայնէն կախուած պաhելով մեծ ու պզտիկ հաւասարապէս։

Երգին ատեն հիւրը գետին կը նայէր, միշտ թաշկինակը ձեռքին։ Քիթը այլեւս մեզի համար կորսնցուցած էր շահեկանութիւնը։ Առանց բան մը հասկնալու կատարուածէն, կը զգայինք թէ ծանր ու ծնծող մթնոլորտ մը հեւքի մէջ կը պահէր սիրտերը։ Որոշ կերպով կը տեսնէինք, թէ հիւրին աչքերուն մէջ արցունք կար եւ թաշկինակով կը սրբէր թարթիչները, քիթը մաքրելու շարժումով մը։

Մայրիկներու շարքը տրտում էր բոլորովին։ Անոնց մէջ ալ թաշկինակ գործածողներ կային։ Երկու ամերիկացի օրիորդները փսփսուքով բաներ մը կ՚ըսէին իրարու։ Օրիորդ Զապէլ կը շարունակէր երգել։ Միակ անտարբեր ու խաղաղ մնացողը բեմին վրայ, Հայրիկն էր, որ կը պահէր սովորական դէմքը։

Դէպքը պատաhեցաւ այսպէս. – Երբ երգը հասած էր այնտեղ, ուր կ՚ըսուի.

6. Կունկ։ "crane"; title of a popular Armenian song.
7. Պարզի՛ր Աղբիւր։ title of a popular Armenian song. *Literally:* "become clear, O spring."

Աղքիւր գիտա̃ս, թիւրդը մեգի ինչ կ'անէ,[8]

Կը հալածէ, կը կոտորէ, կը սպաննէ...

Այստեղ, օրիորդ Զապէլին ձայնը թրթռաց, դանդաղեցաւ ու յանկարծ փոծկումով մը կանգ առաւ։ Մեր եռեւէն մեծ աղջիկներուն մէջ, լսուեցաւ հեկեկանքի ձայն մը, յետոյ ուրիշ մը, երրորդ մը... Քանի մը խոպոտ ու թալ հեծկլտուքներ ալ լսուեցան ուրիշ անկիւնէ մը, արհեստաւոր տղոց խումբէն։ Հեզգհետէ անջատ լացերը միացան, խառնուեցան ու վերածուեցան աննկարագրելի քանի մը։ Հսկայ բազմութիւնը կարծես բռնուեցաւ հալաբակ զառանցանքի մը դողով։

Բեմին վրայ ամէն մարդ կուլար, նոյնիսկ ամերիկացի օրիորդները, բացի հայրիկէն։ Տեսնելով որ թուլրը կուլ լան, փոքրերը սկսան իրենք ալ լալ եւ քարբրաձայն ծէալ, աներեւոյթ երկիւղէ մը բռնուած։

Դեռ երկար պիտի տեւէր այդ ահտելի խառնաշփոթութիւնը, եթէ Հայրիկ ուձգին-ուձգին զարնելով զանգակը, չհրամայէր մայրիկներուն որ բաժնեն նուէրները։ Կարգով սկսանք տողանցել բեմին առջեւէն, ամէն մէկս ստանալով լեցուն գուլպայ մը։ Հսկիչները գործի վրայ[9] էին։ Կը-պոռային, կը յանդիմանէին, Քանալով քով քովի բերել գրուած խումբերը։

Հիւրը քաշուած էր բեմին մէկ կողմը ու կը խօսէր ամերիկացի օրիորդներուն հետ։ Հայրիկը, մտրակը ձեռքը, կը հսկէր բաժանումի գործողութեան, լուռ ու հանդիսաւոր։

Մենք ամէնէն առաջ ստացողներն էինք ու ճամբայ հանեցին մեզ դէպի տուն։ Դուրսը՝ մոգցուած էր արդէն հիւրը եւ իր զարմանալի ընթացքը։ Ծայր տուած[10] էին վեճերը, օրեր առաջ ծախուած նուէրներուն շուրջ։ Կային, որ չէին ուզեր յարգել կնքուած համաձայնութիւնը ու պահանջատէր

---

8.   Կ'անէ = Կ'ընէ.

9.   գործի վրայ: "busy."

10.   ծայր տալ: "to begin."

Կը սպառնային, կ'աղմկէին։ Հսկիչները մեծ դժուարութեամբ կը յաջողէին վերակացմել տեւաբար խանգարուող շարքերը։

Մութ ու նեղ փողոցներէ հասանք Մանկավարժ։ Անեւտուրի վեճերը մեղմացած էին զանազան ձեւի փոխադարծ զիջումներով կամ սպազային վերապահուած ոխակալ սպառնալիքներով։ Խումբ մը կը վիճէր օրուան հիւրին շուրջ։

— Խաբեց, չխղացուց, կը դգդ̂ɡɛր տղայ մը։

— Քիթին նայէիր ու խնդայիր, կը պատասխանէր ուրիշ մը։

— Օրիորդ Զապէլին նշանած էր, մէջ ինկաւ[11] մէկը։

— Օրիորդ Զապէլը չ'առներ այդ մարդը, վճռեց Գող Թորոսը իմաստուն լրջութեամբ։

— Կ'առնէ՛, հարուստ է։

— Չ'առներ։

— Չ'առներ... Քիթը խոշոր է, գլուխը մաɡ չկայ...

— Օրիորդ Զապէլը Հայրիկը պիտի առնէ...

— Է՛չ, Հայրիկը ամուսնացած է...

— Էƨ̂ը դո'ւն եսɪ, քուրակ ... Ɓ̆ս գիտեմ ...

Այդ երկուքը շարունակեցին հայհոյել ու վիճիլ սպազայ հարսին ու փեսային շուրջ, մինչեւ որ պարկելու զանգակը հնƨ̂եց, սովորականէն կանուխ, ու փակեց մեր բացօթիկ կաղանդին օրը։ Անկողնիս մէջ, երկա՜ր մտածեցի օրուան հիւրին եւ օրիորդ Զապէլին մասին։ Մանաւանդ օրիորդ Զապէլին լացը ամէնէն աւելի կը ծնƨ̂ɛր սրտիս։ Վարժուած էինք միƨ̂տ ժպտուն տեսանել զինք եւ շատ տխուր ու զարմանալի բան մըն էր իր լալը, առանց պատճառի։ Թերեւս ծիƨ̂դ էր ըսուածը, խոշոր քիթով մարդուն

<hr>

11. մէƨ̂ իյնալ: "to break in" (into a conversation).

Նշանածն էր ու չէր ուզեր անոր ետ Ամերիկա երթալ։ Ու յետոյ, այդ
ֆիլըը։ Պիտի խնդար ու չխնդաց, պիտի խնդացնէր ու չխնդացուց։ Բարի
մարդ մըն էր սակայն։ Լացաւ ու լացուց բոլորս։ Որոշեցի ֆակիչ
ՅառուԹիւնին ֆարցնել ու միտքս պաֆել իր անունը, քանի որ մեծ մարդ
մըն էր։

Յաջորդ օրը, մոցայ ֆարցնել ու երբեք չգիտցայ անոր անունը։

Տարիներ ետք, նախակրԹարանի սեղանիս վրայ, տարեգիրք մը կը-
ԹրքԹատէի։ Մատներս անփոյԹ կը դարձնէին ֆատ գիրքին էջերը։ ԲազմաԹիւ
նկարներուն մէջ, մէկը գրաւեց ուշադրուԹիւնս։ Սեւ ֆագուստով, սեւ
փողկապով ու ճաղատ գլուխով դէմք մըն էր։ Ինծի այնպէս Թուեցաւ, Թէ
տեղ մը տեսած եմ այդ դէմքը, անոյշ, բարի ժպիտով եւ ֆայկական
նայուածքով։

Ինքն էր, այն ֆեռաւոր ու տարորինակ մեր կաղանդին նոյնքան
տարորինակ ֆիլըը։ Յիշեցի իր նշանաւոր բանախոսուԹիւնը, արցունքները,
մեր ֆաւաքական ողբը։ Չկրցայ ըմբռնել միայն, Թէ ամբողջ կեանքը
խնդալով անցընող մարդը ինչո՞ւ լացած էր մեր աոջեւ, Թէ տասնեակներով
գիրքերու ֆեղինակ գրագէտը ինչո՞ւ երկու խօսք չէր գտած մեզի ըսելիք։

Հիմա կարդացած եմ իր գրած բոլոր գիրքերը։ Կը ճանչնամ իր գործը
արժէքը, արունեստը։ Հասկցած եմ նաեւ, Թէ ինչո՞ւ չկրցաւ խօսիլ ու
միայն լացաւ։ Ի՞նչ կրնար ըսել Տէր-Զօրէն[12] նոր դարձող տառապած ֆայ
գրագէտ մը իր ցեղին ֆազարաւոր որբերուն, որոնց ծնողքները, ամէն
զարունի, վարար Եփրատը դուրս կը նետէր, ոսկոր աո ոսկոր իր աչքերուն
դէմ, աւազին վրայ...

---

12. Տէր-Զօր։ "Deir Zor," on the Euphrates in the Syrian desert - the final
    destination of Armenian deportations in 1915.

Տպեցոյցի նկարին տակ գրուած էր - Երուանդ Օտեան... [13]

Ա. Ծառուկեան

---

13. *Երուանդ Օտեան:* a famous novelist, satirist and journalist, 1869-1926.

Zahrad is a contemporary poet living in Istanbul. The poems below are taken from the following collections: Մեծ Քաղաքը (Istanbul 1960); Բարի Երկինք (Istanbul 1971); Կանանչ Հող (Paris 1976).

ՕՏԱՐ

Քաղաքին այդ կողմերը օտար էին կիկոյին

Բարձր բարձր շէնքերը օտար

Մարդիկը - գեղեցիկ կիները օտար

Գողնց հագած աղջիկ մը եկաւ

Հինգ դրուշ[1] դրաւ ափին -

Օտար էին մարդիկը - օտար -

Կիկո մուրալու չէր եկած

ԱՅՑԵԼՈՒԹԻՒՆ

Դուռը բացի որ Կիկոն էր - Հրամմէ ըսի - նստեցանք

Կիկո ըսաւ թէ շատ կարօտցեր էր զիս

Ես ըսի թէ շատ կարօտցեր էի զինք

Յետոյ խորհեցայ թէ զինք որքան շուտ մոռցեր էի

Յետոյ խորհեցաւ թէ զիս որքան շուտ մոռցեր էր ինք

Ըսի որ աւելի յաճախ կ'ուզեմ տեսնել զինք

Ըսաւ որ աւելի յաճախ կ'ուզէ տեսնել զիս

Որոշեցինք աւելի յաճախ տեսնել զիրար

Գնաց - դրան մէկ կողմն ես - դրան միւս կողմն ինք -

Արդէն իսկ զիրար մոռցեր էինք

---

1. դրուշ: "kurush," small coin.

ԱՐԿԱԾԱՆՆ ԴՐՈԻԹԻԻՆ

Կիկոյի միտքը ման կուգայ[2] քաղաքէ քաղաք

— Կիկօ աշխարհի մասին կը խորհի —

Կիկոյի միտքը կը սաւառնի մոլորակէ մոլորակ

— Կիկօ կը մտածէ արեգակնային դրութեան[3] վրայ —

Կիկոյի միտքը կը ճախրէ աստղէ աստղ

— Կիկօ տիեզերք մը կ'երեւակայէ

Լոյսէն ալ արագ

— Կիկոյի միտքը կ'ուզէ սլանալ աւելի անդին[4]

— Կը մոլորի — չի կրնար

Զրի ճամբորդելն այսքան

ՄԺԵՂԻ ՀԱՇԻԻ

Երբ ամունանցաւ

Կիկօ խորհեցաւ

Սենեակին մէջէը որքան մժեղ կայ

Կէսն իրեն երբ զայ

Կէսն ալ իր կնոջ կ'երթայ — Կը կիսուի —

Բայց մժեղները — աշունն էր — շատցան

Ու հիմա նորէն

Մժեղը նոյնքան

Կին մ'ալ աւելի

---

2. ման գալ : "to tour, wander around."
3. արեգակնային դրութիւն: "solar system."
4. անդին : "farther, beyond."

ՀՈԳ

Ես Կիկոն եմ –

Կորաքամակ

քանի որ

Աշխարհի հոգը շալկած –

Կամ աշխարհն եմ –

Խուճապահար

քանի որ

Կիկոյին հոգը շալկած

ԿԻԿՕ ՄԵՌԱՒ

Բացօթեայ շատ պառկեցաւ

Թող քիչ մրն ալ հողին տակ քնանայ

Հանգիստ իր կոշիկներուն

ՁԵՐՕ

Մէկ անգամ մէկ մէկ

Մէկ անգամ Կիկօ զերo

Երկու անգամ մէկ երկու

Երկու անգամ Կիկօ զերo

Տասն անգամ մէկ տասը

Տասն անգամ Կիկօ զերo

Հարիւր անգամ մէկ հարիւր

Հարիւր անգամ Կիկօ մենք

ԱՅՍՊԷՍ ԱՄԷՆ ԱՌԱՒՕՏ

Այսպէս ամէն առաւօտ

Հրաժեշտ կ'առնեմ կը բաձնուիմ ես ինձմէ

Տանս դուռը երբ կը փակեմ ետեւէս
Գիտեմ թէ
Եսս ներսն է - եւ ամէն քայլ զիս կ'անշատ իմ եսէս

Այսպէս ամէն առաւօտ

Հրաժեշտ կ'առնեմ կը բաձնուիմ ես ինձմէ -

Կը խառնուիմ ուրիշներով շիևուած ևակայ ծովուն մէջ

Ու կը տեսնեմ - պատուևանին ետեւէն

Եսս կեցեր զիս կը դիտէ մտատանջ

Իսկ ես ամէն առաւօտ

Կ'երթամ ծուլլուիլ ուրիշներով շիևուած ևակայ ծովուն մէջ
Մինչդեռ եսս պաան երեսին նատեր կուլյայ ետեւէս -

Հրաժեշտ կ'առնեմ կը բաձնուիմ ես ինձմէ -
Առաւօտուն - ես մանաւանդ առաւօտուն դժբախտ եմ

ՊՈՉ

Թովմասի սիրտր կը նեղանար
Տեսաւ կատուն որ կը խաղար պոչին ևետ
Վեր նայեցաւ - Տէր ըսաւ
Ինչ կ'ըլլար[5] եթէ զիս ալ պոչով ստեղծէիր

---

5. Ինչ կ'ըլլար: "would that."

ՀԱՅԿԱԿԱՆ ԱՌԱԾՆԵՐ

1 Աման միսք համ չունենար ։

2 Ադէկ կին, չունի գին ։

3 Աղուէսէն վկայ ուզեցին, պոչը ցոյց տուաւ ։

4 Աղքատը հացի կարոտ է,
   Հարուստը ամէն բանի ։

5 Աղքատն ունի հաց ու պանիր,
   Գիշերը քունը չի տանիր ։

6 Ամէն քարել տուլողը իրեն քարեկամ կը կարծէ ։

7 Ամէն մարդ ցաւ մը ունի ։

8 Ամէն սեւ հագնող քահանայ չէ ։

9 Անամօթի երեսին թքեր են, ըսեր է
   Փանք քեզ Աստուած, անձրեւ կու գայ ։

10 Անէծքը անիծողին կը դառնայ ։

11 Անխելքի հացը խելոքի փորն է ։

12 Անծրեւն ինչ ընէ քարին,
   Խրատն ինչ ընէ չարին ։

13 Անունը կայ, ինքը չկայ ։

14 Ապրողին ապրանք,
   Մեռնողին պատանք ։

15 Աշով տուր որ ծախով առնես ։

16 Առանց փուշի վարդ չկայ ։

17 Արջէն ազատեց, գայլին կերցուց ։

. . .

18 Թախտին անիւը միշտ կը դառնայ :

19 Բարկացող մարդը շուտ կը ծերանայ :

20 Բերնէ բերան կ՚ըլլայ գերան :

○ ○ ○

21 Գիտունին մէկ, անգէտին հազար :

22 Գիրքին երկու երեսն ալ կարդալու է :

23 Գլուխդ պաղ պահէ, ոտքերդ տաք :

24 Գող, սիրաք դող :

• • ○

25 Դուն քեզ մի՛ գովեր, թող ուրիշը գովէ :

26 Դուն քեզի օգնէ, Աստուած ալ քեզի կ՚օգնէ :

27 Դուրսը քաշանայ, ներսը սատանայ :

• • •

28 Ես կ՚ըսեմ, ես կը լսեմ :

29 Ես տանձ կ՚ըսեմ, դուն զանձ կը հասկնաս :

30 Երկաթը տաք տաք կը ծեծեն :

• • •

31 Էշը հեծեր, էշ կը փնտռէ :

32 Էշն ինչ գիտէ նուշը, կ՚երթայ կ՚ուտէ փուշը :

• • •

33 Ընդդ ես, զատնդ ես :

• • •

34 Թան չէ, մածուն չէ,
    Ամէն մարդու քանը չէ :

35 Թող չըսեն՝ թէ էշ է,
    Թող ըսեն՝ թէ գէշ է :

○ • •

36 Ինչ որ ցանես, զայն կը հնձես ։

37 Ինքը պզտիկ՝ լեզուն մեծ է ։

38 Ինքն իր շուքէն կը վախնայ ։

. . .

39 Լացը լաց կը բերէ ։

40 Լեզու կայ անոյշ է, լեզու կայ՝ լեղի ։

41 Լեզուն արդար, սիրտը չար ։

. . .

42 Խելքը տարիքին մէջ չէ, զլխուն մէջ է ։

43 Խելօքին հետ քար կրէ, խենթին հետ հաց մի՛ ուտեր ։

44 Խենթը զինովեն վախցեր է ։

45 Խենթը ըսաւ, խելօքը հաւատաց ։

46 Խենթին հետ խենթ չեն ըլլար ։

47 Խրատն ինչ ընէ չարին ։

. . .

48 Կամաց կամաց բամպակը կ'ըլլայ մանած ։

49 Կատու չեղած՝ մուկ կը բռնէ ։

. . .

50 Հազար անգամ թուք ու մուր,
    Մէկ անգամ օրինակ տուր ։

51 Հազարին կէսը հինգ հարիւր է ։

52 Համբերութիւնը կեանք է ։

53 Հաց ու գինի ունիս՝ իմ սէրը դուն ես,
    Հաց ու գինի չունիս՝ իմ դեռը դուն ես ։

54 Հաւկիթին մէջ մազ կը փնտռէ ։

55 Հոգը ցաւ կը բերէ, ցաւը՝ մահ ։

. . .

56 Չերքը գոց է :

57 Չեւել չի գիտեր, մկրատը ձեռքէն չի ձգեր :

.   .   .

58 Մարդ կայ էշ է, մարդ կայ գէշ է,

Մարդ կա՛յ սատկած շունէն ալ գէշ է :

59 Մարդ մարդու թանայ,

Մարդ մարդու սատանայ :

60 Մարդուն քաշածը իր խելքէն է :

61 Մարդուս աշքը ծակ է :

62 Մէկ աշքը միւսին օգուտ չունի :

63 Մէկ թշնամին հազար բարեկամէն շատ է :

64 Մէկ խոսէ՛, տաս լսէ՛ :

Հազար չափէ՛, մէկ կտրէ՛ :

65 Մուկ չեղած պատ կը ծակէ :

.   .   .

66 Շատ անոյշ է, տակը փուշ է :

67 Շատ ապրողը շատ բան կը տեսնէ :

68 Շատ մի՛ սիրեր, ատել կայ,

Շատ մի՛ ատեր, սիրել կայ :

69 Շատը գնաց, քիչը մնաց :

70 Շիտակ մարդը ծուռ բան չի սիրեր,

ծուռին ալ շիտակ չ'րսեր :

71 Շո՛ւն, շո՛ւն, եկո՛ւր գիս խած :

72 Շունը կը հաչէ, քամին կը փչէ :

73 Շունը յիշէ՛, փայտը քաշէ՛ :

74 Շունը տիրոջ կը ձանչնայ :

°   •   •

75 Ով որ կ՚ըսէ ուզածը, կը լսէ չուզածը ։

76 Որբին հաց տուող չկայ, խրատ տուող շատ կայ ։

77 Որդը ծառէն կ՚ելլէ՛ ծառը կ՚ուտէ ։

78 Ուտող, ուրացող ։

. . .

79 Չառաւ իր գիւղին գէշը,
Առաւ օտարին էշը ։

. . .

80 Պարտքը տալով, մեղքը լալով ։

. . .

81 Ջուրը զացող՛ ծարաւ դարձող ։

82 Ջուրը չտեսած չէն բոպիկնար ։

83 Ջուրը տեսնայ՛ ծուկ կ՚ըլլայ ։

. . .

84 Սուտ խենթ է եղեր, վանքին հաղը կ՚ուտէ ։

. . .

85 Վա՜յ քեզ քաղաք, Թագաւորդ մանուկ է ։

86 Վեր թքնեմ՛ պեխերս է,
Վար թքնեմ՛ մօրուքս է ։

87 Վերի յարկը տապակ է ։

. . .

88 Տուն շինողին, աղջիկ կարգողին
Աստուած հետը կ՚ըլլայ ։

. . .

89 Քաղցր լեզուն օձը ծակէն կը հանէ ։

90 Քանի լեզու գիտես՛ այնքան մարդ ես ։

VOCALIC ALTERNATION

In classical Armenian the loss of stress entailed certain vowel changes.
E.g. from the noun սէր (love) is derived the verb սիրել (to love), because
stress (nearly) always falls on the last full syllable of a word. Such changes
are no longer fully operative in modern Western Armenian. E.g. the genitive
of հանդէս (celebration; review) is հանդէսի, not * հանդիսի as one might
expect (see §3 below). But many classical forms have been retained in the
literary language, which makes it impossible to draw up regular rules for
vocalic alternation based on *modern* Armenian usage only. However, a summary
of these alternations will help in elucidating many declined forms and compounds.

1. ի > zero or (unwritten) ը: գիր (script), but գրել (to write; two

     syllables).

        ամուսին (husband) but ամուսնանալ (to marry)

     Note: In the declension of some nouns with ի in the last syllable two patterns

          are found. Thus գիրք (book) has gen.: գրքի or գիրքի: ուսուցիչ

          (teacher) has gen.: ուսուցչի or ուսուցիչի Such variants have

          been noted in the vocabulary.

2. ու > zero or (unwritten) ը: սուտ (false) but ստել (to lie)

3. է > ի: սէր (love) but սիրել (to love)

     որպէս (as) but որպիսի (such)

4. ոյ > ու: լոյս (light) but լուսաւորիչ (illuminator)

5. եա > ե: վայրկեան (minute) but վայրկենական (momentary)

CONSONANTAL ALTERNATION

ɲ > n before ʮ: ηnιn (< ηnιnʮ) but genitive ηɲwʮ (door); ηɲwgɦ

(neighbor)

ɸɓn   (< ɸɓnʮ : load) but ɸɓɲɓɭ (to bring)

Note the very frequent loss of a final ʮ after a preceding consonant in modern

Western Armenian (as in the two preceding examples). But the ʮ reappears in

compound forms.

E.g.   ɭɓn   (mountain) but ɭɓnʮwɟɦʮ (mountainous)

 nιnιɥ (study) but nιnιɥʮwwɛɲ (studious)

ɗnιɥ   (fish) but ɗɥʮwɥwɒwn (fishmonger)

CONSONANTAL CLUSTERS

In Armenian clusters of as many as six consonants pose a problem for syllabification and pronunciation as the vowel ը is often unwritten. The following general rules should be of some help. (For the pronunciation of words plus suffixes, see the end of this section.)

The basic rule is that syllables begin with a consonant, except for words with an initial vowel. (But see 1 A below.) Also, generally, where a vowel in a stem or root has dropped because of a shift in stress ը is pronounced.

1. Clusters of two consonants.

    A. *Initial.* ը follows C¹ except for q and u followed by stops or affricates. I.e. with the combinations զբ, զգ, սթ, սկ, սպ, ստ, սփ, սբ the vowel ը is pronounced in initial position.

Thus:	նման	(similar)	նը-ման
	կրակ	(fire)	կը-րակ
	սրել	(to sharpen)	սը-րել
	սխալ	(mistake)	սը-խալ
	շփոթ	(confusion)	շը-փոթ
But	զբաղիլ	(to be occupied)	ըզ-բա-ղիլ
	զգույշ	(careful)	ըզ-գույշ
	սթափիլ	(to come to one's senses)	ըս-թա-փիլ
	սկիզբ	(beginning)	ըս-կիզբ
	սպաննել	(to kill)	ըս-պան-նել
	ստանալ	(to get, receive)	ըս-տա-նալ
	սփոփել	(to console)	ըս-փո-փել
	սբանչելի	(wonderful)	ըս-բան-չե-լի

The combination շտ also falls into this category:

շտապել (to hasten) ըշ-տա-պել

Note that the apparent exception ստել (to lie) is pronounced սը-տել because the verb is derived from the root սուտ (false), and ը is pronounced where the original vowel ու has been reduced following the shift of stress to the final syllable.

B. *Medial.* c^1 closes the preceding syllable, c^2 begins the next. Thus ապրիլ (to live) ապ-րիլ

տարբեր (different) տար-բեր

The causative verbs in -գնել are apparent exceptions: կարդացնել (to cause to read) կար-դա-ցը-նել; but the ը reflects an earlier ու (cf. the classical form մատուցանել, to offer, Lesson XXX).

C. *Final.* The two consonants are run together with the following exceptions: combinations with final ն or ր, and մ preceded by ղ.
Thus: պետք (need) one syllable

պատերազմ (war) պա-տե-րազմ

սուրբ (holy) one syllable

ջերմ (warm) one syllable

արհեստ (trade, skill) արհ-հեստ

հիւանդ (ill) հի-ւանդ

But: նմն (someone) ն-մըն

մանր (small) մա-նըր

փոքր (small) փո-քըր

այժմ (now) այ-ժըմ

Note that մեղր (honey) is pronounced either մեղր or մե-ղըր.

2. Clusters of three consonants.

A. *Initial.* C³ begins a syllable. ə is pronounced between c¹ and c²; before uy etc. ə must also be pronounced before c¹. ə may also be inserted after c² if an original vowel has dropped.

Thus: *խնդալ*   (to laugh)   *խըն-դալ*

     վստահ   (certain)   *վըս-տահ*

     փրկել   (to save, rescue) *փըր-կել*

Note that *շտկել* (to put straight) is regular (*շըտ-կել*), unlike initial *շտ-* (cf. 1 A above).

But: *պտտիլ*   (to walk)   *պը-տը-տիլ* (cf. the noun *պտույտ*)

     սկսիլ   (to begin)   *ըս-կը-սիլ* (cf. 1 A above)

B. *Medial.* c³ begins a syllable; in most cases c¹ and c² are run to-gether. But if c¹ closes a syllable, ə is pronounced after c².

Thus: *անձրեւ*   (rain)   *անձ-րեւ*

     թարգմանիչ (interpreter)   *թարգ-մա-նիչ*

     պաշտպանել (to defend)   *պաշտ-պա-նել*

But: *հասկնալ*   (to understand)   *հաս-կը-նալ*

     աղմկել   (to make a noise)   *աղ-մը-կել* (cf. the noun *աղմուկ*)

Occasionally c¹ and c² form a syllable with ə:

     ոչնչացնել (to annihilate)   *ն-չըն-չաց-նել* (cf. the noun *ոչինչ*)

     ատրճանակ (pistol)   *ա-տըր-ճա-նակ* (cf. Iranian *atur* - fire)

Note that the negative prefix *ան* is not split:

     անհնար   (impossible)   *ան-հը-նար*

C. *Final.* ə is pronounced between c² and c³, except in words ending with the classical plural -ə .

Thus: դուստր   (daughter) դուս-տրը

          բարձր   (high)   բար-ձրը

But: պարտք   (debt) one syllable

          բռունցք (fist) բը-ռունցք

In modern Armenian աստղ (star) is pronounced as one syllable.

3. Clusters of four consonants.

      Rules are difficult to elaborate, as the position of ը is determined by the word's etymology and history.

     A. *Initial*. C^4 begins a syllable. The following sub-categories may be distinguished: a) CvCC-C

                               b) Cv-CvC-C

                               c) CvC-Cv-C

a) խնդրել (to ask): խրնդ-րել . Note that in this word ը does not occur where the original vowel of խնդիր has been lost; not * խըն-դը-րել .

      գրգռել (to incite): գըրգ-ռել

b)   բժշկութիւն(medicine): բը-ժըշ-կու-թիւն

      մկրտել   (to baptise): մը-կըր-տել

      վռնտել   (to expel):   վը-ռըն-տել

c)   փրցնել   (to break, tear off): փըր-ցը-նել (but cf. 1 B for verbs in

       -ցնել)

Note also the initial ը in սկսնակ (beginner): ըս-կըս-նակ; cf. 1 A.

     B. *Medial*. The standard pattern is C-CvC-C.

Thus: արթննալ   (to wake up): ար-թըն-նալ (cf. արթուն)

երկննալ (to grow longer): եր-կրն-նալ (cf. երկայն)

ընկրկիլ (to fall back): ըն-կրր-կիլ

հանգստանալ(to rest): հան-գրս-տա-նալ (cf. հանգիստ)

խորհրդական (counsellor): խոր-հրր-դա-կան

But note նախանձախնդրութիւն (zeal) նա-խան-ձա-խրնդ-րու-թիւն cf. A a)
above.

Compounds in ան- and ընդ- divide after those prefixes:

    անըմբռնելի (incomprehensible): ան-ըմբռն-նե-լի

    անխղճօրէն (unscrupulously): ան-խղճ-օo-րէն (cf. խիղճ)

    ընդվզիլ (to rebel): ընդ-վզ-զիլ

    C. *Final*. No words end in four consonants unless C^4 is a suffix.

4. Clusters of five consonants.

    A. *Initial*. Several patterns are attested:

        a) CvC-CvC-C

        b) CvCC-Cv-C

        c) Cv-CvC-Cv-C

        d) Cv-CvCC-C

a) ճշգրտութիւն (exactitude): ճշ2-գրր-տու-թիւն (cf. ճշգրիտ)

    հրմշտուք (bustle, pushing): հրր-մշ2-տուք

    մշտնջենական (eternal): մշ2-տրն-ջե-նա-կան (cf. միշտ)

    տրտնջիւն (complaint): տրր-տրն-ջիւն

    փնտռտուք (searching): փրն-տռռ-տուք

b) խղճմտանք (remorse): խղճ-մր-տանք (but cf. 3 B)

c) լմնցնե լ   (to finish): լը-մըն-գը-նե լ (cf. 1 B)

d) բունցքամարթիկ (boxer): բը-ունց-քա-մար-թիկ (cf. բունցքը - fist)

  փունգտալ   (to sneeze): փը-ունգ-տալ

B. *Medial.* These are very rare except in compounds:

E.g. վրէժխնդրութիւն   (vengeance): վը-րէժ-խընդ-րու-թիւն (cf. 3 B)

  անբժշկելի   (incurable): ան-բը-ժըշ-կե-լի

  անկրկնելի   (unrepeatable): ան-կըրկ-նե-լի (cf. կրկին)

Note also անսկզբունք   (unprincipled): ան-ըս-կըզ-բունք (cf. 1 A).

C. *Final.* Do not exist.

5. Clusters of six consonants.

There are very few examples which are not easy to categorize.

A. *Initial.*

  բռթմնջալ   (to grumble, complain): բըրթ-մըն-ջալ

  հրմշտկել   (to push): հըր-մըշ-տը-կել (cf. 4 A a)

B. *Medial.*

  անմշտնջենական (not eternal): ան-մըշ-տըն-ջե-նա-կան (cf. 4 A a)

C. *Final.* Do not exist.

6. Suffixes

The demonstrative suffixes -ս, -դ, -ն form one syllable with a preceding vowel.

E.g. կատու (cat), կատուս (my cat) կա-տուս

A single final consonant forms one syllable with the suffix with (unwritten) ը.

E.g. *մատիտս* (my pencil) *մա-տի-տըս*, *մա-տի-տըդ*

    After two or three final consonants, the suffix forms one syllable with the last (plus unwritten *ը*).

E.g. *գիրքս* (my book) *գիր-քըս*, *գիր-քըդ*

    արհեստս (my trade) *ար-հես-տըս*, *ար-հես-տըդ*

    պարտքս (my debt) *պարտ-քըս*, *պարտ-քըդ*

    դուստրդ (your daughter) *դուս-տըրդ* (but cf. *դուս-տըր* , 2 C above).

COUNTRIES AND PEOPLES

1. *The five continents* (գամաքամասերը):

Ամերիկա, -յի; ամերիկեան	America; American
Ասիա, -իոյ; ասիական	Asia; Asian
Աւստրալիա, -իոյ; աւստրալիական	Australia; Australian
Ափրիկէ, -ի; ափրիկեան	Africa; African
Եւրոպա, -յի; եւրոպական	Europe; European

The columns give the Armenian for the country, the people, the language, and the adjectival form.

2. *suffix* աստան (gen. -ի):

Հայաստան	Հայ, -ու	Հայերէն	Հայկական	Armenia
Յունաստան	յոյն, -ի	յունարէն	յունական	Greece
Չինաստան	չինացի, -ի	չինարէն	չինական	China
Պարսկաստան	պարսիկ, -ի	պարսկերէն	պարսկական	Iran
Վրաստան	վրացի, -ի	վրացերէն	վրացական	Georgia

3. *suffix* իա (gen. -իոյ):

Անգլիա	անգլիացի	անգլերէն	անգլիական	England
Աւստրիա	աւստրիացի		աւստրիական	Austria
Գերմանիա	գերմանացի	գերմաներէն	գերմանական	Germany
Զուիցերիա	զուիցերիացի		զուիցերիական	Switzerland
Թուրքիա	Թուրք	Թրքերէն	Թրքական	Turkey
Իտալիա	իտալացի	իտալերէն	իտալական	Italy

4. *Miscellaneous:*

Ամերիկա,-յի	ամերիկացի		ամերիկեան	America
Եգիպտոս,-ի	եգիպտացի	արաբերէն	եգիպտական	Egypt

իսրայէլ, -ի	իսրայէլցի*	եբրայեցերէն	իսրայէլեան	Israel
Լիբանան, -ի	լիբանանցի		լիբանանեան	Lebanon
Հոլանտա, -յի	հոլանտացի		հոլանտական	Holland
ճափոն, -ի	ճափոնցի	ճափոներէն	ճափոնական	Japan
Միացեալ Նահանգներ, -ու	ամերիկացի			U. S.
նոր Զելանտա, նոր -յի	զելանտացի		նոր զելանտական	New Zealand
Ուրուկուէյ, -ի	ուրուկուէյցի		ուրուկուէյական	Uruguay
Պելճիքա, -յի	պելճիքացի		պելճիքական	Belgium
Քանատա, -յի	քանատացի		քանատական	Canada
Ֆրանսա, -յի	ֆրանսացի	ֆրանսերէն	ֆրանսական	France

5.

Արեւելեան Գերմանիա, -իոյ   East Germany

Արեւմտեան Գերմանիա, -իոյ   West Germany

Հարաւային Ափրիկէ, -ի   South Africa

Հիւսիսային Ափրիկէ, -ի   North Africa

6. *Some names indicating Armenian communities in the diaspora* (սփիւռք):

ամերիկահայ, -ի   American-Armenian

լիբանանահայ, -ի   Lebanese-Armenian

պարսկահայ, -ի   Iranian-Armenian

ֆրանսահայ, -ի   French-Armenian

սփիւռքահայ, -ի   one who lives in the diaspora

Armenians born in Soviet Armenia are called հայաստանցի, -ի.

*But հրեայ: Jew.

THE CONJUGATION OF REGULAR VERBS

Infinitive	սիրել	խօսիլ	կարդալ
Present stem:			
Pres. Indic.	կը սիրեմ	կը խօսիմ	կը կարդամ
Pres. Subj.	սիրեմ	խօսիմ	կարդամ
Imperf. Indic.	կը սիրէի	կը խօսէի	կը կարդայի
Imperf. Subj.	սիրէի	խօսէի	կարդայի
Future	պիտի սիրեմ	պիտի խօսիմ	պիտի կարդամ
Conditional	պիտի սիրէի	պիտի խօսէի	պիտի կարդայի
Aorist stem:			
Aor. Indic.	սիրեցի	խօսեցայ	կարդացի
Perfect stem:			
Perf. Indic.	սիրած եմ	խօսած եմ	կարդացած եմ
Perf. Subj.	սիրած ըլլամ	խօսած ըլլամ	կարդացած ըլլամ
Pluperf. Indic.	սիրած էի	խօսած էի	կարդացած էի
Pluperf. Subj.	սիրած ըլլայի	խօսած ըլլայի	կարդացած ըլլայի
Future Perf.	սիրած պիտի ըլլամ	խօսած պիտի ըլլամ	կարդացած պիտի ըլլամ
Perf. Conditional	սիրած պիտի ըլլայի	խօսած պիտի ըլլայի	կարդացած պիտի ըլլայի
Imperative:			
Positive	սիրէ, սիրեցէք	խօսէ, խօսեցէք	կարդա՛, կարդացէք
Prohibitive	մի սիրեր, մի՛ սիրէք	մի՛ խօսիր, մի՛ խօսիք	մի՛ կարդար, մի՛ կարդաք

Participles:

Present	սիրող	խօսող	կարդացող
Future	սիրելու,	խօսելու,	կարդալու,
	սիրելիք	խօսելիք	կարդալիք
Perfect	սիրած, սիրեր	խօսած, խօսեր	կարդացած,
			կարդացեր

THE MOST COMMON DECLENSIONS OF NOUNS

(Forms are given in the order: Nom/Acc, Gen/Dat, Abl, Instr.)

1. Genitive in -ի : ուսանող, ուսանողի, ուսանողէ, ուսանողով

    Plural: ուսանողներ, ուսանողներու, ուսանողներէ, ուսանողներով

2. Genitive in -ու: ծով, ծովու, ծովէ, ծովով

    Plural as for 1.

3. Abstracts in -ութիւն: Հարութիւն, Հարութեան, Հարութենէ, Հարութեամբ

    Plural as for 1.

4. Nouns of kinship. a) Հայր, Հօր, Հօրմէ, Հօրմով

    b) կին, կնոջ, կնոջմէ, կնոջմով

    Plurals as for 1.

5. Genitive in -ան. a) անուն, անուան, անունէ, անունով

    b) բացում, բացման, բացումէ, բացումով

    c) աղջիկ, աղջկան, աղջիկէ, աղջիկով

    Plurals as for 1.

6. Genitive in -ուան: օր, օրուան, օրուընէ (or օրէ), օրով

    Plural as for 1.

This vocabulary is simply an *aide mémoire* for the exercises. It does not contain the vocabulary of the reading material (Lessons 32-36), nor does it include: countries, languages or nationalities; days of the week or months; personal names or pronouns; numbers; comparative or superlative adjectives. Only basic forms have been given. All irregularities and difficulties must be elucidated from the lessons or from the *Armenian-English Vocabulary*, which is fully inclusive and gives all unpredictable declined forms of nouns and the aorist stems of irregular verbs. Note that different meanings of the same English word do not have separate entries.

a, an	մը	to admire	հիանալ
able	կարող	adorable	պաշտելի
to be able	կարենալ	advice	խրատ
about	մասին	to be afraid of	վախնալ
absent	բացակայ	after	ետք
acceptable	ընդունելի	afterwards	յետոյ
accident	արկած	again	դարձեալ, կրկին, նորէն
to accompany	ընկերանալ	against	դէմ
according to	ըստ	age	տարիք
account	հաշիւ	ago	առաջ
acquaintance	ծանօթ	to agree to	համաձայնիլ
to be acquainted with	ծանօթանալ	in agreement with	համաձայն
address	հասցէ	air	օդ
to adjust oneself	յարմարիլ	airplane	օդանաւ

255

airport	օդակայան	to approach	մօտենալ
all	ամէն, բոլոր	approximately	մօտաւորապէս
all of them	բոլորն ալ	army	բանակ
almost	գրեթէ	to arrive	ժամանել, հասնիլ
alone	առանձին,	art	արուեստ
	մինակ	article	յօդուած
aloud	բարձրաձայն	artist	արուեստագէտ
already	արդէն	as	որպէս, պէս
also	ալ	as long as	քանի (որ)
although	թէեւ, թէպէտեւ	as much	ինչ քան
always	միշտ	as...so	ինչպէս..նոյնպէս
amicable	բարեկամական		(or այնպէս)
amount	գումար	to be ashamed	ամչնալ
and	եւ, ու	to ask	խնդրել; հարցնել
to become angry	բարկանալ	to astonish	զարմացնել
animal	կենդանի	at all	բնաւ
annual	տարեկան	at least	առնուազն
answer	պատասխան	to attend	յաճախել
to answer	պատասխանել	attention	ուշադրութիւն
any	որեւէ	author	հեղինակ
apology	ներողութիւն	autumn	աշուն
to appear	երեւիլ, թուիլ	to avoid	խուսափիլ
appearance	տեսք	back (adv.)	ետ
appetite	ախորժակ	bad	գէշ, չար
apple	խնձոր	ball	գնդակ
to apply to	դիմել	barber	սափրիչ

to beat	ծեծել	body	մարմին
beautiful	գեղեցիկ	book	գիրք
to become beautiful	գեղեցկանալ	to be bored	ձանձրանալ
beauty	գեղեցկություն	to be born	ծնիլ
because	որովհետեւ	both	երկուքն ալ
because of	պատճառաւ	bottle	շիշ
to become	ըլլալ	box	տուփ
bed	անկողին	boy	մանչ, տղայ
beer	գարեջուր	branch	ճիւղ
to begin	սկսիլ	bread	հաց
beginning	սկսեալ	to break	կոտրել
to behave	վարուիլ	breakfast	նախաճաշ
behind	ետեւ	to have breakfast	նախաճաշել
believe	հաւատալ	breath	շունչ
to belong to	պատկանիլ	bright	փայլուն
benevolent	բարեսէր	to bring	բերել
beside	քով	to bring in	մացնել
between	միջեւ	brother	եղբայր
bicycle	հեծանիւ	to build	շինել
big	մեծ	building	շէնք
birthday	տարեդարձ	to burn	այրել, այրիլ
black	սեւ	bus	հանրակառք
blood	արիւն	busy	զբաղած
blow	հարուած	but	բայց, իսկ,
to blow	փչել		սակայն
blue	կապոյտ	to buy	գնել

car	ինքնաշարժ	classroom	դասարան
care	խնամք	clean	մաքուր
to take care of	խնամել	to clean	մաքրել
to be careful	զգուշանալ	clear	յստակ
to carry	տանիլ	to climb	բարձրանալ
cat	կատու	clock	ժամացոյց
to catch	բռնել	close	մօտիկ
cause	պատճառ	to close	գոցել
to cause	պատճառել	closed	գոց
caution	զգուշութիւն	to clothe	հագցնել
cent	սենթ	clothes	հագուստ
century	դար	cloudy	ամպոտ
certainly	անպատճառ	club	ակումբ
chair	աթոռ	coast	եզերք
to change	փոխել	coffee	սուրճ
character	նկարագիր	cold	պաղ
cheap	աժան	to collect	հաւաքել
chicken	հաւ	color	գոյն
chief	գլխաւոր	to comb one's hair	սանտրուիլ
child	երախայ, զաւակ	to come	գալ
choice	ընտիր	to come off	փրթիլ
to choose	ընտրել	comfortable	հանգիստ
church	եկեղեցի	compatriot	հայրենակից
circle	շրջանակ	compatriotic	հայրենակցական
circumstance	պարագայ	to complete	լմնցնել
city	քաղաք	concert	համերգ

condition	պայման	day	օր
confidence	վստահութիւն	daytime	ցերեկ
consequently	հետեւաբար	dear	սիրելի
to continue	շարունակել	death	մահ
contrary to	հակառակ	debt	պարտք
conversation	խօսակցութիւն	to deceive	խաբել
cost	ծախք	to decide	որոշել
to count	համրել	decision	որոշում
country	երկիր	deep	խորունկ
courage	քաջութիւն	degree	աստիճան
course	դասընթացք,	demand	պահանջք
	ընթացք	to demand	պահանջել
cow	կով	demonstration	ցոյց
to cry	լալ	demonstrator	ցուցարար
culture	մշակոյթ	to deny	ուրանալ
cup	գաւաթ	to descend	իջնել
to cure	բժշկել	desire	փափաք
to curse	հայհոյել	to desire	փափաքիլ
to cut	կտրել	to despair	յուսահատիլ
dance	պարահանդէս	to detach	փրցնել
to dance	պարել	to die	մեռնիլ
daily	օրական	difference	տարբերութիւն
dangerous	վտանգաւոր	different	տարբեր
to dare	համարձակիլ	difficulty	դժուարութիւն
dark	գոց; մութ	dirty	աղտոտ
date	թուական	to disappear	անհետանալ;
			կորսուիլ

dissatisfied	դժգոհ	easy	դիւրին
distance	հեռաւորութիւն	to eat	ուտել
to divide	բաժնել	education	կրթութիւն
to do	ընել	election	ընտրութիւն
doctor	բժիշկ	end	վերջ
dog	շուն	to end	վերջանալ
dollar	տոլար	to endure	դիմանալ
donkey	էշ	enemy	թշնամի
door	դուռ	to be engaged in	զբաղիլ
doubt	կասկած	to enlarge	մեծցնել
doubtless	անկասկած	to enter	մտնել
down	վար	entrance	մուտք
to draw	գծել	enough	բաւական
dream	երազ	to be enough	բաւել
drink	խմելիք	equal	հաւասար
to drink	խմել	equally	հաւասարապէս
to drive	քշել	to escape	փախչիլ
to drop	ծգել	especially	մանաւորապէս
duty	պարտականութիւն	even	նոյնիսկ
each	ամէն,	evening	երեկոյ, իրիկուն
	իւրաքանչիւր	event	դէպք
each other	իրար	ever	երբեք
early	կանուխ	examination	քննութիւն
to earn	շահիլ	example	օրինակ
earthquake	երկրաշարժ	except	բացի
eastern	արեւելեան	excessively	չարաչար

to exist	գոյութիւն, ունենալ	to feed	կերցնել
existence	գոյութիւն	to feel	զալ
to expect	ակնկալել	fight	կռիւ
expensive	սուղ	to fight	կռուիլ
to explain	բացատրել	to fill	լեցնել
explanation	բացատրութիւն	finally	վերջապէս
to express	արտայայտել	financial	նիւթական
to extinguish	մարել, մարիլ	to find	գտնել
extremely	չափազանց	finger	մատ
eye	աչք	to finish	վերջացնել
face	երես	fire	կրակ
factory	գործարան	first	առաջին
faith	հաւատք	fish	ձուկ
to fall	իյնալ	to flee	փախչիլ
false	կեղծ, սուտ	floor	յարկ
family	ընտանիք	flower	ծաղիկ
famous	յայտնի, նշանաւոր	to follow	հետեւիլ
far	հեռու	following	հետեւեալ
fast	արագ	food	ուտելիք, սնունդ
father	հայր	foot	ոտք
fatherland	հայրենիք	for	համար
fault	յանցանք	force	ոյժ
favor	լաւութիւն	to force	ստիպել
fear	վախ	foreign	օտար
feast	տօն	forest	անտառ
		to forget	մոռնալ

to forgive	ներել	gladly	սիրով
to form	կազմել	glance	նայուածք
former	նախկին	glass	բաժակ
fortunately	բարեբախտաբար	glasses (eye-)	ակնոց
free	ազատ, ձրի	glove	ձեռնոց
to freeze	սառիլ	to go	երթալ
fresh	թարմ	to go up	ելլել
friend	բարեկամ, ընկեր	God	Աստուած
(girl-)friend	բարեկամուհի,	good	աղէկ, բարի, լաւ
	ընկերուհի	good-bye	ցտեսութիւն;
friendship	ընկերութիւն		Մնաս բարով
to be frightened	սարսափիլ	(response:)	Երթաս բարով
in front of	առջեւ	to govern	կառավարել
fruit	պտուղ	government	կառավարութիւն
full	լեցուն	gradually	աստիճանաբար
future	ապագայ	grandfather	մեծ հայր
game	խաղ	grandmother	մեծ մայր
garden	պարտէզ	to grasp	ըմբռնել
general (adj.)	ընդհանուր	greatness	մեծութիւն
general (n.)	զօրավար	to greet	բարեւել
generally	ընդհանրապէս	ground	գետին
giant	հսկայ	to grow	մեծնալ
gift	նուէր	guest	հիւր
girl	աղջիկ	to guide	առաջնորդել
to give	տալ	habit	սովորութիւն
glad	ուրախ	hair	մազ

half	կէս	history	պատմութիւն
hand	ձեռք	to hit	զարնել
to hang	կախել	holiday(s)	արձակուրդ
to happen	պատահիլ	honest	պարկեշտ
happiness	երջանկութիւն	honesty	ազնուութիւն
happy	երջանիկ	hope	յոյս
hard	դժուար	to hope	յուսալ
hardly	հազիւ	horse	ձի
hat	գլխարկ	hospital	հիւանդանոց
to have	ունենալ	hot	տաք
head	գլուխ	hotel	պանդոկ
health	առողջութիւն	hour	ժամ
in poor health	վատառողջ	hourly	ժամական
healthy	առողջ, առողջարար	house	տուն
to hear	լսել	how?	ինչպէս
heart	սիրտ	how many?	քանի̃
heavy	ծանր	how much	որքան
height	բարձրութիւն;	human	մարդկային
	հասակ	hungry	անօթի
hello	բարեւ	to hurry	աճապարել
help	օգնութիւն	to hurt	վիրաւորել; ցաւիլ
to help	օգնել	husband	ամուսին
here	հոս	husband's brother	տագր
here (it is)!	ահա, ահաւասիկ	husband's father	կեսրայր
to hide	պահլւրտիլ	husband's mother	կեսուր
high	բարձր	husband's sister	տալ

ice-cream	պաղպաղակ·	interesting	հետաքրքրական
idea	զաղափար	to introduce	ծանoթացնել,
if	եթէ		ներկայացնել
ill	հիւանդ	involuntarily	ակամայ
to fall ill	հիւանդանալ	iron	երկաթ
illness	հիւանդութիւն	jacket	բաճկոն
to imagine	երեւակայել	job	գործ
immediately	անմիջապէս	joy	ուրախութիւն
impatience	անհամբերութիւն	to judge	դատել
important	կարեւոր	just	արդար
to improve	լաւանալ	to keep	պահել
in	մէջ, ներս	key	բանալի
to increase	աւելնալ	to kill	սպաննել
indifferent	անտարբեր	kilometer	քիլոմեթր
to inform	իմացնել,	kind (adj.)	ազնիւ
	տեղեկացնել	kind (n.)	տեսակ
information	տեղեկութիւն	king	թագաւոր
inhabitant	բնակիչ	to kiss	համբուրել
inner	ներքին	knife	դանակ
inside	ներսը	to know	գիտնալ
instead of	փոխանակ	lacking	կարoտ
intelligence	խելք	language	լեզու
intelligent	խելացի	last	վերջին
to intend	մտադրել	to last	տեւել
interest	հետաքրքրութիւն	late	ուշ
to be inter-	հետաքրքրուիլ	to be late	ուշանալ
ested in			

lately	վերջերս	lip	շրթունք
to laugh	խնդալ	to listen to	մտիկ ընել
law	օրէնք	liter	լիտր
lazy	ծոյլ	literature	գրականութիւն
leader	առաջնորդ	little	փոքր
leaf	տերեւ	a little	քիչ մը
leap year	նահանջ տարի	liturgy	պատարագ
to learn	սորվիլ	to live	ապրիլ, բնակիլ
to leave	մեկնիլ	long	երկայն, երկար
lecture	դասախոսութիւն	to long for	կարօտնալ
lecturer	դասախոս	to look at	նայիլ
left	ձախ	to look for	փնտռել
less	պակաս	to look like	նմանիլ
lesson	դաս	to lose	կորսնցնել
let	թող	loss	կորուստ
letter	գիր, նամակ	loud	բարձր
liberty	ազատութիւն	love	սէր
library	գրադարան	to love	սիրել
to lie down	պառկիլ	low	ցած
life	կեանք	luck	բախտ
to lift	բարձրացնել	man	մարդ
light (adj.)	բաց, թեթեւ	manner	կերպով
light (n.)	լոյս	many	շատ (մը)
like	նման	market	շուկայ
to like	հաւնիլ	marriage	ամուսնութիւն
likewise	նոյնպէս	to marry	ամուսնանալ

matter	խնդիր; նիւթ	money	դրամ
meal	ճաշ	month	ամիս
to mean	նշանակել	more	աւելի
meaning	նշանակութիւն	morning	առաւօտ, առտու
means	միջոց	mother	մայր
measure	չափ	motion	շարժում
meat	միս	mountain	լեռ
medicine	բժշկութիւն	mouth	բերան
to meet	հանդիպիլ	to move	շարժել, շարժիլ
meeting	ժողով	Mr.	պարոն
member	անդամ	Mrs.	տիկին
meter	մէթր	museum	թանգարան
mid-day	կէսօր	name	անուն
middle	մէջտեղ	to name	կոչել
midnight	կէսգիշեր	narrow	նեղ
mile	մղոն	nation	ազգ
milk	կաթ	national	ազգային
mind	միտք	natural	բնական
minute	վայրկեան	nature	բնութիւն,
mirror	հայելի		բնաւորութիւն
Miss	օրիորդ	naughty	չարաճճի
to miss	փախցնել	near	մօտ
mistake	սխալ	need	պէտք
by mistake	սխալմամբ	negligence	անհոգութիւն
modern	արդի	negligent	անհոգ
moment	պահ	neighbor	դրացի

neighborhood	շրջակայք	old age	ծերություն
neither...nor	ոչ...ոչ (ալ)	on	վրայ
new	նոր	once	անգամ մը
news	լուր	only	միակ; միայն
newspaper	թերթ, օրաթերթ	open	բաց
next	յաջորդ	to open	բանալ
night	գիշեր	opening	բացում
no	ոչ, չէ	opinion	կարծիք
no longer	այլեւս + neg. verb	opponent	հակառակորդ
no one	ոչ ոք	opposite (n.)	հակառակ
noise	աղմուկ	opposite (post-	դիմաց
nothing	ոչ ինչ	pos.)	
to notice	նկատել	or	կամ; թէ
to notify	ծանուցանել	order	հրաման
novel	վէպ	organization	կազմակերպություն
now	այժմ, հիմա	oriental	արեւելեան
number	թիւ	other	այլ, ուրիշ; միւս
occasion	առիթ	otherwise	այլապէս
on the occasion of	առթիւ	out	դուրս
of course	անշուշտ	outside	դուրսը
to offer	հրամցնել	owner	տէր
office	պաշտոն	page	էջ
officer	սպայ	pain	ցաւ
official	պաշտոնեայ	to paint	ներկել
often	յաճախ	paper	թուղթ
old	ծեր; հին	parents	ծնողք

part	մաս	plan	ծրագիր
to participate	մասնակցիլ	to play	խաղալ
partly	մասամբ	pleasant	հաճելի
party	կուսակցութիւն;	to be pleased	հաճիլ
	հանդէս	pleasure	հաճոյք
to pass	անցընել, անցնիլ	politeness	քաղաքավարութիւն
past	անցեալ	political	քաղաքական
patience	համբերութիւն	poor	աղքատ; խեղճ
to pay	վճարել	population	բնակչութիւն
peace	խաղաղութիւն	position	դիրք
pen	գրիչ	possible	կարելի
pencil	մատիտ	post office	նամակատուն
people	ժողովուրդ	to praise	գովել
perfect	կատարեալ	to prefer	նախընտրել
to perform	կատարել	to prepare	պատրաստել
perhaps	թերեւս	presence	ներկայութիւն
person	անձ, հոգի	present	ներկայ
in person	անձամբ	president	նախագահ
personal	անձնական	pretty	սիրուն
phenomenon	երեւոյթ	price	գին
photograph	լուսանկար	priest	քահանայ
picture	նկար, պատկեր	prince	իշխան
to pick	քաղել	to print	տպել
piece	կտոր	profession	արհեստ
place	տեղ	profit	շահ
to place	տեղաւորել	to prohibit	արգիլել

to promise	խոստանալ	to recognize	ճանչնալ
to pronounce	արտասանել, հնչել	red	կարմիր
pronunciation	հնչում	with regard to	հանդէպ
proposal	առաջարկ	regarding	նկատմամբ
to propose	առաջարկել	regular	կանոնաւոր
to protect	պաշտպանել	relative	ազգական
public	հանրային	reliable	ստոյգ
to pull	քաշել	to remain	մնալ
to punish	պատժել	to remember	յիշել
pupil	աշակերտ	to remove	վերցնել
purpose	նպատակ	to repeat	կրկնել
to put	դնել	representative	ներկայացուցիչ
to put to bed	պառկեցնել	respect	յարգանք
quarter	քառորդ	rest	հանգիստ
question	հարց, հարցում	to rest	հանգչիլ,
quickly	արագօրէն, շուտ		հանգստանալ
quiet	հանդարտ	restaurant	ճաշարան
rain	անձրև	result	արդիւնք
to rain	անձրևել	to resume	վերսկսիլ
rainy	անձրևոտ	return	վերադարձ
rare	հազուագիւտ	to return	վերադառնալ
to read	կարդալ	to reveal	յայտնել
ready	պատրաստ	review	հանդէս
reality	իրականություն	rich	հարուստ
really	իսկապէս	to ride	հեծնել
to receive	ընդունիլ, ստանալ	ridiculous	ծիծաղելի

rifle	հրացան	science	գիտութիւն
right (adj. & adv.)	աջ; անսխալ, ճիշդ, շիտակ	sea	ծով
		seashore	ծովեզերք
right (n.)	իրաւունք	season	եղանակ
to be right	իրաւունք ունենալ	to seat	նստեցնել
ring	մատանի	to see	տեսնել
to ring	հնչել	to sell	ծախել
river	գետ	to send	ղրկել
road	ճամբայ	sentence	նախադասութիւն
role	դեր	sentiment	զգացմունք
room	սենեակ	separate	զատ
round	շուրջ	serious	լուրջ
row	կարգ	to serve	ծառայել
rule	կանոն	service	ծառայութիւն
to run	վազել	to settle	բնակութիւն հաստատել
sad	տխուր		
sadness	տխրութիւն	severe	խիստ, սաստիկ
safe	ապահով	shade	շուք
saint	սուրբ	to shape	ձեւել
salary	ամսական	sharp	սուր
same	նոյն	ship	նաւ
satisfied	գոհ	shoe	կօշիկ
to satisfy	գոհացնել	shop	խանութ
to save	փրկել	short	կարճ
to say	ըսել	to shorten	կարճցնել
school	դպրոց	to shout	պոռալ

to show	ցոյց տալ, ցուցըներ
side	կողմ
to silence	լռեցներ
silent	լուռ
to be silent	լռեր
silver	արծաթ
simplicity	պարզություն
simple	պարզ
simply	պարզապես
since	ի վեր
sincerity	անկեղծություն
to sing	երգեր
singer	երգիչ, երգչուհի
sister	քոյր
to sit	նստիր
to be situated	գտնուիր
situation	կացություն
sky	երկինք
to sleep	քնանալ
slow	կամաց
small	պզտիկ
to smile	ժպտիր
snow	ձիւն
so	այդպես, այնպես; ուրեմն

so much	այդքան, այսքան, այնքան; որքան
so that	անանկ որ, որպեսզի
softly	մեղմորէն
soldier	զինուոր
solution	լուծում
some	քանի մը
somebody	մէկը
someone	ոմն
sometimes	երբեմն
son	որդի
song	երգ
soon	շուտով
source	աղբիւր
souvenir	յիշատակ
to speak	խօսիր
specialist	մասնագէտ
speech	խօսք, ճառ
speed	արագություն
to spend	ծախսեր
to spill	թափեր, թափիր
to spread	տարածեր
spring	գարուն
stairs	աստիճաններ
to stand	կենալ

to stand up	ոտքի կենալ	suitable	յարմար
state	վիճակ; նահանգ;	summer	ամառ
	պետություն	summit	գագաթ
station	կայարան	sun	արև
to steal	գողնալ	sunny	արևոտ
step	քայլ	supper	ընթրիք
still	դեռ	to suppose	ենթադրել
stone	քար	supposedly	իբր թե
stop	կայան	sure	վստահ
to stop	կեցնել	to be surprised	զարմանալ
story	պատմություն	surprising	զարմանալի
straight	ուղղակի	surprisingly	զարմանալիորեն
straight ahead	շիտակ	suspect	կասկածելի
strange	տարորինակ	to swim	լողալ
stranger	օտար	table	սեղան
street	փողոց	tailor	դերձակ
strong	զորավոր	to take	առնել
student	ուսանող	to take place	տեղի ունենալ
study	ուսում	to talk	խոսակցիլ
to study	ուսանիլ	tall (people)	բարձրահասակ
to succeed	յաջողիլ	taste	համ
such	այսպիսի, այդպիսի,	tea	թէյ
	այնպիսի	to teach	սորվեցնել
suddenly	մէկէն, յանկարծ	teacher	ուսուցիչ,
to suffer	տառապիլ		ուսուցչուհի
sugar	շաքար	tear	արցունք

telephone	հեռաձայն	for a long time	շատոնց
to telephone	հեռաձայնել	times	անգամ
to tell	պատմել	tip	ծայր
tennis	թենիս	to get tired	յոգնիլ
than	քան	tobacco	ծխախոտ
to thank	շնորհակալ ըլլալ	today	այսօր
thanks	շնորհակալութիւն	together	միասին
thanks to	շնորհիւ	tomorrow	վաղը
that	թէ, որ	tool	գործիք
that (adj.)	այդ, ատ, ատի,	totally	բոլորովին
	ատիկա, այն,	to touch	դպչիլ
	ան, անի, անիկա	towards	դէպի
theater	թատրոն	trade	առեւտուր
there	հոն	train	շոգեկառք
there is,	կայ, կան	traitor	դաւաճան
there are		to travel	ճամբորդել
thief	գող	tree	ծառ
thin	բարակ	trouble	նեղութիւն
thing	բան	trousers	տաբատ
to think	կարծել; խորհիլ,	true	ճշմարիտ
	մտածել	to trust	վստահիլ
this	այս, աս, ասի,	truth	ճշմարտութիւն
	սա, ասիկա	try	փորձ
to throw	նետել	to try	ջանալ, փորձել
ticket	տոմսակ	to turn	դառնալ, դարձնել
time	ատեն, ժամանակ	unacceptable	անընդունելի

uncle	հօրեղբայր,	wall	պատ
	մօրեղբայր	walk	պտոյտ
under	տակ	to walk	քալել
to understand	հասկնալ	to want	ուզել
undoubtedly	անկասկածօրէն	war	պատերազմ
unfortunate	դժբախտ	to wash	լուալ
unfortunately	դժբախտաբար	to watch	դիտել
union	միութիւն	water	ջուր
university	համալսարան	weak	տկար
until	մինչեւ	to weaken	տկարանալ
up	վեր	to wear	հագնիլ
to use	գործածել	week	շաբաթ
to get used to	վարժուիլ	well-behaved	խելօք
usual	սովորական	western	արեւմտեան
usually	սովորաբար	what?	ի՞նչ
value	արժէք	when	երբ
various	զանազան	whence	ուրկէ
to verify	ստուգել	where	ուր
very	շատ	which	որ
view	տեսարան	white	ճերմակ
village	գիւղ	who?	ո՞վ
visit	այցելութիւն	whoever	ոեւէ
to visit	այցելել	whole	ամբողջ
voice	ձայն	why?	ինչո՞ւ
to wait for	սպասել	wickedness	չարութիւն
to wake up	արթննալ	wide	լայն

wife's father	աներ	work	աշխատանք
wife of hus- band's brother	ներ	to work	աշխատիլ
		workman	գործաւոր
will	կամք	world	աշխարհ
to win	յաղթել	worry	մտահոգութիւն
wind	հով	to be worth	արժել
window	պատուհան	would that	երանի (թէ)
wine	գինի	to write	գրել
winter	ձմեռ	writing	գրութիւն
wisdom	իմաստութիւն	wrong	սխալ
wish	մաղթանք	to be wrong	սխալիլ
with	հետ	year	տարի
without	առանց	yes	այո
woman	կին, կնիկ	yesterday	երէկ
wonderful	հրանալի, սքանչելի	yet	տակաւին
		young	երիտասարդ
wood	փայտ	young lady	օրիորդ
word	բառ	youth	երիտասարդութիւն

This vocabulary contains all the words used in the exercises and the reading material. It does not contain words used merely for examples, i.e. words in brackets [ ] or those in the *Appendixes*.

The genitive singular of nouns and any other unpredictable forms have been given; for verbs the aorist stem has been given, except for regular aorists of verbs in *-ել, -իլ, -ալ, -ցնել* The cases governed by postpositions and prepositions have been indicated, as have also the cases other than the accusative governed by verbs. Special usages and idioms have been explained. However, only those meanings appropriate to the given context have been noted in this vocabulary. For further reading, a proper dictionary will be required.

ազատ	free	ալ	also, too
ազատել	to save	Ալպեանները	The Alps
ազատիլ	to escape, be saved	ախորժակ, -ի	appetite
ազատութիւն, -եան	liberty, freedom	ախորդիլ	to like
ազգ, -ի	nation	ակամայ	involuntarily
ազգական, -ի	relative (n.)	ակնկալել	to expect
ազգային	national	ակնոց, -ի	(eye) glasses
ազդել	to influence	արեւի ակնոց	sunglasses
ազնիւ	kind	ակնոցաւոր	wearing glasses
ազնուութիւն, -եան	honesty	ակումբ, -ի	club
աթոռ, -ի	chair	ահա, ահաւասիկ	here (it) is
աժան	cheap	ահնելի	horrible
		աղբիւր, -ի	source; fountain
		աղէկ	good; well

276

աղմուկ, -ի	noise	ամուսին, -ի,	husband
աղմկել	to make a noise,	ամուսնի	
	disturb	ամուսնանալ (+	to marry
աղուէս, -ի	fox	հետ and dat.)	
աղջիկ,	girl, daughter	ամուսնութիւն,	marriage
աղջկան (or -ի)		-եան	
աղտոտ	dirty	ամչնալ, ամչցայ	to be ashamed
աղքատ	poor	ամպոտ	cloudy
աճապարել	to hurry	ամսական, -ի	monthly salary
Հրաչեայ	Hrachia Ajarian	այդ	that
Աճառեան	(famous Armenian	այդպէս	thus, so
	scholar)	այդպիսի	such (like that)
ամառ, -ուան	summer	այդքան	so (much), that much
ամավերջ, -ի	year's end	այժմ	now
ամբողջ	whole, complete,	այլ	other
	entire	այլապէս	otherwise
ամենալաւ	best	այլեւս	still, even,
ամենավերջին	latest	with neg. verb	no longer, not any more
ամենատկար	weakest	այն	that
ամենէն	superlative adverb	այնպէս	so
ամերիկացի	American (person)	այնպիսի	such (like that)
ամէն	each, every, all	այնքան	so (much), that much
ամէնը,	each one, everyone,	այո	yes
ամէնքը	all	այս	this
ամիս,	month	այսպէս	thus
ամսուան, ամսու		այսպիսի	such (like this)

այստեղ	here	աներ, -ոջ	wife's father
այսքան	so (much), this much	աներեւոյթ	invisible
այսօր, -ուան	today	անէծք, -ի	curse
այտ, -ի	cheek	անընդունելի	unacceptable
այրել	to burn (tr.)	Անի, -ի	Ani (fem. name)
այրիլ	to burn (intrans.)	անիծել	to curse
այցելել (+ dat. for persons)	to visit	անիկա	he, she, it
		անիմաստ	senseless, meaningless
այցելու, -ի	visitor	անիւ, -ի	wheel
այցելութիւն, -եան	visit	անխելք	senseless, stupid
		անխուսափելի	inevitable
ան	he, she, it	անծանօթ	unfamiliar, foreign
ան, անի	that	անկասկած	without doubt, doubt-
Անահիտ, -ի	Anahid (fem. name)		less
անամօթ	shameless	անկասկածօրէն	undoubtedly
անանկ	so	անկարգապահու-	indiscipline
անանկ որ	so that	թիւն, -եան	
անբաժան	inseparable	անկեղծ	sincere
անգամ	time, occasion; even	անկեղծութիւն, -եան	sincerity
անգամ մը	once		
անգէտ	ignorant	անկիւն, -ի	corner
անգլերէն	English	անկողին, -ի,	bed
Անգլիա,	England	անկողնի	
Անգլիոյ		անկում, -ի	fall, depreciation
անգլիացի, -ի	Englishman	անհամբեր	impatient
անդամ, -ի	member	անհամբերութիւն,	impatience
		-եան	

անհանգիստ	uncomfortable	անվերապահօրէն	unreservedly
անհասկնալի	unintelligible	անվերջանալի	endless
անհետանալ,	to disappear,	անտառ, -ի	forest, wood
անհետացայ	vanish	անտարբեր	indifferent
անհոգ	negligent	անցեալ	last, past
անհոգութիւն,	negligence	անցեալ օր	the other day
-եան		անցընել	to pass (tr.)
անձ, -ի	person, self	անցնիլ	to pass, cross
անձամբ	in person	անփոյթ	careless
անձական	personal	անօթի	hungry
անձրեւ, -ի	rain	աշակերտ, -ի	pupil
անձրեւել	to rain	աշակերտիլ	to study under
անձրեւոտ	rainy	աշխատանք, -ի	work
անմիջապէս	at once, immediately	աշխատիլ	to work; try
աննկարագրելի	indescribable	աշխատցնել	to make (someone)
աննշան	insignificant		work; put into
անշուշտ	of course, certainly		action, start
անոնք	they	աշխարհ, -ի	world
անոյշ, անուշ	sweet	աշխարհագրու-	geography
անուն, -ի,	name	թիւն, -եան	
անուան		աշուն, աշնան	autumn; fall
անպատճառ	certainly, by all	աչք, -ի	eye
	means	ապա	then
անջատ	separate	ապագայ, -ի	future
անջատել	to separate, detach	ապագային	in the future
անսխալ	right, correct	ապահով	safe, secure

ապրանք, -ի	goods	առողջարար	healthy (promoting health)
ապրիլ	to live		
Ապրիլ	April	առողջութիւն, -եան	health
աջ, -ի	right (hand)		
առած, -ի	proverb	արջել (postpos. + gen.)	before, in front of
առանձին	alone		
առանց (prepos. + dat.)	without	արջի օր	the day before yesterday
առաջ (postpos. + abl.)	ago, before	առտու, առտուան	morning
		աս, ասի	this
առաջանալ, առաջացայ	to move forward	ասանկ	such
		ասեղ, -ի	needle, syringe
առաջարկ, -ի	proposal, suggestion	ասիկա	this (pron.)
առաջարկել	to propose, suggest	աստիճան, -ի	degree, grade
առաջին	first	աստիճաններ	stairs
առաջնորդ, -ի	leader; Prelate	աստիճանաբար	gradually
առաջնորդել	to lead, guide	աստղ, -ի	star
առավոտ, -եան	morning	Աստուած,	God
առևտուր, -ի	trade, commerce	Աստուծոյ	
առթիւ (postpos. + gen.)	on the occasion of	Աստուած չընէ	God forbid!
		ատ, ատի	that
արիթ, -ի	occasion, opportunity	ատել	to hate
		ատեն, -ուան	time
առնել, առի	to take, get, receive	(or -ի)	
առնուազն	at least	ատիկա	that (pron.)
առողջ	healthy	արագ	fast

արագութիւն, -եան	speed
արագօրէն	quickly, fast (adv.)
Արարատ (also Մասիս)	Ararat
արարք, -ի	act, deed
Արաքս, -ի	Araxes (river)
արգիլել	to prohibit
արդար	fair, just
արդեօք	is it that?, I wonder
արդէն	already
արդի	modern
արդիւնք, -ի	result, effect
արեւելեան	eastern; oriental
արեւմտեան	western
արեւոտ	sunny
արթննալ	to wake up
արթուն	awake
արժել	to be worth, cost
արժէք, -ի	value, worth
արիւն, -ի, արեան	blood
արծաթ, -ի	silver
արկած, -ի	accident
արկածախնդրու-թիւն, -եան	adventure
արհեստ, -ի	profession, trade
արհեստաւոր, -ի	craftsman
արձակել	to release, pronounce
արձակուրդ, -ի	holiday(s)
արձանագրել	to register, inscribe
արուեստագէտ, -ի	artist
արջ, -ի	bear
Արսէն, -ի	Arsen (male name)
արտայայտել	to express
արտասանել	to pronounce, recite
արտասանութիւն, -եան	recitation
արտօնել	to permit
արցունք, -ի	tear
աւազ, -ի	sand
աւելի	more
աւելնալ, աւելցայ	to increase (intr.), be left over
աւելցնել	to increase (tr.), add
աւետիս, -ի	good news
ափ, -ի	palm; shore
բազմաթիւ	numerous
բազմապատկել	to multiply
բազմութիւն, -եան	multitude

բաժակ, -ի	drinking glass	բարեկամուհի,	(girl) friend
բաժանում, -ի	distribution	-ի	
բաժին, -ի	share	բարեսէր	kind, benevolent
բաժին հանել	to give a share	բարերար, -ի	benefactor
(+ abl.)	in/of	բարեւ	hello
բաժնել	to divide, distrib-	բարեւել (+	to greet, salute
	ute	dat.)	
բախտ, -ի	luck, fate	բարի	good
բաղնիք, -ի	bath (house)	բարկանալ,	to become angry
բաճկոն, -ի	jacket	բարկացայ	
բամպակ, -ի	cotton	բարկութիւն,	anger
բայց	but	-եան	
բան, -ի	thing	բարձ, -ի	pillow
բանալ, բացի	to open	բարձր	high, loud
բանալի, -ի	key	բարձրահասակ	tall (people)
բանախօսութիւն,	speech	բարձրաձայն	aloud; loudly
-եան		բարձրանալ,	to rise, go up, climb
բանակ, -ի	army	բարձրացայ	
բանաստեղծ, -ի	poet	բարձրացնել	to lift, raise (tr.)
բանաստեղծու-	poetry	բարձրութիւն,	height
թիւն, -եան		-եան	
բառ, -ի	word	բաց	open; light (in color)
բարակ	thin, fine	բացակայ	absent
բարեբախտաբար	fortunately, luckily	բացառաբար	exceptionally
բարեկամ, -ի	friend	բացառիկ	exceptional
բարեկամական	amicable, friendly	բացառութիւն,	exception
		-եան	

բացատրել	to explain	բնակիչ, -ի	inhabitant
բացատրություն, -եան	explanation	բնակություն հաստատել	to settle
բացի (prepos. and postpos. + abl.)	except, besides	բնակչություն, -եան	population
բացում, -ի, բացման	opening	բնաւ	at all
բացօթեայ	in the open air	բնաւորություն, -եան	nature, character
բաւական	enough (adj., adv.), quite, considerably	բնություն, -եան	nature
		բոլոր	all
բաւել	to be enough, suffice	բոլորն ալ	all of them
		բոլորովին	entirely, totally
բեմ, -ի	stage	բոպիկնալ	to take off one's shoes
բերան, -ի	mouth		
բերել, բերի	to bring	բուժարան, -ի	sanatorium
բժիշկ, -ի	doctor, physician	բուժուիլ	to be healed, cured
բժշկական	medical	բռնել	to catch; hold
բժշկապետ, -ի	chief physician		
բժշկել	to cure	գագաթ, -ի	summit, peak
բժշկություն, -եան	medicine	գալ, եկայ	to come; (as adj.) next
բիւրաւոր	myriad	գաղափար, -ի	idea
բլուր, -ի	hill	գաղտնի	secret
բնական	natural	գայլ, -ի	wolf
բնակիլ	to live, reside, dwell	գանձ, -ի	treasure
		գարեջուր, -ի	beer

գարուն, գարնան	spring
գաւաթ, -ի	cup
գգուել	to caress, fondle
գեղեցիկ	beautiful, pretty
գեղեցկանալ, գեղեցկացայ	to become beautiful
գեղեցկութիւն, -եան	beauty
գետ, -ի	river
գետին, -ի, գետնի	ground, floor; earth
գերան, -ի	beam
գէշ	bad
գիծ, -ի	trait
գին, -ի	price
գինի, -ի	wine
գինով	drunk
գիշեր, -ուան	night
գիշերապահ, -ի	night-watchman; on night duty
գիտեմ, see գիտանալ	I know
գիտանալ, գիտացայ	to know
գիտութիւն, -եան	science, knowledge
գիտուն	learned
գիր, -ի	letter, script
գիրք, -ի	book
գիւղ, -ի	village
գլխարկ, -ի	hat
գլխաւոր	chief, prime
գլուխ, -ի, գլխու	head
գծել	to draw
գնդակ, -ի	ball
գնել	to buy
գոգնոց, -ի	apron
գոհ, often with մնալ (+ abl.)	satisfied (with)
գոհար, -ի	jewel
գոհացնել	to satisfy, please
գող, -ի	thief
գողնալ, գողցայ	to steal
գոյացնել	to bring about, effect
գոյն, -ի	color
գոյութիւն, -եան	existence
գոյութիւն ունենալ	to exist
գովել	to praise
գործ, -ի	work, job, task; business

գործածել	to use	գրատախտակ, -ի	blackboard
գործածութիւն,	usage	գրաւել	to take, occupy
-եան		գրեթէ	almost
գործարան, -ի	factory	գրել	to write
գործաւոր, -ի	workman	գրիչ, -ի	pen
գործիք, -ի	tool	գրկել	to embrace
գործողութիւն,	operation	գրութիւն,	writing, literary
-եան		-եան	piece
գոց	closed, shut; dark	գրպան, -ի	pocket
	(of color)		
գոց սորվիլ	to learn by heart	դադար, -ի	pause, recess
գոցել	to close, shut	դադրիլ	to cease, stop
գուլպայ, -ի	stocking	դահիճ, -ի	executioner
գումար, -ի	amount, sum	դանակ, -ի	knife
գուրգուրալ	to have great	դանդաղ	slow (adj. and adv.)
	affection for	դանդաղիլ	to slow down
գուրգուրանք, -ի	great affection	դառնալ,	to turn, become
գտնել, գտայ	to find (+ abl. of	-դարձայ	
	place found)	դաս, -ի	lesson; class
գտնուիլ	to be situated	դասընթացք, -ի	course
գրագէտ, -ի	writer, man of	դասագիրք, -ի	textbook
	letters	դասախօս, -ի	lecturer
գրադարան, -ի	library	դասախօսութիւն,	lecture
գրականութիւն,	literature	-եան	
-եան		դասարան, -ի	class (room)
գրասենեակ, -ի	office	դաստիարակ, -ի	instructor, class-
			master

դար, -ու	century	դիմաց (postpos. + gen.)	across, opposite, facing
դարձեալ	again		
դարձնել	to turn (trans.)	դիմել (+ dat.)	to apply to
դարմանուիլ	to be treated (medically)	դիրք, -ի	position
		դիւրահաղորդ	sociable
դաւաձան, -ի	traitor	դիւրաւ	easily
Դեկտեմբեր, -ի	December	դիւրին	easy
դեռ	still, yet	դնել, որի	to put, place
դեր, -ի	part, role	դող, -ի	trembling
դերձակ, -ի	tailor	դուն	you (s.)
դեւ, -ի	demon, devil	դուռ, -ի,	door
դէմ (postpos. + dat.)	against	դրան; pl.	
		դուռեր, դռներ	
դէմք, -ի	face	դուրս (postpos. + abl.)	out of
դէպի (prepos. + acc.; + dat. with pronouns)	towards		
		դուրսը	outside
		դուք	you (pl.)
դէպք, -ի	event, occasion	դպչիլ (դպնալ, դպիլ), դպայ (+ dat.)	to touch
դժբախտ	unfortunate		
դժբախտաբար	unfortunately		
դժգոհ (+ abl.)	dissatisfied (with)	դպրոց, -ի	school
դժգոհիլ	to be dissatisfied	դպրոցական	school (adj.)
դժուար	hard, difficult	դրամ, -ի	money
դժուարութիւն, -եան	difficulty	դրացի, -ի	neighbor
դիմանալ (+ dat.)	to endure, stand up to	եզերք, -ի	coast, shore, edge

եթէ	if	երբեք	ever
ելլել, ելայ	to go up, out; to rise	երգ, -ի	song
		երգել	to sing
ելnյթ, -ի	performance	երգիչ, -ի	singer (male)
եկեղեցի, -ի	church	երգչունի, -ի	singer (female)
եղանակ, -ի	season, weather; tune, melody	երեկոյ, -եան	evening
		երեu, -ի	face
եղբայր, եղբoր	brother	երեսունն	thirty
եղերաբախտ	tragic	երեւակայել	to imagine
ենթադրել	to suppose, assume	երեւակայութիւն, -եան	imagination
եռուզեռ, -ի	bustle		
եu	I	Երեւան, -ի	Erevan (capital of Armenian SSR)
ետ	back (adv.)		
ետեւ (postpos. + gen.)	behind	երեւիլ, երեւցայ	to appear, seem
		երեւnյթ, -ի	phenomenon; appearance
ետք (postpos. + abl.)	after	երեք	three
		երեքշաբթի, -ի	Tuesday
երազ, -ի	dream	երէկ, -ունն	yesterday
երախայ, -ի	child	երէկ գիշեր	last night
երանաւէտ	blissful	երթալ, գացի	to go
երանի (թէ)	I wish that, would that	երթաս բարnվ	good-bye (response)
		երիտասարդ	young
երբ (rel. and interr.)	when	երիտասարդnւ-թիւն, -եան	youth (abs. n.)
երբեմն	sometimes, occa-sionally	երկաթ, -ի	iron
		երկայն	long

երկար	long	Զապէլ, -ի	Zabel (fem. name)
երկարորէն	at length	զառանցանք, -ի	delirium
երկինք, -ի	sky, heaven	զատ (+ abl.)	separate, apart; be-
երկնքի			sides
երկիր, -ի,	country	Զատիկ,	Easter
երկրի		Զատկուան	
երկիւղ, -ի	fear	զարմանալ,	to be surprised,
երկննալ,	to grow longer	զարմացայ	astonished at
երկնցայ		զարմանալի	surprising, amazing
երկու	two	զարմանալիօրէն	surprisingly, amazingly
երկուքն ալ	both	զարմացնել	to astonish, surprise
Երկուշաբթի, -ի	Monday	զարնել, զարկի	to hit, strike, knock
երկրաշարժ, -ի	earthquake	զաւակ, -ի	child
երջանիկ	happy	զբաղած	busy
երջանկութիւն,	happiness	զբաղիլ (+	to be engaged in,
-եան		instr.)	busy with
եւ	and	զգալ	to feel
Եւրոպա,	Europe	զգացմունք, -ի	sentiment, feeling
Եւրոպայի		զգուշանալ,	to be careful, beware
Եփրատ, -ի	Euphrates	զգուշացայ (+	of
եօթանասուն	seventy	abl.)	
եօթը	seven	զգուշաւորու-	caution
		թիւն, -եան	
զայրացնել	to enrage	զգուշութիւն,	caution, attention
զանազան	various	-եան	
զանգակ, -ի	bell	զերո	zero

զինուոր, -ի	soldier	ընթերցանու-	reading
զիջում, -ի	concession	թիւն, -եան	
զուարթ	gay, joyful	ընթրիք, -ի	supper
զուարծունթիւն,	amusement	ընկեր, -ի, -ոշ	friend, companion
-եան		ընկերակցու-	company
զուր տեղը	in vain	թիւն, -եան	
զօրավար, -ի	general (n.)	ընկերանալ,	to go with, accompany
զօրաւոր	strong	ընկերացայ	
		ընկերութիւն,	friendship, society
էշ, -ի, -ու	donkey, ass	-եան	
էջ, -ի	page	ընկերուհի, -ի	friend (female)
		ընկոյզ, -ի	walnut
ըլլալ, եղայ	to become, be	ընտանեկան	family (adj.)
ըմբոշխնել	to enjoy	ընտանիք, -ի	family (n.)
ըմբռնել	to grasp, comprehend	ընտիր	choice, fine, superb
ընդարձակ	wide, spacious	ընտրել	to choose, select
ընդհանուր	general (adj.)	ընտրութիւն,	election
ընդհանրապէս	in general, gen-	-եան	
	erally	ըսել, ըսի	to say, tell
ընդունելի	acceptable	ըսել ուզել	to mean
ընդունիլ (3	to receive, admit,	ըստ (prepos.	according to
p.s. aor.	accept	+ dat.)	
ընդունեց)			
ընել, ըրի	to do	թագաւոր, -ի	king
ընթացք, -ի	course; conduct	թաղում, -ի,	burial
ընթացքին	during	թաղման	
(postpos. + gen.)			

թան,. -ի	a cold drink made from yogurt	թղթոսկի, -ի	banknote
		թնդացնել	to make resound
թանգարան, -ի	museum	թշնամի, -ի	enemy (adj. and n.)
թաշկինակ, -ի	handkerchief	թող (+ subj.)	let
թատրոն, -ի	theater	թոյլ տալ	to permit, allow
թարթիչ, -ի	eyelash	Թովմաս, -ի	Thomas
թարմ	fresh	թորեալ	distilled
թաւ	thick, husky	թուական,. -ի	year or date
թափել	to spill (trans.)	թուիլ	to appear, look, seem
թափիլ	to spill, overflow (intrans.)	թուղթ,. -ի	paper
		թուք, -ի	spittle, spit
թեթեւ	light (weight)	թրթռալ	to vibrate, shake
թենիս, -ի	tennis	թքնել	to spit
թերահաւատու-	scepticism		
թիւն,. -եան			
թերանալ,	to be remiss	ժամ,. -ուան	hour
թերացայ		ժամական	hourly
թերեւս	perhaps	ժամանակ,. -ի	time
թերթ, -ի	(news)paper	ժամանակին	on time
թէ	that; whether; or	ժամանել	to arrive
թէեւ (...բայց)	although (...yet)	ժամացոյց, -ի	clock, watch
թէյ, -ի	tea	ժխոր, -ի	uproar
թէպէտեւ	although	ժողով, -ի	meeting
թիթեղ, -ի	tin	ժողովուրդ, -ի	people
թիւ, -ի	number, figure	ժպիտ, -ի	smile
թղթատել	to leaf through	ժպտիլ	to smile
		ժպտուն	smiling

իբր թէ	supposedly	իրապէս	really
իբրեւ	as	իրար, -ու	each other
իմաստութիւն,	wisdom	իրաւունք, -ի	right, justice
-եան		իրաւունք	to be right
իմաստուն	wise	ունենալ	
իմացնել	to let know, inform	իրենք	they
իյնալ, ինկաj	to fall	իրիկուն,	evening
ինը	nine	իրիկուան	
իննսուն	ninety	իւրաքանչիւր,	each
ի՞նչ	what?	-ի (adj. and	
ի՞նչու	why?	pronoun)	
ի՞նչպէս	how?		
ինչպէս...	as...so (often =	լալ	to cry, weep
նոյնպէս	both...and)	լայն	broad, wide
(or այնպէս)		լագ, -ի	crying
ինչ քան	so much, as much;	լաւ	good, well
	also interrog.	լաւագոյն	better, best
ինք(ը)	he, she, it	լաւանալ,	to get better, improve
ինքնաշարժ, -ի	car, automobile	լաւացաj	(intrans.)
իշխան, -ի	prince	լաւութիւն,	favor
իջնել, իջաj	to descend, go down	-եան	
իսկ	but, whereas	լեզու, -ի	tongue, language
իսկապէս	really	լեղի	bitter, gall
իրազեկ	informed	լեռ, լերան	mountain
իրական	real	(pl. լեռներ)	
իրականութիւն,	reality, fact	լեցնել	to fill; pour into
-եան			

լեցուն	full	խաբել	to trick, deceive
լիալուսին,. -ի,	full moon	խածնել, խածայ	to bite
լիալուսնի		խաղ, -ի	game
Լիզպոն, -ի	Lisbon	խաղալ, խաղցայ	to play
լիտր,. -ի	liter	խաղաղություն,	peace
լմնցնել	to complete	-եան	
լողցնել	to bathe (trans.)	խանգարել	to disturb, disrupt
լողալ	to swim	խանդավառու-	enthusiasm
լույս, -ի	light	թիւն, -եան	
բարի լույս	good morning	խանութ, -ի	shop
լուալ	to wash (trans.)	խառնաշփոթու-	confusion
լուծում, -ի,	solution	թիւն, -եան	
լուծման		խառնուածք, -ի	character, tempera-
լուռ	silent		ment, nature
լուսանկար,. -ի	photograph	խառնուիլ	to blend, intermingle,
լուսին,. -ի,	moon		mix
լուսնի		խաւարում, -ի	darkening, eclipse
լուր, -ի	news	խելացի	intelligent, clever
լուրջ	serious	խելք, -ի	intelligence
լռել	to be silent	խելոք	well-behaved; wise
լռեցնել	to silence	խեղճ	miserable, poor
լռություն, -եան	silence	խենթ, -ի	fool; crazy
լսել (dat. of	to hear	խենթեցնալիք	inducing madness
person)		խիղճ,. -ի, խղճի	conscience
լրջություն,	seriousness	խիստ	severe; very
-եան		խմբուիլ	to gather (intrans.)

խմել	to drink	խորունկ	deep, profound
խմելիք, -ի	drink, beverage	խուճապահար	alarmed, terrified
խմցնել	to make (someone) drink	խումբ, -ի	group
խնամել	to take care of	խուսափիլ (+ abl.)	to avoid
խնամք, -ի	care, solicitude		
խնամք տանիլ (+ dat.)	to care for	խռնուիլ	to flock together
խնդալ (վրայ)	to laugh (at)	խռպոտ	rough, hoarse
խնդացնել	to make someone laugh	խրատ, -ի	advice, counsel
		խրատել	to advise
խնդիր, -ի, խնդրի	matter, problem, question	խոսակցիլ	to talk, converse
խնդրանք, -ի	request	խոսակցութիւն, -եան	conversation
խնդրել (abl. request; to ask of person asked)	request; to ask of person asked)		
		խոսիլ	to talk, speak
խնծոր, -ի	apple	խոսք, -ի	word, phrase, speech
խոժոռ	frowning		
խոշոր	large, massive	ծախել	to sell
խոստանալ, խոստացայ	to promise	ծախսել	to spend
		ծախք, -ի	cost, expense
խոր	deep	ծակ, -ի	hole
խորհիլ	to think, ponder, reflect upon	ծակել	to bore, make a hole in
		ծաղիկ, -ի	flower
խորհրդաւոր	mysterious	ծայր, -ի	tip, end
խորհրդաւորու- թիւն, -եան	mystery	ծանուցանել	to notify
		ծանր	heavy; grave, serious
		ծանօթ, -ի	acquaintance, known; familiar with

ծանoթանաl, ծանoթացայ (+ dat.)	to know, be acquainted with	ծով, -ու	sea
		ծovեզերք, -ի	seashore
		ծուռ	crooked, perverse
ծանoթացնել	to introduce	ծրագիր, -ի, ծրագրի	plan
ծառ, -ի	tree		
ծառայել (+ dat.)	to serve, wait upon		
ծառայություն, -եան	service	կազմակերպու- թիւն, -եան	organization
ծարաւ	thirsty	կազմել	to form
ծափ, -ի	clapping	կաթ, -ի	milk
ծափահարել	to clap, applaud	կախարդական	magical
ծեծ քաշել	to beat	կախել	to hang, suspend (tr.)
ծեծել	to beat, hammer	Կաղանդ, -ի	New Year
ծեր	old (person)	կամ	or
ծերանալ, ծերացայ	to grow old	կամ...կամ	either...or
		կամաց	slow; slowly
ծերություն, -եան	old age	կամք, -ի	will
		կայ	there is
ծերուկ, -ի	old man	կայան, -ի	stop (for bus, etc.)
ծիծաղելի	ridiculous	կայարան, -ի	station
ծխախոտ, -ի	tobacco	կայծակ, -ի	lightning
ծնիլ, ծնայ	to be born	կանգ առնել	to stop, stand
ծնողք, -ի	parents	կանխիկ	ready; cash
ծոծրակ, -ի	nape of the neck	կանոն, -ի	rule, regulation
ծոյլ	lazy	կանոնաւոր	regular, proper
		կանուխ	early

կանչ, -ի	call, cry	կարճ	short, brief
կանչել	to call	կարճնալ	to become short
կապույտ	blue	կարճցնել	to shorten
կառավարել	to govern	կարմիր	red
կառավարու-թիւն, -եան	government	կարմրիլ	to turn red
կասկած, -ի	doubt	կարող	able, capable
կասկածելի	suspect	կարօտ (+ dat.)	lacking, in need of
կատարեալ	perfect	կարօտնալ,	to long for, miss
կատարել	to perform, carry out; execute	կարօտցայ (+ dat.)	
կատու, -ի	cat	կացութիւն, -եան	situation, state
Կարապետ, -ի	Garabed (male name)	կաւիճ, -ի	chalk
կարգ, -ի	row; class, rank; queue; turn	կեանք, -ի	life
կարգել	to marry	կեդրոնանալ	to concentrate
կարդալ	to read	կեղծ	false, feigned
կարելի	possible	կեղծել	to feign
կարելի եղածին չափ	as much as possible	կենալ, կեցայ	to stop; stand
կարենալ, կրցայ	to be able	կենդանի, -ի	animal; living (adj.)
կարեւոր	important	կեսուր, կեսրոջ	husband's mother
կարծել	to think, reckon	կեսրայր, -ի	husband's father
կարծես թէ	it looks as though; one would think	կերպով	(in) fashion, way, manner
կարծիք, -ի	opinion	կերցնել	to feed
		կեցնել	to stop (trans.); park
		կեցուածք, -ի	posture, attitude

կէս, -ի	half	կոտորել	to massacre
կէսգիշեր,	midnight	կոտրել	to break
-ուան		կրաքամակ	with bent back
կէսօր, -ուան	mid-day; noon	կորով, -ի	vigor, strength, energy
կէսօրէն ետք	afternoon	կորուստ, -ի	loss
or վերջ		կորանցնել	to lose (tr.)
կէտ, -ի	point	կորսուիլ	to get lost, disappear
Կիկո, Կիկոյի	male nickname for	կուսակցութիւն,	party (political)
	Giragos	-եան	
կին, կնոջ	woman, wife	կռիւ, -ի	fight, quarrel
կիսուիլ	to be divided in	կռուիլ	to fight, quarrel
	half	կտոր, -ի	piece
Կիրակի,, -ի	Sunday	կտրել	to cut
կղզի, -ի	island	կրակ, -ի	fire
կմկմալ	to hestitate, stumble	կրել	to carry, bear
կնիկ, կնկան	woman	կրթութիւն,	education
կնքուիլ	to be sealed, con-	-եան	
	cluded	կրկին	again; a second time
կողմ, -ի	side, direction; pl.	կրկնապէս	doubly
	area, region	կրկնել	to repeat
կողմնակի	on the side	կրնամ, see	I can
կոճակ, -ի	button	կարենալ	
կոչել	to name, call	կօշիկ, -ի	shoe
անունով կոչել	to name after		
կով, -ու	cow	հագնիլ, հագայ	to wear, put on
կովու միս	beef	հագուիլ	to wear

հագուստ, -ի — clothes, dress, suit

հագցնել — to clothe, dress

հազալ — to cough

հազար, -ի — thousand

հազարաւոր — in thousands

հազիւ — hardly, scarcely

հազուագիւտ — rare, scarce

հալածել — to persecute

հակառակ — contrary to, de- (postpos. and spite; (n.) the prepos. + dat.) opposite

հակառակորդ, -ի — opponent

հակիլ — to lean

հաղորդել — to communicate, report

հաճելի — pleasant

հաճիլ — to be pleased

հաճոյք, -ի — pleasure

համ, -ի — taste, flavor

համով — tasty

համագումար, -ի — conference

համալսարան, -ի — university

համակրանք, -ի — sympathy

համակրելի — likeable

համաձայն — (to be) in agree- (prepos. and ment with postpos. + dat.)

համաձայնիլ (+ — to agree to, with dat.)

համաձայնու- — agreeement թիւն, -եան

համար (postpos. — for + dat.

համարձակիլ — to dare, be bold

համբերութիւն, — patience -եան

համբուրել — to kiss

համերգ, -ի — concert

Համլեթ, -ի — Hamlet

համրել — to count

հայ, -ու — Armenian (person)

Հայաստան, -ի — Armenia

հայելի, -ի — mirror

հայերէն, -ի — Armenian (language)

Հայկ, -ի — Hayg (male name)

Հայկազեան, -ի — Haygazian (family name)

հայկական — Armenian (adj.)

հայհոյել — to curse

հայր, հօր — father

հայրական — paternal

հայրենակից, -ի — fellow-countryman

հայրենակցական — compatriotic

հայրենիք, -ի — fatherland, country

հայրիկ, -ի	father (dim.)	հաշիւ, -ի,	account, bill
հայցական, -ի	accusative case	հաշուի	
հանգիստ	quiet, comfortable; rest	հաշտութիւն, -եան	reconciliation
հանգչեցնել	to put to rest	հաշտուիլ	to be reconciled
հանգչիլ	to rest	հաչել	to bark
հանգստանալ, հանգստացայ	to rest	հասակ, -ի	height (of a person)
		հասկնալ, հասկցայ	to understand
հանգստեան կոչել	to retire (trans.)	հասնիլ, հասայ	to arrive, reach
		հաստ	thick
հանդարտ	quiet, still	հասցէ, -ի	address
հանդեպ (postpos. + dat.)	with regard to, for	հատ	see Lesson IV sec. 6
		հարազատ, -ի	blood-relation
հանդէս, -ի	celebration, party; review	հարիւր, -ի	hundred
		հարկ, -ի	need, necessity
Հանդէս Ամսօրեայ	Handes Amsorya (scholarly review of Armenian studies)	հարուած, -ի	blow (n.)
		հարուստ	rich, wealthy
		հարս, -ի	bride
		հարսնիք, -ի	wedding
հանդիպիլ (+ dat.)	to meet	Հարվըրտ, -ի	Harvard
		հարց, -ի	question, matter
հանդիսաւոր	solemn, pompous	հարցնել	to ask, inquire
հանել	to take, bring out; remove	հարցում, -ի	question
		հաց, -ի	bread
հանրակառք, -ի	bus, tram	հաւ, -ու	chicken, hen
հանրային	public (adj.)	հաւու միս	chicken (dish)

հաւասար	equal	հետ (postpos. + dat.)	with
հաւասարապէս	equally		
հաւաստի	reliable	հետաքրքրական	interesting
հաւատալ (+ dat.)	to believe (in)	հետաքրքրութիւն, -եան	interest
հաւատարիմ	faithful	հետաքրքրուիլ (+ instr.)	to take an interest (in)
հաւատք, -ի	faith, belief	հետեւաբար	consequently, so, accordingly
հաւաքական	collective		
հաւաքել	to collect, assemble (trans.)	հետեւեալ	following
հաւկիթ, -ի	egg	հետեւիլ (+ dat.)	to follow, pursue
հաւնիլ	to like		
հեզ	mild	հեւք, -ի	gasping
հեծանիւ, -ի	bicycle	հիանալ, հիացայ	to admire, be amazed
հեծկլտուք, -ի	sobbing	(+ վրայ, or instr.)	
հեծնել, հեծայ	to mount, ride	հիանալի	wonderful
հեկեկանք, -ի	sobbing	հիմա	now; just (of time)
հեղինակ, -ի	author	հին	old, ancient
հեռաձայն, -ի	telephone	հինգ	five
հեռաձայնել	to telephone	Հինգշաբթի, -ի	Thursday
հեռանալ, հեռացայ	to move away from	հիւանդ	ill; patient
հեռաւոր	distant	հիւանդանալ, հիւանդացայ	to fall ill
հեռաւորութիւն, -եան	distance	հիւանդանոց, -ի	hospital
հեռու (postpos. + abl.)	far, distant (from)	հիւանդութիւն, -եան	illness

հիւսել	to weave, intertwine	հրաժեշտ առնել	to take one's leave
հիւր, -ի	guest	հրամայել	to command, order
հնազանդիլ (+ dat.)	to obey	հրաման, -ի	order, command
		հրամմէ,	see Lesson XXIX sec.
հնդկահաւ, -ի	turkey	հրամմեցէք	3
հնձել	to reap	հրամցնել	to offer
հնչել	to pronounce, ring	Հրանտ, -ի	Hrand (male name)
հնչում, -ի	pronunciation	հրացան, -ի	rifle
հոգ, -ի	worry, concern	հրաւիրել	to invite
հոգ տանիլ (+ dat.)	to care for, mind	հօրեղբայր, հօրեղբօր	uncle (paternal)
հոգաբարձու, -ի	trustee		
հոգածութիւն, -եան	care, solicitude	ձախ	left (adj. and adv.)
հոգի, -ի	person	ձայն, -ի	voice, sound
հոլովուիլ	to be declined; (fig.) to be mentioned frequently	ձանձրանալ, ձանձրացայ (+ abl.)	to grow weary, tired, bored
Հոկտեմբեր, -ի	October	ձգել	to drop; leave, allow
հող, -ի	land, soil	ձեռնոց, -ի	glove
հոն	there	ձեռք, -ի	hand
հոս	here	ձեռք ձեռքի	hand in hand
հով, -ի, -ու	wind	ձեւել	to form, shape, cut out
հսկայ	giant, enormous	ձի, -ու	horse
հսկել	to watch, supervise	ձիւն, -ի	snow
հսկիչ, -ի	supervisor	ձիւն գալ	to snow
		ձմեռ, -ուան	winter

ծուլունիլ	to melt into	ճիւղ, -ի	branch
ծուկ, -ի, ձկան	fish	ճնշել	to oppress
ձրի	free (without charge)	ճշդապահ	punctual
		ճշմարիտ	true
		ճշմարտութիւն, -եան	truth
ղրկել	to send		
		ճչալ	to cry, shriek
ճախրել	to soar		
ճակատ, -ի	forehead, front	մազ, -ի (often in pl.)	hair
ճաղատ	bald		
ճամբայ, ճամբու	road, way	մածուն, -ի	yogurt
ճամբայ ելլել	to set out	մահ, -ուան	death
ճամբայ ղանել	to send off	մահանալ, մահացայ	to die
ճամբորդել	to travel		
ճանչնալ, ճանչցայ	to know a person, recognize	մաղթանք, -ի	wish (as greeting)
		Մայիս, -ի	May
ճաշ, -ի	meal; dish	մայր, մօր	mother
ճաշարան, -ի	restaurant	մայրիկ, -ի	mother (dim.)
ճատ, -ի	speed	մանաւանդ	especially
ճերմակ	white	մանել	to spin
ճզմել	to crush	մանկապարտէզ, -ի	kindergarten
ճիգ, -ի	effort		
ճիշդ	right, correct; exact, precise (adj. and adv.)	մանուկ, -ի	child
		մանչ, -ու	boy
		մանրամասնու-	detail
ճիպրալթար, -ի	Gibraltar	թիւն, -եան	

մանրամասնօրէն	in detail
մաշիլ	to be worn out
մաս, -ի	part
մասամբ	in part, partly
մասին (postpos.	about, concerning
+ gen.)	
մասնագէտ, -ի	specialist
մասնակցիլ (+	to take part in,
dat.)	participate in
մասնակցող, -ի	participant
մասնաւոր	special
մասնաւորապէս	especially, above
	all
մասնիկ, -ի	particle
մատ, -ի (pl.	finger
մատներ)	
մատանի, -ի	ring
Մատենադարան,	Madenataran (manu-
-ի	script library
	in Erevan)
մատիտ, -ի	pencil
մատուցանել	to offer
Մադրիտ, -ի	Madrid
մարդ (pl.	man
մարդեր ; see	
also *մարդիկ*)	
մարդիկ, մարդոց	men, people
մարդկային	human (adj.)
մարել	to put out, extinguish
մարիլ	to be extinguished;
	faint
մարմին, -ի,	body
մարմնի	
Մարտ, -ի	March
մաքուր	clean, pure
մաքրել	to clean
հաշիւ մաքրել	to settle an account
մեծ	great, big, large
մեծ հայր	grandfather
մեծ մայր	grandmother
մեծագոյն	greater, very great;
	greatest
մեծապէս	greatly
մեծնալ, մեծցայ	to grow, increase in
	size, age
մեծցնել	to enlarge
մեծութիւն,	greatness, size
-եան	
մեկնիլ	to go away, leave,
	depart
մեղմ	soft, mild, gentle
մեղմանալ,	to calm down
մեղմացայ	

մեղմօրէն	softly
մեղք, -ի	sin
մեղքնալ, մեղքցայ	to pity
մենք	we
մեռեալ	dead
մեռնիլ, մեռայ	to die
մեռցնել	to put to death
մերժել	to refuse
մէթր	meter
մէկ, մէկի	one (numeral) *մէկու* (pronoun)
մէկէն	suddenly
մէկը, մէկուն	somebody
մէկիկ մէկիկ	one by one
մէջ (postpos. + gen.)	in, at
մէջտեղ, -ի	middle (noun), space between
մը	a, an
մթնոլորտ, -ի	atmosphere
մժեղ, -ի	mosquito
միակ	only, single
միայն	only (adv.)
միանալ, միացայ	to join, unite

միասին	together
միեւնոյն	same
մինակ (+ per- sonal suffixes)	alone, by oneself
մինչ	while
մինչեւ	until
միշտ	always, ever
միութիւն, -եան	union
միջազգային	international
միջեւ (postpos. + gen.)	between
միջոց, -ի	means
միս, -ի	meat
միտք, մտքի	mind; thought
միւս	other
մկրատ, -ի	scissors
մղոն, -ի	mile
մնալ	to remain, stay
մնաս բարով	good-bye (said by person leaving)
մշակոյթ, -ի	culture
մշակութային	cultural
մոլորակ, -ի	planet
մոլորիլ	to go astray, be con- fused
մոռնալ, մոռցայ	to forget

Մոսկուա, -յի	Moscow	մօտենալ,	to approach, come near
մորթ, -ի	skin	մօտեցայ	
մորֆին, -ի	morphine	մօտեցնել	to bring near
մուխ	dark (adj.)	մօտիկ	close, intimate
մուկ, -ի, մկան	mouse	մօրեղբայր,	uncle (maternal)
մուտք, -ի	entrance	մօրեղբօր	
մուր, -ի	soot	մօրուք, -ի	beard
մուրալ	to beg		
մտադրել	to intend	Յակոբ, -ի	James
մտածել	to think, contemplate, consider	Յակոբեան, -ի	Hagopian
		յաղթել	to win, beat (in a game
մտածկոտ	pensive	յաճախ	often
մտահոգ	worried, anxious	յաճախանք, -ի	recurring (thought,
մտահոգություն, -եան	worry, concern		etc.)
		յաճախել	to attend, frequent
մտատանջ	uneasy, worried, anxious	յայտագիր, -ի	program
		յայտագրի	
մտիկ ընել (+ dat.)	to listen to, pay attention	յայտնել	to express; reveal
		յայտնի	evident, well-known,
մտնել, մտայ	to enter		famous
մտրակ, -ի	whip	յանդիմանել	to reprimand
մցնել	to bring in	յանկարծ	suddenly
մօտ (postpos. + dat.)	near, close to	յանցանք, -ի	fault, misdemeanor
		յաջողիլ (+ abl.)	to succeed; pass (exam, etc.)
մօտաւորապէս	about, approximately	յաջորդ	next

յաշորդաբար	in turn	Յուլիս, -ի	July
յաշորդել	to follow, succeed	Յունիս, -ի	June
յատկութիւն, -եան	characteristic	Յունուար, -ի	January
		յուսալ	to hope
յատուկ	particular, special, specific	յուսախաբութիւն, -եան	disappointment
յարգանք, -ի	respect	յուսահատիլ	to despair, give up hope
յարգել	to respect		
յարկ, -ի	floor, storey	յստակ	clear, plain
յարմար (adj. and postpos. + dat.)	suitable, fitting	յօդուած, -ի	article
		յօրանջել	to yawn
յարմարիլ + dat.)	to adjust (oneself)	նաեւ	also
		նախ	at first
Յարութիւն	Harutiun	նախագահ, -ի	president, chairman
Շմաւոնեան	Shmavonian	նախադասութիւն, -եան	sentence
յետին	least, insignificant		
		նախակրթարան, -ի	primary school
յետոյ	then, afterwards		
յիշատակ, -ի	souvenir, memory	նախաճաշ, -ի	breakfast
յիշել	to remember	նախաճաշել	to have breakfast
յիշեցնել	to remind	նախանձ, -ի	envy
յիսուն, -ի	fifty	նախընտրել	to prefer
յոգնիլ (+ abl.)	to get tired (of)	նախկին	former
յոյս, -ի	hope	նախորդ	previous
յուզում, -ի	emotion	նահանգ, -ի	state

նահանջ տարի	leap-year	ներկայացուցիչ, -ի	representative
նամակ, -ի	letter	ներկայութիւն, -եան	presence
նամակատուն, -տան	post office	ներկել	to paint
նայիլ (+ dat.); with ղեպի	to look at; overlook	ներողութիւն, -եան	apology; excuse me
նայուածք, -ի	look, glance	ներողութիւն խնդրել	to apologize
նաւ, -ու or -ի	ship	ներս, -ի (+ abl.)	inside, interior; into, through
նեղ	narrow	ներսը	inside, indoors (adv.)
նեղանալ, նեղացայ	to become upset, uneasy	ներքին	inner, internal
նեղութիւն, -եան	trouble, difficulty	նիւ Եորք, -ի	New York
նեղուիլ (+ abl.)	to be upset, annoyed (with)	նիւթ, -ի	matter, subject, topic
նետել	to throw	նիւթական	material, financial
ներ, ներոջ	wife of husband's brother	նկատել	to notice
ներարկում, -ի	injection	նկատմամբ (+ gen.)	regarding, toward
ներել (+ dat.)	to forgive, excuse	նկար, -ի	picture, image
ներկայ	present (adj.)	նկարագիր, նկարագրի	character (moral)
ներկայացնել	to introduce; present, perform; represent	նկարագրել	to describe
		նման (+ dat.)	like, alike
		նմանիլ (+ dat.)	to look like, resemble
ներկայացում, -ի	production, performance	նշանած, -ի	fiancé(e)

նշանակել	to mean, signify; appoint	շաբաթ, շաբթուան	week
նշանակութիւն, -եան	meaning	Շաբաթ օր	Saturday
նշանաւոր	famous	շալկել	to shoulder, carry on the back
նշանուած	engaged	շահ, -ու	profit, benefit
նշմարել	to notice, perceive	շահեկանութիւն, -եան	interest
նոյեմբեր, -ի	November	շահիլ	to earn
նոյն	same	շատ	very; (too) much, many
նոյնիսկ	even	շատ մը (+ pl.)	many
նոյնպէս	likewise	շատնալ, շատցայ	to increase
նոյնքան	as many	շատոնց	for a long time now; long ago
նոր	new; as adv.: recently	շարժել	to move (tr.)
նորէն	again, anew	շարժիլ	to move (intrans.)
նորոգուիլ	to be mended	շարժում, -ի,	motion, movement,
նուէր, -ի	gift	շարժման	gesture
նուշ, -ի	almond	շարուիլ	to be lined up in a row
նպատակ, -ի	purpose, aim, goal	շարունակ	continuously
նպատակ ունիմ	I intend	շարունակել	to continue
նստարան, -ի	bench	շարք, -ի	row
նստեցնել	to seat	շաքար, -ի	sugar
նստիլ, նստայ	to sit, sit down; ride (in a car)	շէնք, -ի	building
		շճունկ, -ի	serum

շինել	to make, build	շփանալ, շփացայ	to be spoiled
շիշ, -ի	bottle		
շիտակ	right, correct; straight ahead	ո եւէ	whoever
		ոխակալ	spiteful
շնորհակալ լլալ (+ dat.)	to thank, be grateful to	ողբ, -ի	lamentation
		ոմն	someone
շնորհակալու- թիւն, -եան	thanks	ոյժ, -ի (also ուժ)	force, strength, prowess
շնորհիւ (+ gen.)	thanks to	ոչ	no; not
շշուկ, -ի	whisper	ոչ...ոչ (ալ)	neither...nor
շոգեկառք, -ի	train	ոչինչ, -ի	nothing
շոյել	to caress, stroke	ոչ ոք, -ի	no one, nobody
շուարիլ	to become confused	ոսկոր, -ի	bone
շուկայ, -ի	market	ոսկոր առ ոսկոր	bone after bone
շուն, -ի, շան	dog	ո՞վ	who?
շունչ, -ի	breath	ոտք, -ի	foot
շուտ	quickly	ոտքի ելլել, կենալ	to stand up
շուտով	soon, quickly		
շուրջ (postpos. + gen.)	round	ոտքի հանել	to make someone stand up
շուք, -ի	shade, shadow	որ	which (rel. and inter.)
շրթունք, -ի	lip	որ	that
շրջակայք, -ի	neighborhood	որբ, -ի	orphan
շրջանակ, -ի	circle, set of people	որբանոց, -ի	orphanage
		որդ, -ի	worm
շրջանաւարտ, -ի	graduate	որդի, -ի	son

որեւէ	any, whatever	ուշադրութիւն	to be careful, look
որոնել	to search	ընել	out
որոշ	some, certain	ուշանալ,	to be late (for)
որոշել	to decide, deter-	ուշացայ (+ abl.)	
	mine	ուշի ուշով	carefully
որոշում, -ի	decision	ուսանիլ	to study
որովհետեւ	because	ուսանող, -ի	student
որպէս	as	ուսում, -ի,	study
որպէսզի	so that, in order to	ուսման	
որքան	so much, as much;	ուսուցիչ, -ի,	teacher (male)
	interrog: how	ուսուցչի	
	much, how many?	ուսուցչութիւն,	teaching
ու	and	-եան	
ուզել	to want	ուսուցչուհի, -ի	teacher (female)
ութը, ութի	eight	ուտել, կերայ	to eat
ութսուն, -ի	eighty	ուտելիք, -ի	food
ուժգին (adj.	strong, powerful	ուր	where (rel. and inter-
and adv.)			rog.)
ուղղակի	straight, directly	ուրախ	glad, happy
ունենալ,	to have	ուրախութիւն,	joy, gladness
ունեցայ		-եան	
ունիմ, see	I have	ուրանալ,	to deny, renounce
ունենալ		ուրացայ	
ուշ	late, tardy	Ուրբաթ, -ի	Friday
ուշադրութիւն,	attention	ուրեմն	so, then, therefore
-եան		ուրիշ	other

ուրկէ	whence (rel. and interrog.)	պահել	to keep
		պահուրտիլ	to hide oneself
		պաղ, -ու	cold (adj. and n.)
չամիչ, -ի	raisin	պաղարիւն	cool, calm
չար	bad, evil, wicked	պաղպաղակ, -ի	ice cream
չարաճճի, -ի	naughty	պայման, -ի	condition, circumstance
չարաչար	excessively, extremely		
չարութիւն, -եան	wickedness, evil	պայուսակ, -ի	bag, briefcase
		պայքար, -ի	contest, struggle
չափ, -ի	measure, quantity (+ dat. - as)	պանդոկ, -ի	hotel
		պանիր, -ի	cheese
չափէն աւելի	excessively	պաշտամունք, -ի	service
չափազանց	extremely	պաշտելի	adorable
չափել	to measure	պաշտպանել	protect, defend
չէ	no	պաշտօն, -ի	office, position
Չորեքշաբթի, -ի	Wednesday	պաշտօնականանալ,	to be confirmed, made
չորս, -ի	four	պաշտօնականացայ	official
		պաշտօնեայ, -ի	official
		պառկեցնել	to lay down, put to bed
պակաս	less		
պահ, -ու	moment, while	պառկիլ	to lie down
այս պահուն	at the moment	պատ, -ի	wall
պահանջատէր, -ի, -տիրոջ	creditor	պատահիլ	to happen
		պատանի, -ի	youth
պահանջել	to demand	պատանք, -ի	shroud
պահանջք, -ի	demand	պատասխան, -ի	answer, reply

պատասխանել	to answer, reply	պարզություն, -եան	simplicity
պատարագ, -ի	liturgy, mass	պարկեշտ	decent, honest
պատերազմ, -ի	war	պարոն, -ի	gentleman, sir, Mr.
պատժել	to punish	պարտականություն, -եան	duty, obligation; assignment
պատկանիլ (+ dat.)	to belong to		
պատկեր, -ի	picture, painting	պարտէզ, -ի	garden
պատճառ, -ի	cause, reason	պարտք, -ի	debt
պատճառաւ (postpos. + dat.)	because of, on account of	պարտքի առնել	to borrow money
		պեխ, -ի	moustache
պատճառել	to cause	պետություն, -եան	state
պատմել	to tell, relate		
պատմություն, -եան	story, history	պերճանք, -ի	luxury
պատուհան, -ի	window	պզտիկ	little, small
պատրաստ	ready	Պէյրութ, -ի	Beirut
պատրաստել	to prepare	պէս (postpos. + dat.)	as, like
պատրաստուիլ (+ dat.)	to prepare oneself (for)		
պարագայ, -ի	circumstance	պէտք, -ի	need, want
պարահանդէս, -ի	dance (n.); ball	պէտք է (որ) + subj.	it is necessary that, "must"
պարապ	empty	պէտք ունենալ + dat.	to need, require
պարել	to dance	պնդել	to insist
պարզ	simple, plain	պնդում, -ի	insistence, persistence
պարզապէս	simply	Պոլշոյ, -ի	Bolshoi
		պոչ, -ի	tail

պոռալ (վրայ)	to shout (at)	սարսափիլ	to be frightened
Պոսթոն, -ի	Boston	սաւառնիլ	to soar, fly
պտոյտ, -ի	walk	սափրիչ, -ի	barber
պտոյտի երթալ	to go for a walk	սեղան, -ի	table
պտուղ, -ի	fruit	սենեակ, -ի	room, chamber
		սենթ, -ի	cent
ջանալ	to try, attempt	սեպել	to assume, suppose
ջղայնութիւն,	nervousness	Սեպտեմբեր, -ի	September
-եան		սեռական, -ի	genitive case
ջուր, -ի	water	սեւ	black
		սէր, -ի (սիրոյ)	love
ռուսերէն	Russian (language)	սիրել	to love, like
		սիրելի	dear, beloved
սա	this	սիրով	gladly, willingly
սակայն	but; only	սիրուն	pretty
սահեցնել	to make slide	սիրտ, -ի,	heart
սանտրուիլ	to comb one's hair	սրտի	
սառիլ	to freeze (intrans.)	սլանալ, սլացայ	to dart
սաստիկ	severe, strong	սխալ, -ի	mistake; wrong (adj.), wrongly
սաստկութիւն,	severity		
-եան		սխալիլ	to err, to be wrong
Սատանայ, -ի	Satan	սխալմամբ	by mistake, wrongly
սատկիլ	to die	սկիզբ, -ի	beginning
Սարգիսեան	Sarkisian (family name)	սկսեալ (post-pos. + abl.)	beginning from
սարսափելի	frightful	սկսիլ, սկսայ	to begin, start

սնունդ, -ի	food
սովորաբար	usually
սովորական	usual, customary, ordinary
սովորություն, -եան	habit, custom
սորվեցնել	to reach
սորվիլ	to learn
սուլոց, -ի	whistling
սուղ	expensive, dear
սուտ	false, untrue
սուր	sharp
սուրբ, -ի	saint; holy
սուրճ, -ի	coffee
սպայ, -ի	officer
սպաննել	to kill
սպառնալ	to threaten
սպառնալիք, -ի	threat
սպասել (+ dat.)	to wait for, expect
սպիտակ	white
սպիտակիլ	to grow white
ստանալ,	to get, receive
ստացայ	
ստեղծել	to create
ստիպել	to force, compel, insist

ստոյգ	reliable, real
ստուգել	to verify
սրբել	to wipe
սրուակ, -ի	phial, flask
սքանչելի	wonderful, splendid
վազել	to run
վաթսուն, -ի	sixty
վախ, -ի	fear, dread
վախնալ,	to be afraid of, fear
վախցայ (+ abl.)	
վաղը, վաղուան	tomorrow
վայ	woe, alas
վայելել	to enjoy
վայրկեան, -ի	minute
վանք, -ի	monastery
Վաչէ, -ի	Vache (male name)
վատառողջ	in poor health
վար (postpos. + abl.)	down (adv.)
վարար	overflowing
վարդ, -ի	rose
Վարդան, -ի	Vartan (male name)
վարժուիլ (+ dat.)	to get used to
վարուիլ	to act, behave

վեհանձնութիւն, generosity
  -եան

վեր (postpos. up, above, over-
  + abl.) head (adv.)

ի վեր (post- since (time)
  pos. + abl.)

վերադառնալ, to return
  վերադարձայ

վերադարձ, -ի return (n.)

վերածուիլ to be transformed

վերակազմուիլ to be rebound; re-
  organized

վերահաստատել to re-establish

վերապահել to reserve, save

վերջ, -ի; (+ end, ending; after
  abl.)

վերջը later

ի վերջոյ finally

վերջանալ, to come to an end
  վերջացայ

վերջապէս finally

վերջացնել to finish, bring
  to an end

վերջերս lately

վերջին last, final

վերսկսիլ, to resume, begin
  վերսկսայ again

վերցնել remove; lift

վեց, -ի six

վէճ, -ի quarrel, dispute

վէպ, -ի novel

վիճակ, -ի state, condition

վիճիլ to quarrel, dispute

վիրաբուժական surgical

վիրաւորել to hurt, wound

վկայ, -ի witness

վկայական, -ի certificate

վճարել to pay, settle

վճիռ, -ի verdict, judgment

վճռել to pronounce

վստահ sure, certain

վստահիլ (+ to trust, count on
  dat.)

վստահութիւն, trust, confidence
  -եան

վտանգաւոր dangerous

վրայ (postpos. on, above
  + gen.)

տաբատ, -ի (pair of) trousers

տագր, տագրոջ husband's brother

տաժանելի painful, hard

տալ, տուի to give

տալ, տալոշ	husband's sister	տասնութը,	eighteen
տախտակ, -ի	wood, plank	-ութի	
տակ (postpos. + gen.)	under, beneath	տատանում, -ի	flickering
		տարածել	to spread, extend
տակաւին	yet, still	տարափ, -ի	barrage, shower
տակնուվրայ ըլլալ	to be unsettled, agitated	տարբեր	different
		տարբերութիւն, -եան	difference
տանիլ, տարի	to take, carry; bear		
		տարեգիրք, -ի	year-book, almanac
տանիք, -ի	roof	տարեդարձ, -ի	birthday, anniversary
տանձ, -ի	pear	տարեկան	annual; also used to render age
տանջել	to torment		
տառապիլ	to suffer	տարեշրջան, -ի	(academic) year
տասը, տասի	ten	տարեցոյց, -ի	annual register, almanac
տասնամեակ, -ի	decade		
տասնեակներ	tens	տարի, տարուան	year
տասներեք, -ի	thirteen	տարիք, -ի	age (years old)
տասներկու, -երկուքի	twelve	տարօրինակ	strange, odd
		տաք	hot
տասնեօթը, -եօթի	seventeen	տեղ, -ի; (+ gen.)	place, site, location; in place of
տասնըհինգ, -ի	fifteen	տեղի ունենալ	to take place
տասնըմէկ, -ի	eleven	տեղացնել	to shower down, pour
տասնըչորս, -ի	fourteen	տեղաւորել	to place
տասնըվեց, -ի	sixteen	տեղեկագիր, -ի,	report
տասնինը, -իննի	nineteen	տեղեկագրի	

տեղեկացնե լ	to inform, notify	տկարացնե լ	to weaken (tr.)
տեղեկութիւն, -եան	information	տղայ, -ի, տղու	boy, son
տենդոտ	feverish	տոլար, -ի	dollar
տեսակ, -ի	kind, type, sort	տող, -ի	like
տեսարան, -ի	view, panorama	տողանցե լ	to parade, file
տեսնա լ	see տեսնե լ	տոմսակ, -ի	ticket
տեսնե լ, տեսայ	to see	տոպրակ, -ի	bag
տեսք, -ի	appearance	տուն, տան	house, home
տետրակ, -ի	notebook	տուփ, -ի	box; pack (of cigarettes)
տերեւ, -ի	leaf	տպե լ	to print
տեւաբար	continuously	տրական, -ի	dative case
տեւե լ	to last, continue	տրտում	sad
տէր, տիրոջ	master, lord, owner, Mr. (only in conjunction with տիկին)	տրտունջ, -ի	complaint, murmur
		տօն, -ի	festival, feast
		րոպէ, -ի	minute
Տիգրան, -ի	Dikran (male name)		
տիեզերք, -ի	universe	ցած	low, soft (not loud)
տիկին, տիկնոջ	lady; Mrs., wife	ցանե լ	to sow
տիպար	typical	ցաւ, -ի	pain
տխուր	sad	գլխու ցաւ	headache
տխրութիւն, -եան	sadness	ցաւի լ	to hurt, be painful; be sorry
տկար	weak	ցեղ, -ի	family, tribe, race
տկարանա լ, տկարացայ	to weaken (intrans.)	ցերեկ, -ուան	daytime

ցոյց, -ի	demonstration	փոխադարձ	mutual
ցոյց տալ	to show, indicate	փոխանակ	instead of
ցուցարար, -ի	demonstrator		(prepos. + gen.)
ցուցընել,	to show, indicate	փոխանցուիլ	to be transferred,
ցուցուցի	(tr.)		handed over
ցտեսութիւն	good-bye	փոխել	to change, alter
ցրուիլ	to be scattered	փողկապ, -ի	necktie
		փողոց, -ի	street
փախչիլ (or	to escape, flee	փոր, -ի	belly
փախիլ), փախայ		փորձ, -ի	try, attempt (n.),
փախցնել	to miss (train,		rehearsal
	occasion, etc.),	փորձառութիւն,	experience
	snatch	-եան	
փակել	to close, conclude	փորձել	to try, attempt
փայլուն	bright, shining	փուշ, -ի	thorn
փայտ, -ի	wood	փոքր	little
փառք, -ի	glory	փչել	to blow
փափաք, -ի	desire, wish	փսփսուք, -ի	whisper
փափաքիլ	to desire, want,	փրթիլ, փրթայ	to come off
	wish	փրկել	to save, rescue
փեսայ, -ի	groom	փրցնել	to detach, pick off
Փետրուար, -ի	February		
փղձկում, -ի	bursting into tears	քալել	to walk
փնտռել	to look for, search	քալուածք, -ի	walk, gait
փոթորկիլ	to be tempestuous,	քակել	to untie, unwind
	break out	քահանայ, -ի	priest (married)

քաղաք, -ի	city, town	բիչ մը	a little
քաղաքական	political	Քիւրդ, -ի	Kurd
քաղաքավարու-	politeness,	բմայք, -ի	whim
թիւն, -եան	civility	բնանալ, բնացայ	to sleep, fall asleep
քաղել	to pick	բննութիւն, -եան	examination
քամի, -ի	wind	բշել	to expel, drive (a
քայլ, -ի	step, footstep		car)
քան	than	քոյր, քրոջ	sister
քանի՞	how many?	քոյրիկ, -ի	sister (dim.)
քանի մը	some, a few	քով (postpos.	beside
քանի որ	as long as, since	+ gen.)	
քաշել	to pull; suffer	քով քովի	side by side
քաշուիլ	to withdraw	քուն, -ի	sleep
քաջ	brave, courageous	քուռակ, -ի	colt, foal
քաջութիւն,	courage	քսան, -ի	twenty
-եան		քրտինք, -ի	sweat
քառասուն, -ի	forty		
քառորդ, -ի	quarter	օգնել (+ dat.)	to help, aid, assist
քառուղի, -ի	crossroads	օգնութիւն,	help, aid
քար, -ի	stone	-եան	
քարանալ,	to become petri-	Օգոստոս, -ի	August
քարացայ	fied	օգուտ, -ի	benefit, usefulness
քարտէս, -ի	map	օդ, -ի	air, weather
քիթ, -ի, քթի	nose	օդակայան, -ի	airport
քիլոմեթր, -ի	kilometer	օդանաւ, -ի	airplane
քիչ	little, somewhat	օձ, -ի	snake

oտար, -ի	foreign (adj.); stranger, for- eigner	օրէնք, -ի	law
		օրինակ, -ի	example, copy
		օրինակի համար	for example
օր, -ուան	day	օրիորդ, -ի	young lady; Miss
օրաթերթ, -ի	(daily) newspaper	օրորել	to rock
օրական	daily		